FAMBROUGH · JERRY WAUGH · MARILYNN SMITH · BILL HOUG

B FREDERICK · CURTIS McCLINTON · JOH

JO JO WHITE · NOLAN CROMWELL · GARY KEMPF · DARNELL

NTER · LARRY BROWN · GLENN TRAMMEL · KEVIN PRITCHARD

OLLISON · NICK REID · MARK MANGINO · RUSSELL ROBINSON ·

EVANS · DON FAMBROUGH · JERRY WAUGH · MARILYNN SMITH

BERLAIN · BOB FREDERICK · CURTIS McCLINTON · JOHN HADL

S · JIM RYUN · JO JO WHITE · NOLAN CROMWELL · GARY KEMPF

CHAEL CENTER · LARRY BROWN · GLENN TRAMMEL · KEVIN PRITC

CK COLLISON · NICK REID · MARK MANGINO · RUSSELL ROBIN

RAY EVANS · DON FAMBROUGH · JERRY WAUGH · MARILYNN S

HAMBERLAIN · BOB FREDERICK · CURTIS McCLINTON · JOHN

GGINS · JIM RYUN · JO JO WHITE · NOLAN CROMWELL · GARY K

GE · MICHAEL CENTER · LARRY BROWN · GLENN TRAMMEL ·

AFRENTZ · NICK COLLISON · NICK REID · MARK MANGINO · R

DICK HARP · RAY EVANS · DON FAMBROUGH · JERRY WAUGH ·

RTER · WILT CHAMBERLAIN · BOB FREDERICK · CURTIS McCLIN

ASS · JOHN RIGGINS · JIM RYUN · JO JO WHITE · NOLAN CROM

TRACY BUNGE · MICHAEL CENTER · LARRY BROWN · GLENN TRA

WHAT IT MEANS TO BE A
JAYHAWK

BILL SELF
AND KANSAS'S GREATEST JAYHAWKS

JEFF BOLLIG AND DOUG VANCE

TRIUMPH
BOOKS

This book is available in quantity at special discounts for your group or organization. For further information, contact:

Triumph Books
542 South Dearborn Street
Suite 750
Chicago, Illinois 60605
(312) 939-3330
Fax (312) 663-3557

Printed in U.S.A.
ISBN: 978-1-57243-981-8
Design by Nick Panos.
Editorial production and layout by Prologue Publishing Services, LLC.
All photos courtesy of University of Kansas Athletics unless otherwise noted.
Endsheet artwork by John B. Martin, courtesy of University of Kansas Athletics.

CONTENTS

FOREWORD

by Bill Self

I HAVE ALWAYS ENJOYED WORKING in the college-campus setting. The energy created by the interaction of students, professors, administrators, coaches, alumni, and other supporters is exciting. Without a doubt, it is a stimulating environment.

For that reason, I think people look back at their college days with great pride. There is a sense of accomplishment and a deep appreciation for the experience. I look back on my days at Oklahoma State in that vein. The support and resources there were integral to my personal and professional growth. I am proud to be a Cowboy. But I also consider myself to be a Jayhawk—a proud one at that. You might look at it like marriage. You have your own family and then you join and are accepted by another.

I became a Jayhawk in the summer of 1984. I was working at Coach Larry Brown's basketball camp when I injured my knee in a pickup basketball game. He said if I ever needed anything, just give him a call. I jumped on the offer and asked him if I could serve as a graduate assistant under him if he had an opening. I think he felt sorry for me, so in a weak moment he said yes. I was on cloud nine—I was a member of Larry Brown's staff at the University of Kansas.

To say I was an integral part of the basketball program at Kansas at that time would be an overstatement. I tell people my main job was to read *USA Today* for Coach Brown and let him know what was in the news. I'm sure I did some good for the program, but in reality he was affording me an opportunity to learn from one of the best coaches at one of the best, if not *the* best, basketball programs in the nation.

The 1985–1986 season was almost magical. Coach Brown had built upon the tradition of coaches like Naismith, Hamilton, Allen, Harp, and Owens. The campus and the city were alive, and the atmosphere was great. Growing up in Oklahoma, I had known all about Kansas basketball, but I don't think I gained a true appreciation until I came to work for Coach Brown. I was now meeting the legends I had heard so much about: Clyde Lovellette, Jo Jo White, Bud Stallworth, Darnell Valentine, and so many others. I was sitting on the bench with my feet planted on the Allen Fieldhouse court. I tried to be a sponge and absorb everything that was happening around me. To cap off my year with a trip to the Final Four was more than I could ask for. I returned to Oklahoma State as a full-time assistant coach the next year, having lived one of the best years of my life.

As a young coach, you have goals and you have dreams. Sometimes, they match up. To set a goal of being the head basketball coach at the University of Kansas is really a pretty lofty dream. Heck, through 100 years of basketball, there had only been seven head coaches. Plus, to get to that position, you have to have a pretty good track record. Did I dream of being the head coach at KU? Sure. But as I was coaching my first year at Oral Roberts, losing 18 games in a row, it was the furthest thing from my mind.

Perhaps the best part of athletics is the relationship-building that occurs. I have enjoyed my associations with student-athletes, administrators, coaches, fans, media, and others that have developed over the years. Even though I was at Kansas only a year, some of my most enduring friendships were developed during that time. As they say, once a Jayhawk, always a Jayhawk.

Although I was focused on building my own programs at Oral Roberts, Tulsa, and Illinois, I took an interest in the success of the Kansas program. But then again, the Jayhawks were so good, it was hard not to notice. They were on television every night and in the headlines every day. It was hard not to be impressed. The most amazing thing to me was the continuity of the program. There was really little transition, given the longevity of the coaches. And when one did retire or move on, it seems like the next one had a tie of some sort. Behind the scenes you had longtime administrators, loyal fans, and former players who remained close to the program. Kansas was always rock solid.

I have been fortunate throughout my career. With the support of many, I have had amazing opportunities. But nothing approached what would happen in April 2003. I had just completed my third season at Illinois and had a good thing going. I was vacationing in Florida when I got a message to call

Bill Self, only the eighth coach in the history of Jayhawks basketball, was first exposed to Kansas basketball in 1985 when he was hired by Larry Brown as a graduate assistant coach. Self joins Brown (1988) and Phog Allen (1952) as Kansas coaches who have won NCAA championships.

the University of Kansas. Roy Williams had left for North Carolina, so I had an inkling of what they were calling about. The next few days were a blur. But I was quite happy at Illinois. In the end, however, the allure of Kansas was just too much. I had the opportunity to be head coach at a place I respect so much.

My five years as head coach at Kansas have been great. Sure, there is pressure. But I look at that as a positive. There is just so much passion for the program and the university. I feel I have the responsibility to represent both to the highest of my abilities. It has been everything I thought it would be and more. The people on campus, in the community, and in the state have been tremendous. I have renewed many old acquaintances and have established countless new ones. The fans, most notably the students, have made Allen Fieldhouse the best arena in the nation. Sometimes I wish I could just sit in the student section at a game to get the flavor of the experience. At the same time, there is no better feeling than being in the locker room before a game. You can feel the excitement coming through the walls. Then, when the door opens and you walk through the tunnel, the adrenaline takes over. I'll never get tired of that experience.

What does it mean to be a Jayhawk? Terms such as pride, excellence, passion, and class come to mind. Jayhawks truly care about the university and what it stands for. They treasure the history and the experience it has afforded them. This was never more obvious than this past season, when we celebrated the 110 years of Kansas basketball, experienced an extraordinary Senior Night, and made our march to the NCAA title. There are no better fans in all of college sports than Kansas Jayhawks.

Athletics is just one part of the university, but an important one. It provides a learning opportunity for the student-athletes and the vehicle by which many maintain their ties to the school. I am fortunate that I have the chance to interact with current and former coaches and student-athletes representing all sports at KU. The stories I hear are inspiring, humorous, enlightening, and full of passion. *What It Means to Be a Jayhawk* gives all of us the opportunity to share in those stories. I am sure you will enjoy reading them as much as I have.

—Bill Self

Men's Basketball Coach, 2003–present

Bill Self is only the eighth coach in the long and storied history (110 years) of Kansas basketball. A native of Okmulgee, Oklahoma, he was a four-year letterwinner (1982–1985) at Oklahoma State, earning academic all-conference honors. He got his start in coaching as a graduate assistant at Kansas under Larry Brown in the 1985–1986 season as the Jayhawks advanced to the Final Four. After serving as an assistant coach at his alma mater, he served four years (1994–1997) at Oral Roberts, taking it from a 4–22 mark the year before he arrived to a 21–7 record and an NIT berth his final year. That was followed by an extraordinary three-year run at Tulsa (1998–2000) where he was 74–27, taking his final squad to the NCAA Elite Eight with a 32–5 record. He followed that with a 78–24 mark in three years (2001–2003) at Illinois and a sparkling 142–32 record in five seasons at Kansas. Fueled by the Jayhawks' 37–3 season and 2008 NCAA title, Self has the best winning percentage of any coach in Kansas basketball history, winning 81.6 percent of his games. He has taken three schools to the NCAA Elite Eight (Tulsa 2000; Illinois 2001; Kansas 2004, 2007, and 2008), joining Eddie Sutton, Rick Pitino, and Gene Bartow as the only coaches to accomplish that feat. Self is 349–137 in 15 years as a head coach and has been a four-time finalist for the Naismith National Coach of the Year. *The Sporting News* named him the National Coach of the Year in 2000.

ACKNOWLEDGMENTS

THE DAUNTING CHALLENGE of pulling together the life stories of a selected group of University of Kansas student-athletes and coaches would not have been possible without the generous help of several people who we would like to acknowledge.

First on that list are the coaches and student-athletes who made themselves available for interviews and agreed to participate in the project. They are the stars of this book, and their stories will hopefully continue to inspire future generations of Jayhawks.

The project would not have been possible without the cooperation of the University of Kansas and many of those professionals who lead the athletics department. Athletics Director Lew Perkins along with Associate Athletics Director Jim Marchiony have been supportive of the project and provided assistance in various aspects of making the book a reality.

Assistant Athletics Director Chris Theisen and his staff in the KU media relations office were always there when we needed a historical fact or to provide meaningful direction.

We'd also like to single out Carole Hadl (KU football office), Joanie Stephens (men's basketball office), and Audrey Novotny (Williams Educational Fund) for helping provide valuable contact information.

We would also like to thank good friend Bob Snodgrass for approaching us to serve as authors of this book and for his guidance throughout the project. He's been a great partner in helping us overcome a handful of roadblocks along the way.

Also, to Triumph Books for serving as the foundation of the project and the vehicle for making its publication possible.

Finally, we'd like to thank our respective wives—Laurie Bollig and Sue Vance—who continue to demonstrate remarkable patience with two guys who have a passion for paying close attention to the sports world and, in particular, the one that blossoms each season from Lawrence, Kansas.

DEDICATIONS

To my parents, Marion and Shirley Bollig, who provided guidance and encouragement to chase my dreams. To my siblings, Coleen, Joe, Camille, and John, for being there at all times. And to my wife Laurie, daughter Courtney, and son Kyle, who make following the Jayhawks fun. No amount of words can express my love and appreciation for my family.

—Jeff Bollig

To special friends and coworkers during 20 years at KU: Jennifer Berquist, Ginger Bliss, Jeff Bollig, Laurie Bollig, Dean Buchan, Teri Burtin, Sara Cameron, Crissy Causey, Mitch Germann, Jeff Cravens, Jeff Jacobsen, Donna Klein, Richard Konzem, Janay Leddy, Mason Logan, Janelle Martin, Anne McAlister, Dick O'Connor, Craig Pinkerton, Mike Prusinski, Heather Powell, Beau White, Barb Zeff along with Will Hancock, and many other terrific student assistants.

—Doug Vance

INTRODUCTION

A S ANY SUCCESSFUL ARCHITECT UNDERSTANDS, it's difficult to build a quality building without the direction of a set of blueprints.

And it's equally complicated to write a book like this one without a preconceived plan that gives the author (or authors, in this case) a clear path and understanding of how the message will be delivered.

The University of Kansas boasts an athletic identity that has flourished in a culture of excellence and is defined by a lineage of legends that includes James Naismith, Ray Evans, Clyde Lovellette, Al Oerter, Wilt Chamberlain, John Hadl, Gale Sayers, John Riggins, Jim Ryun, Jo Jo White, Lynette Woodard, and Danny Manning.

It's fitting that the timing of our efforts to document the memories and feelings of those individuals who have shaped the school's history in competition would coincide with a season (2007–2008) in which new legends were born and an unparalleled standard of combined success was established in football and men's basketball.

Among those from our gallery of greats offering reflections on the topic of being a Jayhawk are the respective coaches (Bill Self and Mark Mangino) who orchestrated the monumental seasons in basketball and football and two student-athlete catalysts for those teams, Russell Robinson (basketball) and Todd Reesing (football).

Our major challenge from the outset in writing *What It Means to Be a Jayhawk* was identifying a select group of former student-athletes and coaches who would best represent a cross-section of teams and who offered an

With the Jayhawks down 63–60 and 3.6 seconds left to go in the fourth quarter of the 2008 NCAA finals, Mario Chalmers puts up a three-point attempt. The shot fell in, sending Kansas into overtime against the Memphis Tigers, where the Jayhawks won their third NCAA championship. *Photo courtesy of Getty Images*

intriguing story that would serve to convey the emotion of what the book title suggests.

There are no shortage of high-profile athletes and coaches to choose from when you review the history of KU athletics. The menu of stars who have been Jayhawks is a thick and well-established roster.

In discussing our options, there was also the issue of availability of interview candidates and uncertainty about whether everyone on our list would agree to participate in the project. Our original catalog of names changed slightly as we moved through the project. A few athletes failed to respond to our interview requests and, in just one instance, a former Jayhawk didn't feel his story was worthy of a chapter in the book.

But, beyond those few, we found an assortment of Jayhawks who were eager and honored to share their feelings and be included in these pages.

Our final list includes both the well-known and those who competed but did not receive wide acclaim. We wanted to offer a variety of perspectives, ranging from an assortment of different sports and time periods. We found celebrated standouts such as Al Oerter in Florida, shortly before his death, Willie Pless in Canada, Nick Collison in Seattle, and through an exchange of emails, interviewed Nick Reid between his NFL Europe games in Germany.

Also included are stories from a handful of Jayhawk heroes no longer among the living that we gathered through the memories of their families or friends. Any book designed to honor the past would fall short of that goal without commentary on Jayhawk legends such as James Naismith, Wilt Chamberlain, Ray Evans, Dick Harp, and Galen Fiss.

Suffice it to say, the pride of being a Jayhawk is not solely reserved for those who have dropped sweat on a KU venue of athletic competition. Since the inaugural graduating class of four students received their diplomas in 1873, more than 260,000 degrees have been presented at the University of Kansas.

They are all certified, wheat-waving Jayhawks who lay claim to a unique, but rich heritage. While this book celebrates the stories of former KU athletes and coaches, it is dedicated to the entire family of Jayhawks.

The Jayhawk brand represents a unique badge for those who qualify to wear it in competition or continue to feel it throughout their lives.

There are a wide variety of chest-thumping Wildcats who represent Kansas State, Arizona, Kentucky, or Davidson, and there are more than 40 universities who have Tigers as a moniker, including Memphis, Missouri, Auburn, Fort Hays State, and Grambling. There are also a wide assortment of Eagles, Vikings, Cardinals, and Warriors among the more than 1,700 college nicknames and mascots.

However, there is only one university that produces alumni represented by the mythical bird known as a Jayhawk. And, as the old adage goes, birds of a feather do flock together.

As you will learn in reading the thoughtful perspectives presented in this book, exploring the question of what it means to be a Jayhawk is often a journey with deep roots in a category of sport competition.

While each of the subjects has a unique story to share, we discovered during our months of interviews that most are linked by a set of values that include dedication to sport, the commitment to achievement, the respect of teammates and coaches, and the love and influence of an experience at a special university.

As authors, our assignment was to bring to you, the reader, what these special individuals remember during their journeys to KU and its influence on their lives. Our only regret is not being able to share with you those wide smiles, the moments of laughter, and the intense pride our subjects shared as they looked back and discussed their KU experience.

Included in the pages ahead are the varied thoughts and perceptions of men and women who share one common bond—they are forever Jayhawks.

These are the moments that shaped decades of competition, enhanced the history of the university, and were painted beneath the banner of the several variations of the Jayhawk logo, from its evolutionary stages as a cross-legged, crow-type creature to Harold Sandy's depiction, which surfaced in the late 1940s and continues to serve as the licensed Jayhawk brand.

They all serve to both inspire and remind those who claim membership in the Jayhawk nation of what it means to be a Jayhawk.

The 2007 Kansas football team celebrates a 12–1 record and 24–21 Orange Bowl win over Virginia Tech.

In the
BEGINNING

DR. JAMES NAISMITH
MEN'S BASKETBALL COACH
1898–1907

THE UNIVERSITY OF KANSAS is known worldwide for producing great academicians, respected business leaders, cutting edge technology, and services that benefit all humanity. But some may say the best thing to come out of Mount Oread is the game of basketball. Just seven years after Dr. James Naismith invented the sport in 1891, he brought it to the Sunflower State, where it became an instant hit. As director of chapel and head of the physical education department, Naismith cast a large presence—on campus, in the community, nationally, and worldwide.

Naismith was born November 6, 1861, in rural Ontario, Canada. His parents died of typhoid fever when he was nine, and along with a brother and sister, he was raised by his uncle. He dropped out of high school at age 15 and worked as a lumberjack to support the family. At the age of 20, he returned to finish high school and then went to McGill University to become a Presbyterian minister. He was a passionate sportsman, excelling in a variety of skills. Upon graduation in 1890, he accepted a position with the Springfield YMCA. One year later, he invented basketball, loosely based on the Canadian game "Duck on a Rock." In 1895, he went to Denver to earn a medical degree and work as the director of the YMCA. Three years later, he came to Kansas. On May 4, 1925, he became a naturalized citizen of the United States.

Having invented the game at the age of 30, he saw the game enjoy extraordinary growth—including his lobbying to have it introduced to the Olympics

James Naismith actually played in just two basketball games during his lifetime: the first one ever played at the Springfield YMCA and the first one at the University of Kansas to demonstrate to students how to play the game.

in 1936. He would serve as the first coach of the Jayhawk basketball team, compiling a 55–60 mark in nine years (1898–1907). He remained on the Kansas faculty until 1937 and passed away at the age of 78 on November 28, 1939. Naismith is buried in Lawrence at Memorial Park Cemetery on East 15th Street. The court in Allen Fieldhouse is named in his honor, while the venerable on-campus facility is located on Naismith Drive. In 1968, the Naismith Basketball Hall of Fame opened in Springfield, Massachusetts, in his honor. In 2006, he was named to the inaugural class of the National Collegiate Basketball Hall of Fame.

Not much was written about Naismith until his grandson, Ian (pronounced "yawn"), was joined by his siblings and stepmother to preserve the heritage of the man and the principles of the game he so loved. In 1994, Ian Naismith formed the Naismith International Basketball Foundation to promote the growth of the game internationally and the ideals of sportsmanship. In the following recollection, the younger Naismith, the unofficial historian of the game's inventor, leaves no doubt that the good doctor was indeed a Jayhawk through and through.

★　★　★

My dad says God led my granddad to Kansas. He was attending Gross Medical School at the University of Colorado and worked as the YMCA director. He had a student die in a tumbling accident, and it had a huge effect on him. It was not his fault, but he could not live with what had happened. He didn't sleep much and lost 30 pounds in a short time. He began to question his faith. At the same time, the University of Kansas was looking for a school pastor and physical education director. It had contacted legendary football coach Amos Alonzo Stagg for a recommendation. He was a rugby teammate of my grandfather at McGill College in Canada. Stagg wired a message back to the school saying, "James is a medical doctor, a teetotaler, all-around athlete, nonsmoker, and owner of a vocabulary without cuss words." Kansas hired him immediately.

My granddad fell in love with the place right away. He loved the people. My grandmother was a New England girl and thought of Kansas as the "New Frontier" and would have liked to move back home. But she knew the place meant so much to my grandfather. It gave him a purpose that he lost while in Colorado. He would stay at KU 41 years until his death and be buried there. He liked teaching at KU so much that they waived the mandatory retirement age law for him. He would teach until 1937. My father, James, was born in Lawrence and graduated with an engineering degree. My mother, Frances Pomeroy, was from Holton and the daughter of state senator Frank Pomeroy. In 1933, she became the first female to graduate from the engineering school. I attended KU for two years and finished my engineering degree at Texas A&M. We were all Jayhawks.

Our family likes to say that basketball was born in Massachusetts but raised in Kansas. Oddly enough, nobody in my family played basketball in any organized competition. My grandfather played 11 sports, but basketball was not one of them. He played only two games, the first one ever at the Springfield YMCA and the first one at Kansas to show them how the game was played.

We kind of get a chuckle when people talk about Dr. Naismith being the only coach at Kansas with a losing record. He was very much a tactician and an innovator. However, when my grandfather first coached, his wife became ill with typhoid fever while pregnant with their second child. My grandmother nearly died twice and ended up losing her hearing. He stayed with her and missed many of the games. He would also serve as the official for the games and spent much of the time teaching not only the Kansas team, but the opponent, as well. He was not your typical coach. Many people do not realize he was the co-inventor of volleyball. He and one of his students in Springfield drew the game out on a napkin. They called it "Vrroom Ball" after the sounds airplanes would make. He also invented "Net Ball," which is a sport played by females, largely in the Caribbean.

The first game at Kansas was played in a skating rink, but it burned down. The first on-campus location was at Snow Hall. The ceiling was not high enough, so he had the floor dug out and re-poured. Once they outgrew Snow Hall, they built old Robinson Gymnasium. My grandfather oversaw the design and construction of Robinson. It was designed similar to the Springfield YMCA.

There are many stories out there about my grandfather's relationship with Phog Allen. They got along quite well. They debated about parts of the game, but both were gentlemen. He thought quite highly of Phog Allen. I've been fortunate to know every coach at KU since Allen. I met him when he was quite elderly. I remember I was waiting to get my hair cut. Phog was in the chair, and the barber and the others were talking about how Allen really deserves the credit for making the game popular. It wasn't Phog saying that, but the others. Now I was only 18, but I could not take it anymore. I said, "Hey, I'm James Naismith's grandson. He invented the game and brought it here." Phog smiled and told me I was right. He told me how much my grandfather meant to him, KU, and the game. We ended up doing some joint public appearances and became friends. I value my friendship with all of the Kansas coaches. I always enjoy going back to Allen Fieldhouse for games. It is a great atmosphere.

My grandfather had four doctorates and two master's degrees, but he always said his proudest moment was when the game was introduced as an Olympic sport in 1936. It showed that it was truly an international game. He had done so much to promote the game. He was the head of the rules committee, was the first president of the National Association of Basketball Coaches, and traveled the world to grow the game.

Dr. Naismith was a man of great integrity and treated everyone equally. He designed the game for his male students, but modified it once women showed interest and promoted it as a game for both sexes. My dad told me the story that there were a group of young female teachers who stopped by the Springfield YMCA on December 21, 1891, to watch the first game. Then they would stop by the next few weeks to watch the games. One of them finally got the courage to ask my grandfather why there were no women playing. Three months later, he had games for women, as well. I think that young lady may have had ulterior motives, however. She became my grandmother.

He also was color-blind. One day, a young black man came and stood in Dr. Naismith's office doorway and introduced himself as John McLendon. He said, "My dad said I should come see you, and you would take care of me." My grandfather said, "If your daddy said that, then we will." John was small, maybe 5'8", 130 pounds, but he loved basketball and wanted to coach. Dr. Naismith took him under his wing and taught him the game. He actually got him the job as head basketball coach at Lawrence High School in 1933. It was unheard of to have a black high school coach at that time.

John was the first African American to graduate from the University of Kansas with a physical education degree, doing so in 1936. My grandfather made it a requirement that every physical education major had to be able to swim. John was an outstanding swimmer from Kansas City, Kansas. One day, my father saw the janitor draining the pool and asked them why. He said that they were draining it because a black man had just finished and the white students were going to swim next. That got my father mad. He told the janitor to never drain the pool again for that reason. He had two football players guard the pool to make sure it was not drained and that John was not bothered. Of course, John went on to be an outstanding college coach and was named to the Hall of Fame. John and I were like brothers. He passed away in 1999, and I still miss him dearly.

I never really knew my grandfather, but he did leave his mark on me. I was born in Dallas in August 1938 and he took a train from Lawrence to baptize me. He stayed for three days with my parents and then he went home and passed away three months later. He put his hands on my head, and the family joke is that he called me the first dribbler.

I know what basketball means to the people of Kansas. That makes the whole Naismith family proud. I know it made my grandfather proud. The people of Kansas should know how special KU and Lawrence were to him. He spent 41 years of his life there and was buried there. He was a true Jayhawk.

The Original 13 Rules of Basketball
(written by James Naismith)

1. The ball may be thrown in any direction with one or both hands.
2. The ball may be batted in any direction with one or both hands, but never with the fist.
3. A player cannot run with the ball. The player must throw it from the spot on which he catches it, allowance to be made for a man running at good speed.
4. The ball must be held by the hands. The arms or body must not be used for holding it.
5. No shouldering, holding, pushing, striking, or tripping in any way of an opponent. The first infringement of this rule by any person shall count as a foul; the second shall disqualify him until the next goal is made or, if there was evident intent to injure the person, for the whole of the game. No substitution shall be allowed.
6. A foul is striking at the ball with the fist, violations of Rules 3 and 4 and such as described in Rule 5.

7. If either side makes three consecutive fouls it shall count as a goal for the opponents (consecutive means without the opponents in the meantime making a foul).

8. A goal shall be made when the ball is thrown or batted from the grounds into the basket and stays there, providing those defending the goal do not touch or disturb the goal. If the ball rests on the edges, and the opponent moves the basket, it shall count as a goal.

9. When the ball goes out of bounds, it shall be thrown into the field and played by the first person touching it. In case of dispute the umpire shall throw it straight into the field. The thrower-in is allowed five seconds. If he holds it longer, it shall go to the opponent. If any side persists in delaying the game, the umpire shall call a foul on them.

10. The umpire shall be the judge of the men and shall note the fouls and notify the referee when three consecutive fouls have been made. He shall have power to disqualify men according to Rule 5.

11. The referee shall be judge of the ball and shall decide when the ball is in play, in bounds, to which side it belongs, and shall keep the time. He shall decide when a goal has been made and keep account of the goals, with any other duties that are usually performed by a referee.

12. The time shall be two 15-minute halves, with five minutes rest between.

13. The side making the most goals in that time is declared the winner.

The
THIRTIES

DICK HARP

BASKETBALL ★ ASSISTANT COACH ★
MEN'S BASKETBALL COACH
1937–1940 ★ 1948–1956 ★ 1956–1964

To GAIN FULL APPRECIATION of Dick Harp's legacy in Kansas basketball history, consider the fact that the Jayhawks have played in the NCAA championship game eight times and that Harp was a significant contributor in four of them. No other coach or player in KU history has been on the Jayhawks bench in a national championship game more often. In addition, Harp is one of just six people in history to have played and coached in an NCAA title game.

He was a team captain his senior season and played a meaningful role in leading the Jayhawks to the 1940 NCAA national championship game. Later, as an assistant to Phog Allen, he was an important strategist in guiding Kansas to the 1952 national championship and a return to the national title game in 1953. He later replaced Allen as head coach and, in 1957, added another trip to the national title game to his basketball résumé.

Harp served as head coach of the Jayhawks from 1956 to 1964 and was named Big 8 Coach of the Year in 1960. In eight seasons as head coach at KU, Harp compiled a 121–82 record and led the Jayhawks to a pair of conference titles and two NCAA tournament appearances. He spent 13 years as the director of the Fellowship of Christian Athletes following his coaching career at Kansas. He also served on the staff of Dean Smith at North Carolina from 1986 to 1989. He died March 18, 2000, at the age of 81.

No basketball coach or player in KU history has been on the Jayhawks bench more often in a national championship game than Dick Harp. Of the eight times the Jayhawks played for a title, Harp was a player or coach for KU in four of them.

Note: The following quotes attributed to Harp and former player Al Correll are excerpts from a 1995 interview conducted by author Doug Vance for the book, *Max and the Jayhawks.*

★   ★   ★

"When all of the talk first started about retiring [as head coach at KU], Doc [Allen] didn't give any indication he wouldn't step down," said Harp. "As time went on, however, his close friends kept after him about it. When he finally got involved and made it an issue, he decided that he wasn't going to lose. He wanted one more season to coach. I think he really wanted to have the opportunity to coach Wilt [Chamberlain]. When he lost the battle and was forced to retire, he didn't take the news very well.

"I probably did change when I became head coach [at Kansas]. After the experience with [coaching] Wilt, I was a different person. I was really upset with some of the things [outside the program among boosters] that were done with recruiting. I reached a certain point and decided that I needed to give up the job because I had lost—not my enthusiasm—but my way in life.

"We had lost a home game to Kansas State at the end of the 1963–1964 season. We were having some guests to the house after the game, and I called my wife, Martha Sue, and told her I would be late. I went up and sat down on the grass under the Campanile Memorial. I was looking around and praying a little bit and probably crying a little when it started to rain. I thought, 'Okay, Lord, I recognize what you want me to do now.' So, I got up and went home and told Martha Sue that I'd decided to resign. She wasn't particularly happy with that decision, but it was my decision. That's the way it went."

★   ★   ★

Philadelphia proved to be fertile recruiting territory for Kansas basketball in the 1950s and early 1960s. Wilt Chamberlain and Wayne Hightower came from the "City of Brotherly Love" as did a 6'3" guard/forward named Al Correll.

In his debut season in 1960, Correll played an important role coming off the bench in helping the Jayhawks to a conference cochampionship. Kansas came within one game of advancing to the NCAA Final Four when Oscar Robertson scored 43 points in leading Cincinnati past the Jayhawks in the

Midwest Regional final. In a 1996 interview for the book, *Max and the Jay-hawks*, Correll recalled the pride Harp had in being a part of KU.

"Dick Harp loved KU," said Correll. "I know you are not supposed to love an inanimate object, but Dick truly loved the University. He felt when you put that uniform on, you were following a tradition of some great players, and we owed the players and the fans the very best we could give them.

"I remember a halftime of one game. Coach Harp would always get personal. He might tell Bill Bridges he was going to call his mother and tell her he's not doing this or doing that. We were sitting at halftime of a game, and he was really angry we hadn't played very well. I was there sitting in front of my locker watching Coach Harp, and his top lip was quivering as he looked over at each of us.

"In his own style, he was almost in tears. He was telling us that these people in the stands have been spending their day working out in the fields of Tonganoxie and all these little towns, and they've put up their hoes and they've come up here to Lawrence, down the turnpike, to see their Jayhawks. He asked us to give them our best performance and nothing less. We probably didn't have an appreciation for what he was saying. But we knew he felt it in his heart.

"To Dick Harp, wearing the Kansas uniform has a special significance. One night, we had finished practicing, and we were not doing very well. It was my senior year, and I was the last one out of the locker room. As I was leaving, I looked out on the floor. The whole court was dark, but there was one light on above the big scoreboard shining down on the big *K* on the floor. Coach Harp was sitting there in a chair by himself on the big *K* with that light over his head. It was kind of an eerie thing, and I walked out to check on him. I looked at him and asked, 'Coach, are you all right?' He said he was fine, but he couldn't understand why a player wouldn't give his all and realize how important this game is and what it means to wear a Kansas uniform. He was really serious. I don't think I've ever felt as strange as I did at that moment. It really hurt him."

★   ★   ★

Jerry Waugh enrolled at KU about the same time that Phog Allen hired Harp as his first full-time assistant coach. Later, Harp lured Waugh from his position as basketball coach at Lawrence High School to be his assistant coach. They maintained a close friendship until Harp's death in 2000.

"He was like a lot of us," said Waugh. "He wanted very much to come to KU and play basketball for Phog Allen. To be a part of Kansas basketball was the heart of him.

"He was so proud of being at Kansas, to be a Jayhawk and be a part of all of this. I don't think there has ever been anyone who felt it as deeply as Dick Harp did.

"There is no doubt in my mind that Dick had all the ingredients to be a great coach. He was presented with the opportunity he had wanted all of his life: to come back to the University of Kansas and be the head basketball coach. If anyone had a dream, Dick had that one and saw it fulfilled. Then, when he got that dream, he didn't enjoy it."

★   ★   ★

Harp did live the dream of being a Jayhawk, and his playing and coaching résumé reflects many contributions to the school's basketball heritage. He reached the national championship game as a player, assistant coach, and head coach.

Unfortunately, he concluded his coaching career at Kansas in regrettable fashion as he battled alumni influence in recruiting at KU and the lack of success on the court.

"Dick had a great coaching mind," said Waugh. "As a technician, there were no superiors. I believe without question that Dick had a significant influence on Dean Smith and that influence was also reflected in Roy Williams. Many of the things Dick did as a coach technically were a part of the philosophy of Dean and Roy.

"But Dick didn't have total control of recruiting at KU, and that troubled him. Dick wanted to exclude the involvement of alumni in the recruiting of athletes. He went to the administration at that time and asked for their support. He was turned down. They were people of great influence, not only in athletics, and keeping them away would be a hot potato the administration didn't want to touch.

"In his own eyes, I think Dick saw himself as a failure. I don't think he walked away from all of this feeling fulfilled."

Bill Hougland, a starter on the 1952 national championship team at KU, credits Harp as being the catalyst in the Jayhawks' NCAA title quest.

"I don't think we would have ever won the championship had it not been for Dick Harp," said Hougland. "Doc was great with motivation, and Dick was the one who developed the strategy. I remember that we lost at Kansas State midway through the season, and Dick decided we needed to change our defensive philosophy. We became much more aggressive and overplayed everyone. If someone got by you, Clyde [Lovellette] was in the middle to deny anything easy at the basket. That was all Dick's doing, and it made a big difference in our ability to control the game."

★   ★   ★

Harp was an influence on some of basketball's greatest players and coaches. He was a teammate of Ralph Miller at KU, and among the former players he's coached are Clyde Lovellette, Dean Smith, and Wilt Chamberlain, all inductees in the Naismith Basketball Hall of Fame. Harp also hired as an assistant coach at Kansas Ted Owens, who later guided the Jayhawks to a pair of Final Four appearances after replacing him as head coach.

And, as his last contribution to Kansas basketball history, he was the first person to recommend to then–athletics director Bob Frederick that he consider hiring Roy Williams as head coach.

In tribute to Harp, Dean Smith, the legendary North Carolina coach, called him "one of the most brilliant basketball minds I have ever known." Harp also faced adversity during his coaching career, dealing with public pressures of following Allen as head coach and the racial overtones prevalent in America for college teams with African Americans on their roster.

Harp graduated from Rosedale High School in Kansas City, Kansas, and served in the U.S. Army during World War II. He was also head basketball coach at William Jewell College and spent 13 years (1964–1983) as executive vice president of the Fellowship of Christian Athletes. From 1986 to 1989, Harp served as an assistant to Dean Smith on the North Carolina coaching staff.

After returning to Lawrence, following his stint with the Tar Heels, Harp returned to campus and was a frequent visitor to Allen Fieldhouse and KU practice sessions.

16

Dick Harp (left) played for Phog Allen (right) at Kansas and succeeded him as head coach of the Jayhawks.

The FORTIES

RAY EVANS

FOOTBALL/BASKETBALL

1941–1942 ★ 1946–1947

IT WAS APPROPRIATE THAT, at Ray Evans's funeral, the closing hymn was a medley of "The Rock Chalk Chant," "The Crimson and the Blue" (alma mater), and "I'm a Jayhawk." That, in a nutshell, signified the reverence he had for his school and the spirit in which he supported it. Along with teammate Otto Schnellbacher, he earned the university's first All-America honors in football in 1947. Evans was also a Helms Foundation Basketball All-American in 1942 and 1943. He is the only Jayhawk to have earned such dual-sport honors and to have his jerseys in both sports retired (No. 42 in football and No. 15 in basketball). At 6′1½″, 195 pounds, Evans was an agile, yet powerful force. Though quiet in nature, he was a fierce competitor and respected by all.

In football, Evans led the nation in passing on offense (1,117 yards) and interceptions on defense (10) in 1942. His school season passing mark stood until 1967, and his interception record remains today. He earned the nickname "Riflin' Ray" and "the Kansas Rifle" for his ability to pinpoint his passes. Legendary Minnesota coach Bernie Bierman called him one of the greatest all-around backs he had ever seen, and the *Kansas City Times* labeled him as "the league's [Big 6 Conference] best clutch player." The *New York Sun* selected him as the College Football Player of the Year in 1947, and he was elected to the College Football Hall of Fame in 1964.

"Ray was a natural leader and probably the best athlete I had ever been around. He had it all," said teammate Don Fambrough. "I told him if he wanted me to come to Kansas, I would go. I never regretted that decision. It was the best one I had ever made in my life. I always thought there were two categories of athletes at the University of Kansas—one category was for him and one was for everybody else. When you look at two things—Ray Evans as an athlete and man—he is in a category by himself."

Evans played one year professionally for the NFL's Pittsburgh Steelers, but was also drafted by the NBA's New York Knicks and was offered a baseball contract by the Brooklyn Dodgers. The annual Jayhawk defensive player of the year award and the indoor football practice facility are named in his honor. A successful businessman, he was integral in luring professional sports franchises to Kansas City (the Chiefs and the Kings), was selected by President Eisenhower to the National Council on Youth and was a Board of Regent for the state's universities and colleges from 1954 to 1966. Evans passed away April 24, 1999. His story is told by his son, Ray, who lettered for KU as a defensive back in the 1979–1980 season.

★　★　★

DAD WAS A QUIET AND HUMBLE PERSON, so I know it would not have been his idea to end his funeral with "The Rock Chalk Chant," the alma mater, and "I'm a Jayhawk." But still, I have to believe he was smiling down on us because KU meant so much to him. He never forgot that KU gave him the opportunity to succeed as a student, an athlete, and a person. My grandfather passed away when my dad was a child, and my grandmother had to raise the kids. It was tough back then during the Depression. Had he not received an athletic scholarship, he would not have been able to go to school.

Dad grew up in a very vibrant neighborhood in Kansas City, Kansas. They lived on Barnett Street, and there was always some type of game going on. I remember seeing pictures of my dad and his friends with "Barnett Street AC" (Barnett Street Athletic Club) stenciled on their shirts. He was a great high school athlete and was heavily recruited by KU and Missouri. He always thought of himself as more of a football player than a basketball player, but it was Phog Allen who convinced Dad to go to KU. Phog was so personable and charming, and there was no way Dad was going to turn him down.

When Dad first got to KU for football, they had a wide-open offense. There was a lot of passing. He actually played halfback most of the time. He would receive a pitch and then roll out and throw the ball downfield to Otto

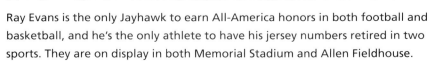

Ray Evans is the only Jayhawk to earn All-America honors in both football and basketball, and he's the only athlete to have his jersey numbers retired in two sports. They are on display in both Memorial Stadium and Allen Fieldhouse.

Schnellbacher most of the time. He told me many stories of how great Otto was as a receiver. Dad was part of that group of guys who had their careers interrupted by World War II. I vividly remember his telling me that they beat Kansas State in the final basketball game of his sophomore year on a Saturday, then on Sunday he and a few of his teammates were driven to St. Joseph, Missouri, where they enlisted in the Air Force. That was a great team that could have won the NCAA title, but everyone went their own separate ways that day. He actually continued to play football in the service as they traveled around the nation. I remember his telling me that the competition was tough just to make the team. The games featured stars from both college and the pros. He even played a game in the Rose Bowl in front of a pretty big crowd. They played the games to raise money to purchase war bonds. He was fortunate he did not have to go overseas, but he was in Cuba for a while. He said his biggest challenge came when he was officer of the day on the last day of the war. He said everyone was taking jeeps and other supplies. It was his job to try to keep order, which was impossible to do.

Don Fambrough tells the story that Dad was the reason he came to KU. Fam went to Texas his first two years, then entered the service and met Dad while they were stationed in Colorado. They played on the same football team and developed quite a bond. Dad was that quiet leader, so I know it was not a "Rah-Rah" speech to get Fam to return with him to Kansas. I think it was more of how Dad talked with great pride about the school, the campus, and the community. He always took such pride in KU. I think that rubbed off on the guys. Some pretty good athletes came to KU after the war, including Fam, Hugh Johnson, and Red Hogan.

My dad told me that coming back to KU was exciting. The war had ended, and college campuses were growing quickly. I think KU tripled in size. Memorial Stadium did not have the upper level at that time, so the games were always packed. They had two great teams under George Sauer, who was the coach. His senior year they qualified for the Orange Bowl, which was Kansas's first bowl game. They lost to Georgia Tech [20–14] when they fumbled going in for the winning score. It was KU's only loss, but they still won the Big 6 Conference title. Sauer left after that [to head coach at Navy], and my dad felt that was a big loss for Kansas. He always thought Sauer could have made Kansas into a national power.

The Orange Bowl was a big deal. It was a national game. I remember Dad telling me about a group of his friends who loaded up a flatbed truck with about 20 guys and drove all the way down to Miami and back. My dad was not only proud of KU, but proud of the state of Kansas. Most of that team was made up of Kansas kids, and I know that meant a lot to him. The other game that meant a lot to him was the Oklahoma game in Norman his senior year. The Sooners were favored to win the league. KU scored late in the game to tie it at 13–13. Oklahoma fought back and was driving for the winning score behind Darrell Royal [future Texas coach] at quarterback and Jack Mitchell [future Kansas coach] at receiver. They were deep in our territory when Dad intercepted the ball on the last play of the game. He ran it back almost all the way and was tackled fairly close to the end zone. He said that was an extremely hard-fought game and the point when they started to receive national attention that season.

Missouri was rival for Dad, and that continued later in life. He wanted to beat Kansas State, but pulled for them when they were playing someone else. Growing up in Kansas City and working there, he lived the KU-MU rivalry. He was a calm guy, but even he got fired up for the Tigers. One of my fondest memories was going to a basketball game at the Hearnes Center when it was fairly new and seeing him and my uncle Roy get a kick out of our beating Missouri. They enjoyed walking out with big smiles while the Missouri fans were complaining. My uncle Roy really stuck the needle in them.

Dad had opportunities to play professionally, but I think he was ready to get on with his life. Pro sports weren't as big as they are now. He wanted to get married, start a family, and get on with his life. He became a banker and got involved in the community and KU. He felt blessed and wanted to give back. As a family, we went to all of the home football and basketball games, and even some of the road games. But he never pressured me or my sisters to go to KU. He wanted to us to do what was best for us. Of course, all I knew was KU. I know it made him proud to see me play for the Jayhawks.

DON FAMBROUGH
FOOTBALL ★ HEAD COACH
1946–1947 ★ 1971–1974, 1979–1982

DON FAMBROUGH, in his deep, gravely voice, will never hesitate to remind anyone within earshot that he's probably the only major-college football coach who has been fired twice from the same school—the University of Kansas. He will quickly add, with a stern conviction, "But, I still love the University of Kansas." It's doubtful that anyone is more loyal to their alma mater. As a guard and kicker for the Jayhawks in 1947, he was a significant force in helping KU to its first Orange Bowl. He earned All–Big 6 honors in 1946 and 1947. He went on to serve as a graduate assistant coach under J.V. Sikes and spent 19 seasons as an assistant coach at KU under Sikes, Jack Mitchell, and Pepper Rodgers. Fambrough was selected as head coach of the Jayhawks twice and led the team to the 1973 Liberty Bowl and the 1981 Hall of Fame Bowl. He was named the Associated Press Big 8 Conference Coach of the Year in 1981. Fambrough, who also served as assistant director of the Williams Fund, has played or coached in five of the 11 bowl games in which the Jayhawks have appeared. "Fam," as he's known, continues to be a regular at Jayhawk practices and consultant to those coaches who walk the home sideline at Memorial Stadium.

★   ★   ★

I GREW UP IN EAST TEXAS and lived on a cattle ranch about 15 miles from town. We lived just outside Longview, a town of 7,500 about 125 miles east of Dallas. Our nearest neighbor was probably 10 to 12 miles down the road, so I didn't have anyone to play with as a kid. My mother was very excited about the prospect of my going to college on scholarship some day and was determined to help me achieve that goal. I would be the first one in the family to attend college.

I loved football. You have to understand that Texas is a state that loves its high school football. In my day, it came before college football, and there was very little pro football at that time.

I was interested in kicking extra points and field goals, so my mother and I made a goal post out of three pine trees. She would get out there and hold the ball for me. She was not only my mother, she was my best friend, and she was my holder for kicking!

My father was just the opposite. He was an old, hard-nosed rancher and figured if you could read and write a little bit, that's all you needed. He was a cattle rancher and foreman of the ranch. He spent his whole life in the cattle business and had no interest in the fact that I wanted to attend college and play football someday. It was all my mother.

The first year I got involved in organized football was in junior high. They furnished all the equipment we needed except football shoes, and my folks couldn't afford to buy me shoes.

I was on the team all year but never played a single down. We only had about 14 or 15 players on the entire team.

We qualified for the league championship and were scheduled to play Henderson, a town that was about 30 miles down the road. My mother was determined that I was going to have a pair of football shoes for that last game, and she baked cakes, did that sort of thing, and finally saved enough money to buy me a pair of shoes. It was like someone had given me the moon.

We went to Henderson and were all in the locker room getting dressed. I was showing off my new shoes, so very proud, when the head coach came up to me and asked what size shoe I wore. As it turned out, our starting quarterback had forgot his shoes.

"Fambrough, you're going to have to give your shoes up," said our coach.

Well, I really didn't mind that much. I was just going to sit on the bench with my uniform on like all season. The only difference was that I sat there barefoot.

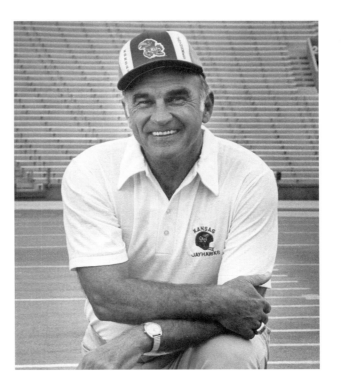

Don Fambrough, who helped KU to its first-ever Orange Bowl appearance as a player in 1948, served two different stints as head coach of the Jayhawks. He has played or coached in five of KU's 11 bowl appearances.

In the beginning of the second half, our running back got hurt. The coach came up to me and said, "Fambrough, you've got to go in." I pointed at my feet and told him, "But, Coach, I don't have any shoes."

He looked me in the eyes and barked, "Son, do you want to play or not?"

Well, I came off that bench like I was shot out of a cannon. Somehow, I ran for three touchdowns in the second half playing barefoot. There were 22 players on the field, and 21 of them had on those long football cleats. We won the game, and after it was over my feet looked like they had been in a meat grinder.

The next day the newspaper made a big thing out of my playing barefoot— one of the statements in the story was that they didn't know if I was that fast or I was just afraid I'd get my feet stepped on.

Pretty soon after that game, Christmas came along. Like I said, the people loved their football and their football players. I received 38 brand new pairs of football shoes from various people in town.

That got me started on the road to being a good football player. Three years later, we won the state football championship, and I was fortunate to make first-team all-state. I was recruited to play at Texas by Coach D.X. Bible, who was a legend at that time.

I played my freshman season for Texas, and we were selected for the Cotton Bowl. Most of us were headed for military duty, and they had put us in the reserves to help keep us from reporting before the bowl game. We were granted a "delay en route" so we could play in the Cotton Bowl game. One day I was in the Cotton Bowl and the next I was in the Air Force, marching on the drill field.

I wanted to be a fighter pilot in the worst way. But I got washed out of that opportunity because I couldn't land the airplane. The instructor knew how much I wanted to be a pilot.

"It's pretty important to know how to land the plane," he reminded me.

That was a great disappointment but proved to be a blessing for me. I was waiting to go to officer candidate school, and that's when I met Ray Evans, the greatest athlete and finest gentleman I've ever been associated with in my life. We were sent to Colorado Springs and, when we arrived, found out we were supposed to report to the football coach. We didn't even know they had a football team in the service.

Ray and I became close friends. He was a captain and I was a sergeant, which meant he was my commanding officer.

He told me once, "Don, if we ever get out of this mess, we're going back to Kansas to play football together."

We had a lot of free time, and someone had given me a book that described William Quantrill's raid on Lawrence. I read about what a sorry so-and-so he was and how he came over and left the city in smoldering ashes, killed all the men, and raped all the women. I read that and developed such a hatred for that person.

When Ray said he wanted me to go back to Kansas, I told him, "Sir, I will follow you to Russia. I will follow you to Germany. But, I will not go with you to Missouri."

He said, "Don, we only go over there once every two years and kick their ass and come back home."

Later, when I was a coach at Kansas, I used to tell my players about what Quantrill did in Lawrence and I then explained that he attended the University of Missouri. It served as good incentive.

After the war, I was back home in Texas. By that time, I was married and had a little boy. I got a call one day from Ray, inviting me to come up to

Lawrence and look over the University of Kansas. I had already told Coach Bible that I was returning to Texas, and I had so much respect for that man that there was no way I could break my word. I told Ray that, but he still insisted that I come up for a visit.

Well, I rode the train to Kansas City, and they picked me up. From the very moment I stepped off that train and started meeting all of the people from the University of Kansas, I fell in love with the school, the people, and the town. I kept thinking that, if I had to do it all over again, this is where I would want to attend school.

KU's head coach at the time was George Sauer, who had played for Coach Bible at Nebraska. I told him that in any other situation, I'd be here in a second. But I couldn't go back on my word to Coach Bible. He understood and indicated he would also have trouble calling his old coach.

The time came for me to catch my train back to Texas. I went by the football office in old Robinson Gym to tell the coaches good-bye. When I walked into Coach Sauer's office, he told me that there was someone on the phone who wanted to talk with me. Of course, it was Coach Bible.

I don't think I've ever been as scared and nervous in my life. I almost melted in my shoes. I picked up the phone and said, "Yes, sir."

He said, "Don, you know I coached George Sauer at Nebraska and he's just like a son to me. We used to play Kansas, and it's a great school. Since it's one of my former players and I know you are going to get a first-class education, then you have my permission to play for the Jayhawks." I told Coach Bible thanks, and that's how I ended up at KU.

I went back and got my family, and we lived in the Sunnyside Apartments for $18.25 a month. I was 26 years old with a wife and a child.

Well, we had a hell of a football team. We were all so thankful to be out of that war and back to normal life. Nobody had to tell us to go to class or see a tutor. I spent four years in the military and didn't like one second of it. I was so happy to get out, go back to school, get my education, and play football.

It's hard to describe how I feel about the University of Kansas. I've probably been to every campus there is and know for a fact there is no place that can compare to KU. I came of age there, and both of my boys graduated from KU. My wife taught school in Lawrence for 30 years. We were so proud, and I'm still so proud that I can tell people I went to school, played football, and coached at the University of Kansas.

JERRY WAUGH

BASKETBALL ★ ASSISTANT COACH
1947–1951 ★ 1957–1960

Jerry Waugh suggests there is no significance to the fact that his birth date (February 12) mirrors that of former president and noted orator, Abraham Lincoln, hall of fame basketball player Bill Russell, or one of the most memorable characters in Kansas basketball history, Scot Pollard.

But spend time with Waugh and you will quickly learn that he is a man of great inspiration, who carved out a basketball career as a defensive specialist and, although nowhere close to the label of "flake," enjoys reminiscing about teammates who shared that characteristic.

Born in Wellington, Kansas, the same year, 1927, that Babe Ruth hit 60 home runs, Waugh was the youngest son of Camille and Joe Waugh. He enrolled at the University of Kansas in the spring of 1947 after spending two years in the service. He started four years for the Jayhawks as a 6′0″, 155-pound guard. He graduated in 1951, just missing the 1952 national championship season. He later served as an assistant coach to Dick Harp from 1957 to 1960, helping tutor the legendary Wilt Chamberlain and the Jayhawks in the 1957 triple-overtime national championship loss to North Carolina. He also served as an assistant athletics director at KU. Later in his career, Waugh was a significant force in amateur golf in Kansas. He was director of the Kansas Golf Association from 1979 to 1991 and was tournament director of the Kansas Open for 18 years. He was inducted into the Kansas Golf Hall of Fame in 1998 and is also a member of the KU Athletics Hall of Fame. He worked as women's golf coach at KU from 1991 until he retired in 1998. He remains a frequent visitor for KU basketball practice and has been known as a source of wisdom and advice to most of the KU head basketball coaches over the years.

★   ★   ★

I WAS RAISED IN A SMALL TOWN where exposure to education and athletics was limited for most of us. It was rural, by and large, and the horizons for young people coming out of that community were not set very high.

We lived modestly in Wellington, and my parents had a limited education—both graduated from high school—so the standards for my future were not too well established. The parameters at that time in my life were not set very high.

Somehow, *sports* stepped into the picture. My dad never coached me, but he presented me with opportunities to learn sports. He put a big backboard on a large elm tree in the backyard and poured sand to level out the ground, and that was my introduction to basketball.

I was about 10 years old at the time and spent many days on that makeshift backyard court. Like any young kid, I was fantasizing about being a star player and making the winning basket in a game at New York City's Madison Square Garden, which, at that time, was the mecca of college basketball.

I practiced and eventually played in high school and KU. My senior year in college, I actually got to play in Madison Square Garden, and we beat St. John's 52–51. They were ranked second in the nation, and we were ranked fourth. I think that's always a good story to tell kids. You have a dream when you are young and it can happen.

My mother, on the other hand, kept me humble. She had two brothers who were athletes, and I believe she was always upset that she did the work around the house while they were out playing. It seemed there was a deep resentment somewhere from her past. I remember when she was mad at me, she would say, "Jerry Waugh, I've never known an athlete that was worth a damn."

In today's environment, it's fair to say that Mother had part of it right!

But, as it is for any young man, I did have a dream. I didn't realize it at the time, but that dream would take me to KU to play basketball.

The road to KU wasn't all that established. I was influenced by several KU alumni in the community who followed sports at Wellington High School.

One of those people was John Stewart, and his family continues to have a long history of support for KU. They were the ones who directed me toward college.

There were no athletic scholarships at the time. I was fortunate because I went directly into the military out of high school for two years and, when I came out, I had financial aid that enabled me to attend college.

Since the war was coming to a close, I didn't have to serve overseas. Most of my duty in the military was at Fort Benning [Georgia], where I was a paratrooper. I played on the parachute-school basketball team. My coach actually attempted to persuade me to reenlist for three more years, but I rejected that life because I didn't feel there was any stability in the military and you were forced to move around the country all the time. Ironically, I became a coach and ended up moving around the country all the time!

I decided to attend KU when I was discharged from the Army. I did have some interest in Oklahoma State and Fort Hays State, where my high school coach—Cade Suran—had gone to coach the basketball team.

It's funny now, reflecting upon it, but neither Henry Iba, head coach at Oklahoma State, nor Phog Allen of KU ever talked with me about coming to school and playing basketball. I was not recruited by the coaches, but that was a normal routine for kids at that time. In fact, I didn't meet Doc Allen until I came out for basketball.

I left the military late in the fall of 1946, enrolled at KU in the spring of 1947, and was added to the basketball roster. At that time, Howard Engleman was the interim head coach because Doc Allen had been knocked to the floor in practice and had a head injury. Engleman took over the team in early January and finished out the season. It was decided that I wouldn't play in any games, so I just practiced with the team. They had a veteran group that included Charlie Black, Ray Evans, and Otto Schnellbacher.

My addition to the team was somewhat political. There was a fellow named Harlan Altman, a football player at KU, who was a classmate of Engleman's. Altman's father was from Wellington and, along with Stewart, was a big influence in my attending KU.

The next year was my first introduction to Doc Allen, and that first practice was a circus. There were more students coming out for basketball—I'd say between 60 and 90 kids—than I had seen in all my life.

Jerry Waugh was known as "the Sheriff of Sumner County" during his playing days at KU. The nickname was bestowed on the Wellington native for his defensive prowess.

Our first game was at Emporia State, and our best returning player—Schnellbacher—had not yet joined the basketball team. He was still playing with the football team, which was preparing for the 1948 Orange Bowl game.

I played in the JV game and a little bit in the varsity game. Emporia had a good team that year, and we lost 67–44. The next game I started and, as it ended up, I started every game the remainder of my career—except for a few games my sophomore season when I had an ankle injury.

The injury was a high ankle sprain that I suffered in practice. I had a hard time recovering and, as a result, saw my starting position lost and my playing time diminish. It started to bother me.

Doc Allen was always quick to say, "My door is always open to my players." So I made an appointment and intended to let him know about my frustration. I never will forget the moment I walked in his office. He immediately raised up from behind his desk to shake hands. Doc was a great handshaker. That's what he would always do…he'd walk in a room with his hand out.

We both sat down and went through the pleasantries, and I finally said, "Doc, I want to talk about my playing time."

That's when he said, "Now, before we start, I want you to know, there is no one that thinks more of you than I do."

And, as I will always remember, he completely disarmed me. I had practiced what I was going to say. I wanted to talk about not being treated properly, that I was a good player, but he never did give me the opportunity to say those things.

I told him, "Well, I just know that I can perform better."

He immediately struck his desk with his hand, pointed at me, and said, "You'll start the next game."

I said, "Doc, I didn't come in here to demand I start. I just want to play!"

He hit desk again, and repeated, "You'll start the next game."

I did start the next game and I actually exceeded all of my previous performances. I played every minute of every game the rest of the way. In retrospect, I always wondered if he manipulated me as a player to that level of play. I pondered that later as coach and wondered if he had those insights to recognize that here was a player who's ready to play. As a coach, I choose to believe that was his approach.

It was Doc's coaching philosophy to use only about six or seven players if the game was in question. He believed in having a big team, but only the top six or seven players saw much action. Everyone was considered a part of the team, and he stressed it was a family.

I had success playing defense and the ability to defend any position with the exception of the post player. If the other team had a guard or forward who was the leading scorer, he would be my responsibility. I took that challenge on early in my career, and that helped me make the team. I could run with people.

KU had a creative sports publicist named Don Pierce. From his typewriter, Pierce would pound out stories and send them to newspapers, and he created the nickname for me, "The Sheriff of Sumner County…He always gets his man." Pierce even arranged for a publicity picture of me in a cowboy hat, guns, and sheriff's badge that he sent out to the newspapers.

I remain extremely proud that the neighborhood in which I grew up produced three players—Ernie Barrett at Kansas State, Harold Rogers at Oklahoma State, and myself—and we were all team captains at our respective schools at the same time. We just lived a few blocks apart in Wellington.

There was a story that appeared in *The Daily Oklahoman*, the newspaper in Oklahoma City, that quoted me as saying, "There's nothing to playing defense. You just hang your nose on the guy's belt buckle and run with him."

Rogers later told me that Coach [Henry] Iba cut that article out of the newspaper, took it to practice, showed it to his players, and said, "They might as well give that young man his degree right now, because he understands how this game is played."

I took pride in being a good defensive player. Defense is all about paying attention to what you are supposed to do. It's not that difficult.

My playing career came to a surprising and disappointing halt at the end of the first semester of my senior year. The fact wasn't clear until near the end of December of the 1950–1951 season. Because I had enrolled a semester early, my eligibility was up, and I didn't get to play the second semester. We had no idea that that was going to happen until the Christmas Tournament when the Iowa State coach, Chick Sutherland, informed Doc about the situation.

That was terribly disappointing.

Early in my coaching career, I sometimes felt I was not totally prepared to develop my team. It seemed that somewhere along the way I had missed something. I noticed the kids were not learning what I was teaching. I didn't know if I was teaching the wrong things or if I was a poor teacher.

I studied Iba's approach to coaching. I noticed his players were indoctrinated from day one about what was expected from them. His rules said, "This is what you do on *day one*, and this is what you do on *day two*." There was never any question in Iba's mind that through this indoctrination, there were no shortcomings in this approach. Everything Iba's teams did was very precise. Eventually, it all fell into place for me as a coach. There was influence from both Coach Iba and Doc Allen. What I learned most from Doc Allen was how to work with people. I believe his success was along those lines more than anything else. He knew how to motivate people.

Doc Allen always said you win on the mistakes of your opponents, not your good play. I'll always remember that. Thus, as a coach, I tried to organize my teaching based on eliminating those mistakes that would get us beat and focus on the little things.

Young coaches, I believe, like to organize practices to teach all of the great plays they can run to win a game. Older coaches look at how they can lose and you coach not to lose. Young coaches coach to win. Of course, you can argue that point all night, but that's what I believe.

I always admired the coaches who stressed discipline—people like Iba and Bobby Knight who demanded a lot from their players.

34

I never saw myself as a great leader or anything special, but I tried to do all the right things. There is a little ego in all of us. To excel, there has to be a little bit of self-importance in you.

Doc Allen taught us to have great pride that we played at Kansas. I recall that, when I was a high school coach in Arizona, my stature was very high because I played at Kansas. I came from a school that had a reputation as being an outstanding basketball program.

It's often said that kids are different today. I don't buy that. If I had to pick two things that are vital for kids, I would say they need love and they need discipline. Young people today are the same as they have always been. They are impacted by a different society than we were when I grew up. But they have those same needs.

I personally don't like the adulation that goes along with college basketball today. Basketball was just a small part of my life at KU, and I was into the mainstream of the student body. I was Jerry Waugh, who belonged to a fraternity, who also played basketball and had lots of friends. That's who I was. That part has changed for today's college basketball player at high-profile schools.

Doc Allen instilled pride in his players about being students. It was not just basketball, but it was the university. I believe the University of Kansas is better than Kansas State University. That was ingrained in me from the very beginning. I don't say that in any way to belittle Kansas State. They talk about Snob Hill. So much of that was feeling good about yourself, and Doc Allen hammered that belief into his players.

Doc Allen spent 39 years at KU and developed those many traditions and that heritage of greatness we all share as players. He did it by telling the same stories over and over again.

I suppose it's like the old Indian chiefs who would gather around the campfire and tell of past victories to the young braves and ingrain a sense of pride in the tribe. This is who we are, this is what we've done, and this is what our future is. Doc did a great job talking about players like Paul Endacott and Tommy Johnson. He would go on and on about players and outstanding achievements. He told those stories to me for four years. I know who those people were and I take great pride in being a part of who they were and a responsibility for the future of the program.

I've learned along the way that it is my responsibility and the responsibility of each player to help protect the heritage of Kansas basketball. If a coach falters, then it is our duty to step forward and say we need to make a change.

35

My experience at KU as a player under Doc Allen launched my coaching career. When I left KU and applied for my first coaching job at Emporia High School, Doc Allen wrote a letter for me to the school superintendent.

He wrote, "This young man is as clean as a hound's tooth."

I was meant to be a coach. I was meant to work with young people. That's who I am.

MARILYNN SMITH
WOMEN'S GOLF
1948–1949

MARILYNN SMITH MIGHT NOT BE the most recognizable name in Kansas Jayhawk athletics, but she may be the most decorated. On October 30, 2006, Smith was inducted into the World Golf Hall of Fame. It marked the eighth hall of fame to which she has been named, including the KU Athletics Hall of Fame in 1999. Ironically, Smith never was an "official" Kansas athlete. The athletic department did not sponsor any sports for women at the time, so she struck out on her own to establish herself as the top collegiate female golfer of her era. Today, the university honors her with the Marilynn Smith Intercollegiate Women's Golf Classic, held annually in Lawrence.

★   ★   ★

"I was a pretty good amateur golfer," Smith said, "and Ohio State hosted a national championship for collegiate women. My dad went to Phog Allen, the athletics director at the time, and asked if he would cover my entry fee ($5) and expenses. He told my dad, 'Mr. Smith, it's too bad your daughter is not a boy.' But I went anyway and finished second in 1948 and won it in 1949.

"I had a wonderful time at KU. I remember when I first went there, the campus and community were beautiful. The fall was especially pretty with all of the trees changing colors. I was a member of the Kappa Alpha Theta sorority and became president of the sophomore class. I had excellent grades

When Marilynn Smith's dad went to KU athletics director Phog Allen to ask if the athletics department would pay his daughter's $5 entry fee and expenses to compete in the national championship golf tournament, Allen turned him down and said, "Mr. Smith, it's too bad your daughter is not a boy."

in high school, but they slipped just a bit in college. There was just so much to do…maybe I was having a little too much fun.

"I played golf at Lawrence Country Club with a few women, mostly with Ruth Hoover, who was the head of the women's physical education department. But I also played with the men and never had any issues. I never sensed that people in the community did not like female golfers.

"There was not a professional golf tour for women, but there were some tournaments and clinics where some money could be made. But my parents and I thought it would be important if I pursued an education first. I wanted to be a physical education teacher. I also took classes in journalism.

"After winning the second national championship, the Spalding equipment company came after me to play in tournaments and do some clinics. My teachers wanted me to finish school. I was one of very few women who Spalding approached. They offered me $5,000. My dad said, 'Opportunity only knocks once,' so I took up the offer and left school. They signed me to 27 one-year contracts, just like Walter Alston of the Dodgers."

Born April 13, 1929, Smith moved from Topeka to Wichita as an infant. She was the typical tomboy growing up, playing sports and mixing it up with the boys. Her dream was to be a pitcher for the St. Louis Cardinals. But one day after a particularly poor performance, she came home and used an expletive in front of her parents. Her mother proceeded to wash her mouth out with Lifebuoy soap, and her father looked for a more ladylike activity for his 11-year-old daughter.

"They took me to take lessons at Wichita Country Club. I really did not want to do it because I thought golf was a sissy sport. I took the lessons the boys did, and it came pretty easy to me. I don't think some of the boys liked me because I got to be better than them."

She went on to compete in several city tournaments and won the Kansas women's amateur state tournament in 1946, 1947, and 1948.

Smith's trailblazing mentality did not stop after signing the first contract with Spalding. In 1950, at Rolling Hills Country Club in Wichita, Smith and 12 other female golfers formed the Ladies Professional Golfers Tour (LPGA). That group included Olympian Babe Didrikson Zaharias. Members of the LPGA played in 13 tournaments with a total purse of $50,000 that first year—compared to today's total prize money of more than $50 million.

"Those early days were fun, but we had some struggles. We didn't have plane tickets, so we would load up in cars and drive around the country. We would drive some 1,600 miles from Spokane, Washington, to Waterloo, Iowa, for a tournament. We played in many small cities.

"But golf opened the world up for me. I played in 36 different countries and with five presidents: Eisenhower, Nixon, Kennedy, Ford, and Bush [Sr.]. I met thousands of people. I don't think I would change a thing."

Smith estimates she taught more than 4,000 clinics during her time. She won 21 LPGA events, including two major championships. In 1973, she became the first female commentator for a men's professional golf event as she worked the 1973 U.S. Open and Colonial Invitational Tournament.

Though she lives in the Phoenix, Arizona, metropolitan area, Kansas is never far from her heart.

"I am proud of being born and raised in Kansas and going to KU. I watch the sports teams on television and keep up with friends whom I went to school with. There are quite a few Kansas graduates here, and we get together often. I still have a Jayhawk decal in my car window and a vanity plate that says 'Kansas Jayhawks.'"

The University of Kansas annually hosts the Marilynn Smith Sunflower Invitational Golf Tournament.

BILL HOUGLAND

BASKETBALL

1949–1952

BILL HOUGLAND DISPLAYS HIS WARM, ever-present smile as he sits proudly behind a large wooden office desk in his Lawrence home.

Surrounding Hougland and occupying most of the available wall space are clusters of framed pictures which present vivid storylines reflecting success in athletic competition, enjoyment of the outdoors, a deep devotion to family, and a commitment to his alma mater.

Anchoring one corner of his desk and casting a shadow across the table-top is a 12-inch-tall bronze Jayhawk statue, a limited-edition casting from the KU Alumni Association that was a gift from his five children. It's obvious that the unique-looking, oversized KU mascot—because of its weight—would be a serious challenge to move from its assigned space on Hougland's desk.

Spend a short amount of time talking with Hougland and you will also learn that the immense bird on his desk is symbolic of the rock-solid feeling he has about KU in his heart. Both the statue and what it represents should be considered permanent fixtures.

Since rising from his small-town Kansas roots to earn a national championship banner for his alma mater and two gold medals for his country, as well as carving a 30-plus-year professional career as president of one of the state's most successful business entities, Hougland has remained dedicated in support of the school that launched him into adulthood.

He has changed home addresses, changed his team uniform, and represented more than one successful business. Throughout it all, however, he's never switched his allegiance to a university that is symbolized by that mythical bird known as a Jayhawk.

Following graduation from Beloit High School in 1948, Hougland arrived at Mt. Oread simultaneously with three other small-town Kansas recruits—Bob Kenney (Winfield), Bill Lienhard (Newton), and John Keller (Page City). Also enrolling at Kansas that season—thanks to the creative recruiting of head coach Phog Allen—was a tall and talented center from Terre Haute, Indiana, named Clyde Lovellette.

Their arrival signaled the start of a quest by Allen and assistant coach Dick Harp that was realized four years later when the Jayhawks captured the NCAA championship and later represented the USA in Olympic basketball competition.

"The most important thing, for me, is the friendships we made along the way," says Hougland, who retired and moved back to Lawrence in 1994, following 30 years as an executive with Koch Oil Company in Wichita. "That's why we wanted to come back to Lawrence. It's a place that's very special, and many of my best friends from KU also are here."

Hougland was known for his all-around skills as a basketball player. His modest career scoring average of 5.9 points per game is more of a statement about a coaching philosophy. "Our job was to play defense, rebound, and get the ball into Clyde," recalls Hougland. "We didn't need to be scorers with Clyde on the team."

★ ★ ★

I WAS BORN IN CALDWELL, KANSAS, but our family moved to El Dorado about six months later. My dad managed a J.C. Penney store and often employed some of the boys part-time who played on the junior college basketball team [Butler County Community College] in town. I often did part-time work around the store while growing up and would enjoy hearing them talk about basketball. As I got older, they included me in their pickup games. They were older, bigger, and more experienced, which probably helped me develop as a basketball player.

We played a lot of basketball around town or wherever we could find a hoop mounted on something. There were kids in my neighborhood who also liked playing basketball. Dad had nailed a goal up on our garage, but we had a gravel driveway. I'd practice there quite a bit.

Our family moved to Beloit just before my junior year in high school, and Dad opened up a hardware store. I played all of the sports and was pretty good in basketball, football, and track. Our basketball team went to the state playoffs both my junior and senior year, but we lost in the semifinals one year and the finals the next year.

Don Fambrough was an assistant football coach at KU, and he actually came to Beloit my senior year and offered me a scholarship to play football. I was quarterback and could throw the ball way down the field. That's what appealed to Don. In those days, they were looking for players who had strong arms and could just heave the ball a long distance and let the receivers go get it.

I never seriously considered playing football in college. I wanted to play basketball for Doc Allen.

Both Dick Harp and Doc Allen had recruited me to play at KU. I know that it has been told many times that Doc instructed Dick to promise some of us whom he recruited that year that, if we came to KU, we would win a national championship and later win an Olympic gold medal. That may have been said, but I don't really remember now if it actually happened. Of course, that prophecy did come true.

42

I enrolled at the university as a freshman and had what you would call a partial scholarship. They paid my tuition and books the first year. I was on a full scholarship the last three years. Of course, we had to work for that scholarship.

One year, I tended to the wire baskets that held students' clothing in the PE locker room. We also had to sweep the stadium after football games and sold programs during the games. By the time I was a senior, I was assigned security detail at the entrance of the football pressbox. That was easy duty because hardly anyone ever came in there.

Doc always brought in a lot of players. I'm not certain why he did it, but we probably had 15 freshmen out for basketball and, at that time, didn't play any outside games. There was no freshman schedule. All we did was practice and scrimmage among ourselves. There were no restrictions on the amount of time you could practice. We had spring practice and, in fact, practiced all year long.

We were a very close team throughout the years and have remained close as time has passed.

Bill Hougland was a starter on the 1952 national championship team at KU and became just the second basketball player ever to win two gold medals in Olympic competition for the U.S.A.

We had modest success our first couple of years. We were cochampions of the Big 7 Conference my sophomore year, going 14–11 overall, and eventually losing to Bradley by two points in the NCAA district playoff game in Kansas City. Clyde [Lovellette] was a force from the very beginning and established himself as one of the best players in the country.

Clyde was very strong and dominated because of his size and skills. He was not known, however, for his leaping ability. I'm not certain if he could dunk the ball. He probably could, but just barely. Of course, it was not legal in those days.

We had a better overall record [16–8] my junior year, but we finished second in the conference so there was no postseason for us. As I recall, we lost a lot of close games that season, including a heartbreaking 39–38 loss at Missouri.

Between my junior and senior seasons, I got married. In fact, there were four of us—[John] Keller, Lovellette, and [Bill] Lienhard—who all were married that summer.

We were all confident we would be a great team by the time we were seniors. The lineup included Lovellette, [Bob] Kenney, Lienhard, Dean Kelley—who, along with his brother, Al, were important players also from a small Kansas town [McCune].

We got off to a great start and won our first 13 games of the season. Our first defeat, however, was in Manhattan against Kansas State in our 14th game. Four nights later, we traveled to Stillwater and lost by four points to Oklahoma State.

When we returned for practice the following day, Dick Harp changed our strategy on defense, and from that point on, we overplayed everything. If someone got past us, Clyde was there to clean up. It was a great strategy. We didn't lose another game the rest of the year, including the win over St. John's for the national championship in Seattle. We never would have won the title had it not been for Dick Harp.

I had injured my leg in the Kansas State game, and by the time we got to Seattle, it was really bothering me. In fact, I told Doc that I didn't think I could play. Doc had his son, Bob Allen, who was a doctor, look at it. He pulled out a long needle and numbed it. I don't know if it actually helped the injury, but I could play free of pain. I got in early foul trouble and had to sit on the bench for a while, as it turns out.

In those days, winning the national championship was not quite as big a deal as it is today. It was a great accomplishment, but I'm more proud of what happened after the tournament when we were selected to play on the USA Olympic team.

I guess marching into the stadium in Helsinki representing my country is one of my all-time great thrills. We played Russia in the gold-medal game, and they were not very good. But they stalled, and I hit a shot at the end of the first half to give us a two-point lead going into the locker room. We took over in the second half and won the game easily.

I was in the Air Force ROTC while at KU and was scheduled to report for duty right after I graduated. They actually delayed my reporting date so I could play in the Olympics. From the Air Force's point of view, I was representing the service when I played in Helsinki. A week after I returned, I reported to Mitchell Air Force Base in Long Island.

I spent time in Korea, but I was not a pilot. I worked what was called the "flight line" and did things like help haul the wounded from planes. As part of my duty in the service, I was also assigned to a base basketball team.

I went to work for Phillips Petroleum in Bartlesville, Oklahoma, following my stint overseas. In fact, a lot of KU people worked for Phillips. Doc played a role in that because one of his former players, Paul Endacott, was a high-ranking official with the company. K.S. "Boots" Adams, another influential KU grad with Phillips, was also anxious to have KU alumni work there.

45

The Phillips 66ers, of course, were a successful AAU basketball team that was sponsored by the company to help promote its name. Working at Phillips meant I would play on the team. We played about 50 games a year all around the country. We would play anyone we could schedule.

Being a part of that team opened up another opportunity for me to represent the country in Olympic competition in 1956. In those days, the Olympic team was determined by a round-robin tournament that featured the AAU champions, a college all-star team, and a service team.

We won the tournament, which qualified us to represent the country in the Olympic Games in Melbourne, Australia. They added three players to the roster from the college all-star team, including a pretty good center from San Francisco by the name of Bill Russell.

Before we left for Melbourne, we toured around the country and played all-star teams. We spent two weeks training at Bunker Hill Military Academy in Indiana, and I roomed with Bill. He was obviously a great player. One thing that sticks out in my mind is that Bill always seemed to get sick before games. It was his nerves, as I remember.

We won the gold at the Olympic Games. Once again, it was such a great thrill to be a part of that experience.

I was only the second USA basketball player to win two gold medals in Olympic competition. Bob Kurland [Oklahoma State] did it in 1948 and 1952. My kids used to take the two gold medals to school for "show and tell," and once one of them actually lost one of the medals on the playground. Thankfully, they were later able to find it.

I turned the medals over to the KU athletic department to display in its hall of fame in Allen Fieldhouse. I think that's the best place for them.

I left Phillips in 1961 because I wanted to live in Kansas. As I advanced up the ranks, it appeared I might be transferred to another state, and we wanted to live in Kansas. I went to work for Koch Industries in Wichita, where I spent 30 years. I retired in 1991, and we decided to come back to Lawrence.

The opportunities and friendships that resulted from my days at KU had a lasting impact on my life. From a business perspective, it opened up a lot of doors for me. There are so many other KU grads out there in the business world.

I was fortunate to foster friendships that have lasted a lifetime. I wouldn't trade my experience at KU for anything. It made a real difference in my life.

Hougland (back row, third from right) was a member of the 1952 NCAA championship team.

The
FIFTIES

CLYDE LOVELLETTE

BASKETBALL

1950–1952

KANSAS HEAD BASKETBALL COACH Phog Allen had a dream. In four years, the Olympics would be conducted, and that team would include members of the NCAA championship squad. Allen had enticed the top high school basketball players from the state of Kansas to commit to KU, but to realize that dream, Allen knew he needed a big man in the middle. He targeted 6′9″ Clyde Lovellette. To get the nation's top frontline recruit, he would have to get him to leave the shadows of the University of Indiana. Persistence paid off as "Cumulus Clyde" chose Kansas and became the first person ever to win an NCAA, NBA, and Olympic title. He fell short of winning a high school championship by one point at Garfield High School in Terre Haute, Indiana.

Lovellette was dominant at Kansas. As a senior, he led the nation in scoring at 28.6 points per game and was named the college player of the year as the Jayhawks defeated St. John's 80–63 to win the 1952 NCAA title. He was also the leading scorer on the United States' gold medal–winning Olympic team. He was the Big 7 Player of the Year three years in a row, leading the league in scoring each season.

Lovellette had a solid pro career, playing 11 seasons (Minneapolis Lakers, Cincinnati Royals, St. Louis Hawks, and Boston Celtics) and appearing in three NBA All-Star Games. He played a key role for NBA championship teams in 1954 (Minneapolis) and in 1963 and 1964 (Boston). In 704 games, he averaged 17.0 points and 9.5 rebounds. He played both forward positions and center, extending his shooting range beyond the paint.

Lovellette currently resides in the small town of Munising in the Upper Peninsula of Michigan. He has served as the varsity basketball assistant coach at Munising High School and is currently serving on the city council.

★ ★ ★

THERE WAS NO DOUBT I WAS GOING to Indiana. All of the coaches in my high school went to Indiana—the track coach, the baseball coach, the football coach, the basketball coach. If you were a hometown boy and you were good in basketball, you just were expected to go to Indiana. They never thought you would look at other places. Here is the thing about recruiting: when you don't show interest in the person, in addition to the athlete, you are doing the kid an injustice. I am not saying you need to wine and dine them. But Indiana just assumed I was going there. So I took a look at all of the schools in Indiana. I just did not want to be taken for granted. I visited North Carolina, Purdue, North Carolina State, Michigan State, Georgia, and some others. I went to quite a few places.

You have to remember that, in 1948, television was not in every household. I don't think we had one. All you heard or read about in Indiana was the Big Ten. You never heard about Kansas or anyone in the Big 6 or Big 7. So Kansas was never on the radar for me until Bob Nelson, who was a student reporter for the *Daily Kansan* and [assistant coach] Dick Harp came to visit. They were going to Chicago, I believe, but had heard about me, so they went a bit out of their way. It was during my senior year in high school. I really did not know about Kansas. Phog Allen was a legend, but not to me, because I had never heard of him. They [Harp and Nelson] just talked. They did not press me, however. They invited me to come to Lawrence for a visit and meet Phog Allen.

Gosh, I thought. *Kansas is a long way—three states away, and we don't do that.* I did not accept their offer. I told them I was probably going to Indiana. Later, I learned that Phog was going to St. Louis to make a speech. He asked me to take a train to meet him there. I did not want to do that, but I sort of said yes. But I sent my brother-in-law, Charlie. I had a hard time telling anyone no, even when I wanted to do so. So Charlie went to St. Louis, met Phog, and told him that I would not be coming. Phog said, "We're going to

Clyde Lovellette (shown here with coach Phog Allen) became the first person ever to win an NCAA, NBA, and Olympic title and also the first to lead the nation in scoring and take his team to the NCAA championship.

Terre Haute." Charlie told him I was going to Indiana. But Phog didn't take no for an answer.

So one day, I was sitting on the front porch with my father and I saw this huge Cadillac, or maybe it was a Chrysler New Yorker, coming down the road. It was the biggest car I had ever seen. I just knew it was Phog. I could see Charlie sitting on the passenger side. I told Dad I was going in the house and to tell Phog I was going to Indiana just to get rid of him. So when Phog came to the porch and asked if he could talk to me, my dad said I was in the house. Phog found me on the back porch. We talked. I don't know how long it was. But we talked and we talked and we talked. Phog was a marvelous talker. He said, "You know, we have this good group of kids at Kansas, and we have a few more coming in from Illinois. We have the nucleus of a great ballclub, but I am lacking someone inside. I think we can accomplish a lot with someone like you. I think we can do two things. I think we can win the national championship, and I believe we can go to the Olympics. But I don't think we can do it without someone like you in the middle. I've never seen you play. I'm taking the chance. I would like you to come to Kansas, see what we've got. Then you can make a decision."

I told him I did not want to go. But the next thing I knew I was in his car headed to Kansas. I had never been away from Mom and Dad for a very far distance or a long time. I wanted them to go, but they couldn't. This was summertime, and I stayed a few days. The campus was about 7,000 students, so it was not as big as Indiana's. I visited the campus and met some of the other kids from Kansas—Bill Hougland, Bill Lienhard, and Bob Kenney. I went back on the train. When I got on the train, I still thought I was going to Indiana. I got off the train at Terre Haute and met my parents. We talked about it. I told Mom and Dad that it would be a nice place to go, but we all thought it was too far away. They told me I could make the choice. I went back to Indiana one more time for a visit. I really never paid attention to this before, but it was a huge campus, and I seemed to get lost among all the people. I thought, *Good gosh, this is huge.* I met with Branch [McCracken, Indiana's head coach] to talk. He had no idea I went to Kansas for a visit. I came back home, and that is when I gave Kansas serious consideration.

51

We called Phog and told him it was between Indiana and Kansas. He asked if my parents and I could come for a visit. Mom was impressed by Phog. He was ever the charmer. Dad liked the farm country and became comfortable. I did not know the tradition of Kansas, but after you go there, you can feel it. It meant so much to the people there. These guys were honest. They weren't blowing smoke. They weren't giving us anything other than the love they had for Kansas. There were not inducements. All they were selling was an education and a chance to play. Phog had great confidence in what he was doing and he transferred that to his players. He was a special person. I miss him to this day.

I committed to Kansas during that visit. Phog wanted me to stay because school was going to start soon. But I had to get clothes and other stuff. So he drove us back to Terre Haute. I got my belongings, and then we turned around and headed back to Lawrence. I think he did not want to let me out of his sight. He probably thought that, if he wasn't around, that I would go to Indiana. I don't know who told Branch McCracken that I was not going to Indiana—it was probably my mom. I still think that there are a lot of powerful people in the sports world in Indiana who don't think highly of me. They don't say it. They treat me well, but the underlying current is that I let them down. It took me a long, long time to make the Indiana Hall of Fame. I think it's too long to let stuff like that hold on.

The people were so genuine in Lawrence. That is one reason I really loved Kansas so much. The people did not seem so phony. At a lot of the colleges, the people seemed fake. They really tried to flatter you. They never seemed sincere. I never had that feeling at Kansas. They wanted to be friends with me, not just the ballplayer. I met so many wonderful people who became lifelong friends.

Lawrence was perfect for me. I did have asthma as a kid, and that concerned my parents. Phog always said there was something healthy about Lawrence. He said that it had this rarified air. He told my mom, "You'd be surprised how much the air would help him." He said that "by my treating him, Clyde will not have asthma." And I didn't. Doc treated all of his players. He was a tremendous osteopath. He also treated many of the top professional athletes who came from all over to see him.

I really think I fit in well with the team because they were all from small towns. I think we were the same type. I felt a very good relationship with the Kansas boys, which is what we predominantly had. We had one thing in mind, and that was to win the NCAA championship and the Olympics. As far as meshing, I had a great relationship with the guys and still do.

I've always said that Phog was like a second father to the boys. I never saw his door shut. You could always find him to talk. But, if you weren't doing something right, then Mom or Dad would be on your case, and he would be on your case. He would write your mom. One time, he wrote Mom about my not paying a bill. He wanted to make sure Mom knew what was going on. I just forgot to do it. I thought that it was great he chose to write to our parents. I still have a few of the letters.

He was ahead of his time in a lot of respects. We experimented on a 12-foot goal sometimes. He said it would not make any difference, because if you are a big man, you are still closer to the rim. He said, "Don't worry about it. You just have to adjust your shot." That was a big adjustment. It was terrible. You felt stupid and clumsy. I did not like it. I even tried it in the pros. The people in the stands were laughing. He was always trying things out on us. The foot arch normalizer was another one. It was a rolling pin that was for your arches. It hurt. I got smart and instantly said my feet felt good so I would not have to use it. I do think some guys said it helped them.

Hoch Auditorium was an interesting home court. You had the curved wall on one side with bleachers on the stage, and then permanent seats on the other. We practiced in old Robinson and dressed there for games, too. We'd run to Hoch for the games—it seemed like a few hundred yards. We had a little room for halftime. It was so small. I think they stored chairs there. It was junky, but we did not know any better. The floor was directly on concrete. It was hard. Shin splits are the worst injury a player could have. It was painful. We put a piece of felt and wrapped it around the shin, then wrapped a piece of rubber around it to keep the muscle together. I knew he [Allen] had plans to build a fieldhouse, but there was no talk of its being ready for us. I did play one game there, however. It was an exhibition game between St. Louis and Philadelphia, when I played for the Hawks and Wilt [Chamberlain] for the Warriors. We had a great crowd, and it was good to come back. Wilt was an awfully, awfully good player.

The bad part of playing in Hoch is there weren't enough seats for all of the students. There was a lottery where they could get tickets for only half of the games. If we had an arena like Allen, we would have filled it. The fans were great when I played. I loved the fans. They are still great. That is what is special about coming back. They either remember who you are, or they have learned about you. I had my family with me, all five kids, grandkids, and nephews, when we went out on the court, and they introduced each ballplayer for the 100th anniversary celebration. When I stepped out, the applause seemed to go off the scale. It gave me goosebumps. After it was done, my youngest daughter, Shari, said to me, "You know, Dad, you're quite famous, aren't you?" It meant quite a bit to me to receive that reception.

The 1952 season was great. I almost missed the championship game, however. At the Final Four in Seattle, we beat Santa Clara the first night. Fig Newton was a Coast Guard officer and was a Sigma Chi fraternity brother from KU. He wanted to know if I could have dinner on the boat. Phog said yes, but I needed to get back to the hotel to have a good night's rest. This was the day before the championship game against St. John's. So I went out in the Puget Sound. It was a cutter or a buoy tender. There was huge fog. We had to sit out there. We did not have the radar equipment that they have today. It was getting late. So, finally, we got back to port. It was close to or after

53

midnight, I am not sure. But the lobby was empty except for a news reporter. He looked up at me and then looked down. I slipped into bed, and it was not very long that there was a rap on the door for breakfast. My tardiness was not printed, nobody said a word. I had a great game. I don't know how it got out, but the story of my adventure became known. I was worried. I thought people might have thought I was out carousing and drinking. I never took a drink. Good thing I had a good game and we won.

We came back to Lawrence for a parade. There were thousands and thousands of people. I asked if I could drive the fire truck. They said, "Sure, you can do anything. You just won the national championship." It was neat. Of course, the students had collected every issue of *Look* magazine they could and built a bonfire. They burned them all because that was the only publication that did not pick me as an All-American.

Phog was vocal on a lot of issues. He was probably one of the more prominent people of his time in college basketball. He did not spare any words if he was displeased. He called New York the snake pit of college basketball. I remember our sitting in the lobby of the Muehlbach Hotel in Kansas City, waiting to go to the airport. We were to play LaSalle in Madison Square Garden. The two officials were from the East. We weren't going to go until we got a Big 7 official. The phone lines were burning up, but we finally got one and we were off.

He was also concerned about gambling and point-shaving. We were not approached because we could not be approached. We moved as a unit. Phog, Dick [Harp], and [sports information director] Don Pierce kept us together. We were not allowed to get phone calls directly. They had to call Phog or Dick to get us. Everything went through Phog. He ordered all of our meals and made our travel plans.

I never regretted my decision to attend KU one bit. I enjoyed my time there. I enjoy my time when I get back. KU has always treated us well. Roy Williams was always good about connecting us with the new guys. I remember they gave rings to the 1988 national championship team. We didn't get rings when we played. I got a call from either [Bill] Hougland or [Bill] Lienhard, and he asked if I would pay for a ring if we had some made. I said sure. We got the rings, and then soon after I got the money back. Roy wrote a letter and said the athletics department was not going to let us pay for our rings. That was nice of him and [athletic director] Bob Frederick.

KU has always been a special place to me and it always will be.

GALEN FISS
FOOTBALL/BASEBALL
1950–1953

THEY SAY YOU JUDGE A MAN by the company he keeps. Galen Fiss was a roommate of basketball hall of famer Dean Smith, a teammate of the legendary Roger Maris, and shared a locker room with perhaps the greatest running back of all time, Jim Brown. Not bad for a kid who grew up in Johnson, Kansas, a town of 400 located in the extreme southwest corner of the state. Fiss may have rubbed elbows with some of the sporting elite, but in his words, his most valuable experience was that he was a Kansas Jayhawk. Fiss played on the freshman basketball team, was a member of the baseball team (catcher), and played football (fullback and linebacker). An All–Big 7 performer as a senior in 1952, he went on to play minor league baseball in 1953 and then served in the Air Force. In 1956, he signed with the Cleveland Browns, playing 11 seasons, highlighted by his captaincy of the 1964 NFL championship team. Fiss passed away July 17, 2006, at the age of 75 in Kansas City. His story is told through the words of his sons, who both played offensive line for the Jayhawks, Bob from 1977 to 1980 and Scott from 1983 to 1985.

★ ★ ★

"I remember my dad telling me the stories of when he was growing up, being huddled around the radio with my grandfather and uncle, listening to Kansas games on the radio," Bob Fiss said. "Being a Jayhawk meant everything to my dad. It was the center of our family's life. Even when my dad played for Cleveland, we'd pack up and move back to Kansas City for the offseason. He didn't want to be too far away from KU. When he retired from the Browns and we moved back for good, he made sure we made it to every home game—and quite a few of the road trips."

"Dad must have made a deal with the YMCA when he coached us in football," Scott Fiss said. "Every one of our games was at 8:00 AM so we could make it to the KU games on time. I can tell you that I changed out of my pads and into my clothes as we drove over to Lawrence quite a few times."

"Don Fambrough and Red Hogan came out to recruit my dad," Bob said. "They really did not have to sell my dad too much. They were also recruiting Ollie Spencer out of Ulysses, just 20 miles away. So it was kind of neat to have two small-town kids grow up just a few miles away and become NFL players. I remember Dad telling me that he and Spencer drove up to Lawrence together before their freshmen year and did not know a soul. So they stopped and called the head coach, J.V. Sikes. Mrs. Sikes invited them over for a piece of pie. I think that calmed their nerves. Dad said they each had quite a pit in their stomachs as they came over the hill and approached the campus. He said that if one of them said, 'Let's turn around,' then those two farm boys would have hightailed it back home."

"You have to understand where Dad came from," Scott said. "When he played high school football, the people would park their cars around the field and turn on their lights. That was their stadium. In basketball, he would play the first half and then go up in the stands and play in the pep band for halftime."

"I think after those first few days at KU, he felt he belonged because he proved he could play," Bob said. "It didn't matter where he came from once they saw him play. His nickname was 'Earthshaker' which I believe the *Daily Kansan* [student newspaper] gave him because he hit so hard. I think he surprised people because he wasn't that big [6', 208 pounds]."

"It was the thrill of my career to be associated with Galen," Don Fambrough said. "I guess if you had to write out the prerequisites of what you're looking for in a football player and person, it'd pretty much fit him."

While Fiss was a standout as a collegian, he made his mark in professional sports. Signed by major league baseball's Cleveland Indians, he was selected by the NFL's Cleveland Browns in the 13th round later that year. Fiss was never tendered a contract by the Browns because he was already playing

Galen Fiss was a product of the small town of Johnson, Kansas (population 400), but that didn't stop him from having a big impact in both college and professional football. He was an All–Big 7 performer at KU and played 11 seasons with the Cleveland Browns in the NFL.

baseball. He was assigned to the Northern League's Duluth-Morehead Indians, were he teamed with future New York Yankees All-Star Roger Maris. They went on to win the league title that year as Fiss hit .275 with three home runs and 27 RBIs. They became good friends and remained in touch as both called Kansas City home for a period of time.

Fiss's baseball career ended as he served a two-year stint in the Air Force, returning to try his hand at football with the Browns. His 11-year career included Pro Bowl selections in 1962 and 1963, and a title in 1964 with a 27–0 win over Johnny Unitas and the Baltimore Colts. Teammates called Fiss's performance in that contest "the perfect game," despite playing in the shadow of greats Jim Brown, Frank Ryan, Lou Groza, and Vince Costello. At a team reunion, the mild-mannered Fiss talked about his professional career with the Cleveland media:

"I played both sports in college, but never really thought about liking one or the other. It just so happened the Browns' contract offer after that one year in the Indians' organization was just better for me, so I signed with them. I enjoyed that one year in baseball. I was real nervous [joining the Browns as a rookie after the team won the NFL title], actually a little frightened because I just didn't really know what to expect. [Head coach] Paul Brown took care of that right away. He roomed me with [Hall of Fame offensive lineman] Mike McCormack. I knew Mike from my days at Kansas, and he showed me the ropes. I owe Mike for that."

It should come as no surprise that the Kansas football program bestows an annual award in Fiss's honor upon a student-athlete for exemplary service on the campus and in the community. Fiss's support of the university continued after his retirement from the Browns as he presided over the letterman's club, served on the university's athletic board, and on several search committees for coaches, including the one for basketball coach Roy Williams.

"I know Dad enjoyed being involved because he felt he needed to give back," Bob Fiss said. "He was intensely loyal to the coaches. He supported them in every way he could. I think they appreciated him for that. All the stories you hear about the Roy Williams hire are pretty much accurate. Roy was meeting with the committee and was just bawling about his love for North Carolina and how tough it would be for him to leave [as assistant coach at UNC]. All of a sudden, he turned and looked at my dad, who was tearing up, too. Roy stopped, and my dad blurted out, 'Roy, I respect you even more now. Nobody loves Kansas more than I do, and I know you can come to love Kansas, too. I want you as my head coach.' I always said my dad would cry at a perfectly hit 5 iron. He was such a passionate person and wore his emotions on his sleeve."

Shortly after Fiss passed away, *Kansas City Star* writer Joe Posnanski shared the thoughts of those who were friends and teammates of the unassuming man who grew up in the days of the Dust Bowl in rural Kansas:

Fiss had something inside him, something special, something they alternately call character and integrity, and gentleness and ferocity—though none of those single words captures it. He was the best man they knew. He was their captain. He was, simply, their closest friend.

Let John Wooten explain: "He was so strong. So right. He didn't waver. He was captain of our team in a very turbulent time in this country. It was black and white. But we always stayed together. That was Galen. When Galen talked, you never thought he was talking to you as a white man or a black man. He was talking to you as a man."

Let Vince Costello explain: "I was thinking about this. I knew Galen for 50 years. We were friends for 50 years. And during that time, I don't think we ever had an argument."

Let Mike Brown, Cincinnati Bengals owner and son of legendary Browns coach Paul Brown, explain: "Galen would look you in the eye. I remember he came to one of our games after he retired. My father introduced him to the team. He said, 'Here's my old captain.' And I could just tell from his demeanor that my father was proud to have coached Galen."

Let Paul Wiggin explain: "In society, we want greatness to be goodness. That was Galen Fiss."

Everybody loved Galen. After he played for the Browns, he settled in Kansas City, raised a family, and opened an insurance company his sons still run today. On Mondays after he retired, Fiss and Costello would meet a bunch of old-timers at The Other Place, and they would swap stories and lies, and Fiss held a contest to see who got stuck with the check. Everybody loved Galen.

AL OERTER

TRACK

1956–1958

Aᴌꜰʀᴇᴅ Aᴅᴏʟꜰ "Aʟ" Oᴇʀᴛᴇʀ Jʀ. didn't forget his days as a track athlete and student at the University of Kansas, but he didn't have any Jayhawk mementos on display at his home in Fort Myers Beach, Florida.

"I don't want to live in a museum," noted Oerter, when interviewed a few months before his death in early October 2007. "But, I certainly have good feelings toward the University of Kansas and my days in Lawrence."

Instead of reminders of the past, Oerter spent much of his later years in life creating works of art for the future. His abstract art was exhibited in shows around the country with a price tag that reached as high as $5,000. Oerter created a series of unique paintings he called "Impact Paints," which were created by the impact of an Olympic-weight discus. The result was dramatic and colorful, and freezes the moment of impact.

Oerter estimates he's thrown the discus more than 500,000 times in his lifetime. Four of those throws earned him Olympic gold and established him as one of the great American heroes of the Olympic Games. He won his first gold medal in 1956 at the Melbourne Games while he was a student at KU, upsetting fellow American Fortune Gordien and setting an Olympic record of 184'11". He also won gold in 1960 (Rome), 1964 (Tokyo), and 1968 (Mexico City).

Oerter, along with sprinter/long jumper Carl Lewis, is the only Olympic athlete to win four gold medals in the same event. During his career, he also

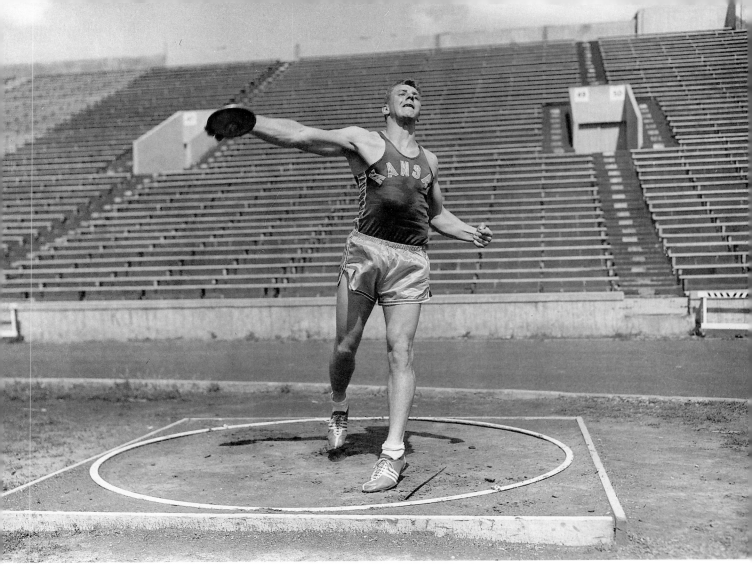

Al Oerter estimated he'd thrown the discus more than 500,000 times in his lifetime, and four of those throws earned him Olympic Gold. He carried the Olympic flame into the stadium for the opening ceremonies at the 1996 Atlanta Olympic Games.

set world records four times and set Olympic records in each of his four Olympic Games. At KU, he won the conference discus title three straight years and won two NCAA titles and six AAU championships. He graduated from KU with the 38 best discus throws in Big 7 Conference history.

His success is somewhat remarkable considering he was never trained by a discus coach.

"If I would have had a coach, I never would have stayed in sports. I made my own training schedule and didn't need anyone telling me what to do. If I was sick, I went home and didn't train; if I felt bad, I didn't train. If I felt like training for seven hours, I trained for seven hours. I didn't have a coach, but I trained harder than anyone else in the world. I think many great athletes fail because they depend on their coaches and not on themselves."

Oerter's teammate at KU and also an Olympian in the shot-put, Bill Nieder, called him "the finest competitor that had ever been in track and field."

Oerter retired from athletics after the 1968 Olympics. He did make an attempt to qualify for the American team in 1980, but finished fourth in the trials. However, he set his overall personal record of 69.46 meters (227′ 103¾″) that year at the age of 43.

Oerter carried the Olympic flame into the stadium at the 1996 Atlanta Olympic Games.

He has been inducted into the U.S. Olympic Hall of Fame and the U.S. Track and Field Hall of Fame. He returned to his alma mater in 2004 and was inducted into the Kansas Relays Hall of Fame.

★   ★   ★

MY PARENTS WOULD OFTEN SUGGEST that I was born with a stubborn streak. They would joke that, had I not needed someone to put a baby bottle in my mouth, I would have been out of the house right after I came into the world.

I was born in 1936 in Astoria, Queens, New York. My father owned a family plumbing business, later a construction business, that had been started by his grandfather. My mother, Mary, worked in film distribution for Paramount Pictures. She could tell you all the populations of all the cities in the country, and how many movie screens they had. My family, including my younger sister, Marianne, and I lived behind the plumbing store. I would often play stickball under the El of the Ditmars Boulevard train station.

When I was eight years old, I started lifting weights in the basements of some of the families from the old country that had immigrated to New York City. As they described it, lifting was a sport in itself in the old country, and they brought some of the lifting apparatus with them to the United States. As kids, we didn't try to get stronger for some sport. Lifting was almost a recreational activity. We thought it was great fun, and that continues today.

My father played semipro baseball and once played alongside future major leaguer Tony Cuccinello. Cuccinello was a third-base coach for the Cincinnati Reds and once evaluated me as a prospect. I pitched and played center field in sandlot ball. I could throw the ball right through you, but when I played center field, instead of throwing it to the catcher or shortstop, I threw it right over the stadium.

My mom died of cancer when I was 16 years old, and my heart just wasn't in sports for a while. I quit high school football, but I still loved to run. I lived roughly two miles from school and would run home every day after school and enjoyed doing that. I decided to go out for the track team in the spring of 1952.

I started out as a sprinter and then became a miler for a few months. But I kept growing. I was a horse. I'd run, and the discus kept skipping onto the track during practice as I ran past, so I'd throw it back. I threw it farther than the guy who was our regular in the discus. After that, the coach told me I was no longer a miler. It was one of those magic moments in my life.

My coach gave me a discus and a flipbook on techniques for throwing the discus. The book had progressive pages, so if you flipped the pages as fast as you could, you would see how the discus was thrown. On each page was a description on each individual move. I would sit in my English class and put my discus book over my English book and study it.

It paid off for me. I set a state discus record that stood for 13 years. People have asked how a New York City kid ended up at the University of Kansas. Well, there was no recruiting involved. My high school coach, Jim Fraley, was a graduate of Emporia State University and sent all of his good athletes to school there. If he had some that were really good, he'd send them to KU.

He contacted Bill Easton, the KU coach, and I was sent a one-way ticket to Lawrence. I actually went on an academic scholarship. At that time, if you attended college on an athletic scholarship and got hurt, you lost your scholarship. I was a good enough student, and I didn't want to be on an athletic scholarship. Obviously, Lawrence was a lot different than New York. You could actually walk out of town in 15 minutes. That's something I couldn't do in New York!

The Midwest was a difficult adjustment for me, and I actually tried to leave KU when I was a sophomore. I went to see Coach Easton and told him I had decided to go home. We had an argument about it. I made the long drive back home at semester break and contacted the coach at Penn State. He told me that he could arrange the same academic scholarship for me. Right before it came time to sign, I changed my mind. I told Penn State that I just couldn't do that to KU.

When I came back, I believe they put me on a football scholarship. That was done in those days because football didn't have a limit on scholarships. The football coach was Chuck Mather, and he kept trying to pressure me to play football. He even went to the *Lawrence Journal-World* and said some things about me and how strange it was that a guy with my size and strength wasn't playing football. I went out to watch football practice. It was the third or fourth day, and it was in the 90s. Really hot. They were in full pads and jarring the fillings loose in each other. That was enough for me. I couldn't see it.

I always told them that they make All-Americans in football every year, but they only make Olympic gold medalists once every four years.

Coach Easton didn't have any impact on me in terms of my progression as a discus thrower. Neither he nor his assistants really knew that much about the techniques, so they basically left us alone. He ran the team, of course, but we had our own regimen at practice. That was a good thing, because he used to have all of his runners on that toast-and-honey diet, which was not going to work for me at all.

There have been some things written that I used to arm wrestle Wilt Chamberlain when we were at KU. That never happened. Can you imagine where my hand would come next to Wilt's if we both had our elbows on the table?

But I got to know Wilt. He was actually a pretty good track athlete. I remember once in our locker room, which was under the stadium, a man came to see Wilt. His locker was next to mine. After he left, Wilt told me it was Abe Saperstein, the owner of the Harlem Globetrotters. Later, of course, Wilt left KU early to play for the Globetrotters.

After I graduated from KU, I went back to Long Island and took a job at Grumman Aerospace in computer programming, where I worked for 26 years.

I've had five or six careers in my life, including being a husband and father. I was involved with computers, a motivational speaker, I did some things at the Olympics, and now I'm an abstract artist.

The painting career took off when my wife got me a set of paints around 2002 or 2003. But I've always been fascinated by abstract art. My parents used to take me to museums in New York when I was young, and abstract artists became heroes of mine. I didn't know anything about athletes in New York until I was maybe 12.

I have done somewhere in the range of 250 paintings, and I'm active in selling art. I'm strictly an abstract artist.

Painting is much like training for the Games. You have to be very inventive. You have to persevere. You are constantly thinking about how to make things a little better. It's the same thing in art. You stare at a four-foot-square piece of white canvas. It's a thrill to put the first color on it, the first stroke, the first whatever. Then you watch something emerge out of that canvas. But it's a lot easier on the knees.

My wife, Cathy, and I have organized a group of athletes who are also artists. We call it Art of the Olympians, and it's a group of 14 Olympians representing seven different countries. We're taking our art show on tour.

I've had some health issues in recent years. I had congestive heart failure, but I'm doing better now. Doctors have indicated I need a new heart, but I ruled out heart surgery. I came into the world with one heart and I want to leave it with the same one.

I'm back working out in the gym and walking on the beach. I'm enjoying life.

WILT CHAMBERLAIN

BASKETBALL/TRACK

1956–1958

Wilt Chamberlain never sat down with the authors to tell them "what it means to be a Jayhawk." Instead, he told it to the world. On January 17, 1998, Chamberlain returned to his alma mater to help celebrate its 100th anniversary of basketball. Wearing the same letterman's jacket he donned as student, Chamberlain spoke from the heart in expressing his feelings for the school and its people. His address was part of the halftime ceremonies in which his No. 13 was retired. The Jayhawks went on to defeat intrastate rival Kansas State 69–62 that day. Sadly, Chamberlain would pass away just 18 months later, October 12, 1999, due to heart failure. What follows is his halftime speech:

A little over 40 years ago, I lost the toughest battle in sports in losing to the North Carolina Tar Heels by one point in triple overtime [national championship game]. It was a devastating thing to me because I let the University of Kansas down and my teammates down.

But when I come back here today and realize, not a simple loss of a game, but how many people have shown such appreciation and warmth, I'm humbled and deeply honored.

I've learned in life that you have to take the bitter with the sweet, and how sweet this is, right here! I'm a Jayhawk and I know now why there is so much

66

tradition here and why so many wonderful things have come from here, and I am now very much a part of it by being there [pointing to his jersey hanging from the rafters] and very proud of it.

Rock Chalk, Jayhawk.

Perhaps no University of Kansas student-athlete cast as large a shadow, both literally and figuratively, as Wilton "Wilt" Norman Chamberlain. Lured by the prospect of playing for the legendary Forrest C. "Phog" Allen, the 7′ Chamberlain matriculated to Lawrence from Overbrook High School in Philadelphia in 1955.

Allen gushed with excitement as Chamberlain announced he was coming to Kansas but, true to his witty nature, told friends and media alike, "I hope Chamberlain comes out for basketball."

Despite the racial tensions that existed during that time, Chamberlain was active in the community and on campus, and was well-liked by his classmates. He was dean of his pledge class and would eat at many segregated restaurants, waiting until he would be served. He took immense pride in his efforts to break down the barriers faced by blacks at that time.

Chamberlain was a person of many interests, as evidenced by his having his own 30-minute, weekly radio show on the student radio station KUOK. *Flippin' with Dipper* featured popular hits as well as commentary from Chamberlain. He would invite his teammates to join him on occasion. One such episode featured him playing the bongo drums and his teammates the spoons.

67

Freshmen were not eligible to play in varsity basketball competition, but Chamberlain's first year on Mount Oread attracted followers from afar. He debuted before 14,000 fans at Allen Fieldhouse November 18, 1955, leading his team to an 81–71 win over the varsity on Allen's 70th birthday. He had 42 points and 29 rebounds. After the game, Allen deadpanned that "Chamberlain could team with two Phi Beta Kappas and two coeds and give us a battle." It would be the last season Allen would coach Chamberlain, as a mandatory state law forced him to retire at age 70.

In two years on the varsity squad, Chamberlain was dominant. He averaged unreal stats of 29.9 points and 18.3 rebounds per game, and led Kansas to one Big 7 championship. His first game, played before an oversold Allen Fieldhouse (capacity 17,000) on December 3, 1956, saw him register Kansas single-game records of 52 points and 31 rebounds in a win over Northwestern. That

In his two varsity seasons as a Jayhawk, Wilt Chamberlain averaged 29.9 points and 18.3 rebounds per game in leading KU to two conference championships. The "Big Dipper" scored 52 points with 31 rebounds in his varsity debut versus Northwestern.

year, the Jayhawks advanced to the 1957 NCAA title game, falling in triple overtime to North Carolina 54–53 at Kansas City's Municipal Auditorium.

But Chamberlain was more than just a talented basketball player. In his freshman track season, he set the Big 7 freshman indoor record in the high jump, placed fourth at the Kansas Relays in the triple jump, and captured third in the Big 7 at the shot put. He went on to tie the Big 8 indoor record in the high jump with a leap of 6'6¼" during his junior year at KU in 1957–1958. He was a three-time league champion in the high jump.

Chamberlain left Kansas after his junior season and joined the Harlem Globetrotters for one year. He was then drafted by the Philadelphia Warriors of the NBA. It began an outstanding 14-year professional career that saw him garner Rookie of Year honors in 1960; earn four NBA MVP awards (1960, 1966, 1967, and 1968); win two NBA championships (1967 and 1972); be named to seven All-NBA first teams (1960, 1961, 1962, 1964, 1966, 1967, and 1968); be elected to the Naismith Memorial Basketball Hall of Fame (1978); and be honored as one of the 50 Greatest Players in NBA History (1996). He averaged 30.1 points and 22.9 rebounds per game, retiring as the NBA's all-time leading scorer and rebounder. He holds the NBA's single-game scoring record as he collected 100 points in a 169–147 win over the New York Knicks on March 2, 1962, in Hershey, Pennsylvania.

Chamberlain's return to Lawrence was long overdue. There were reports of a "few" visits to friends over the years, but no one realized his absence was due to the fact that he felt he let the fans down with the loss in the 1957 NCAA title game.

Former Kansas athletics director Monte Johnson and the late Bob Billings were teammates of Chamberlain's, and both were instrumental in luring him back. Though Johnson knew Chamberlain's health was failing, he sensed the weekend was emotionally and physically uplifting.

"Bob [Billings] and I spent Friday, Saturday, and Sunday with him," recalled Johnson. "We met him at a hotel in Kansas City, and I remember seeing him get off the elevator. In my mind, he looked as if he could still play the game. We later found out that Wilt was terribly sick. His sister, Barbara, later told us he had no business making the trip because of his health.

"But he was so committed. He was so sick with heart problems and bothered with his hip problems. He was almost deathly ill.

"He told Bob and I just before he left [back home to Los Angeles] that it was one of the most—if not the most—meaningful days of his life," recalled

Johnson. "And if you think about all of the meaningful days he had in his life—that is quite a statement."

Chamberlain clearly enjoyed himself during his return visit. It was his time to connect and reconnect. A media conference lasted approximately one hour, which was followed by more than another hour of one-on-one media conferences. He used the time to dispel any negative feelings about the university.

"A lot of people thought there was something missing between me and the University of Kansas in a negative way," said Chamberlain to a packed room of media types and fans. "But it was a great building block for me. It helped prepare me for life. I'm negligent in not being here sooner."

At the game that Saturday, plans were made to escort Chamberlain from the arena before the game ended for fear he would be mobbed by interview requests. He would have none of that. Instead, he asked administrators to put out a table so that he could sign autographs for fans who wanted one. He would remain after the game for more than two hours, signing and conversing with every fan who stood in the line that ringed the court.

Chamberlain left quite a legacy, but his last act was to give something that he could be remembered by and something that could benefit those less fortunate than he. He donated his prized letterman's jacket that he wore most of the weekend. In addition, his estate donated $650,000 to assist the athletics department in conducting an annual clinic for members of the Special Olympics.

"On Friday night, Bob hosted an event for Wilt at Alvamar Country Club, and he came over to my house to change clothes," said Johnson. "He brought in his suitcase, and I remember seeing him open it. Right on top of everything was his letter jacket. How many people would think to come back like that and bring their letter jacket? He had kept that, and his sister told us it was one of his prized possessions."

BOB FREDERICK

BASKETBALL ⋆ ASSISTANT COACH
ATHLETICS DIRECTOR
1959–1962 ⋆ 1963–1964, 1972 ⋆ 1987–2001

Bob Frederick, soft-spoken and always dapper, fidgets with the 1988 NCAA championship basketball ring on his right finger as he reflects on his life in sports. Boyhood memories of suburban St. Louis in the 1950s spill out, where his heroes played for the Cardinals and Hawks, and his mentors were a father who dreamed his son might some day play professional baseball and a high school coach who placed an emphasis on education and character.

Drama and disappointment enter the story when he transitions from high school to college, and the roadmap for his career in sports is established. It starts with the discovery of an astigmatism in his eye that leads to a last-second change in his college basketball plans and triggers a phone call from an obscure college assistant coach named Dean Smith to his old college coach at KU, Dick Harp. The altered career path now detours to the University of Kansas where, once again, he faces a setback. A freak knee injury limits him to just a brief appearance in one varsity game during his playing career. But the values he gained from his father and high school coach help him to persevere, and he remains committed to finishing his education and using the experience as the foundation to help launch his involvement in sports.

Those early experiences planted the seeds for a long, successful career for Frederick as a coach, administrator, and teacher. While his early involvement in athletics at KU lacks distinction, his status as significant leader in the school's proud athletic history is unquestioned.

During his eventful 14-year tenure as athletics director at the University of Kansas (1987–2001), Frederick hired a football coach (Glen Mason) who led his team to a pair of bowl victories, a basketball coach (Roy Williams) who guided teams to the Final Four four times, and hired coaches in baseball (Dave Bingham) and softball (Kalum Haack) who advanced their respective teams to College World Series championship tournaments. He also presided over a national championship in men's basketball.

During the 1992–1993 season, KU became the first school in NCAA Division I history to win a bowl game, participate in the men's basketball Final Four, and play in the baseball College World Series.

He orchestrated a $31 million improvement at Memorial Stadium. Also, under his watch, a new competition volleyball/basketball practice facility was built, and the $8.1 million Wagnon Student Athlete Center was constructed.

He significantly increased funding for women's sports, including the addition of rowing and soccer, and broadened emphasis on academic support in the athletics department. His influence was national in scope as he served as chairman of the prestigious NCAA Division I Men's Basketball Committee and as chairman of the NCAA Committee on Sportsmanship and Ethical Conduct.

Frederick's résumé also includes stints of coaching and teaching at high schools in Russell and Lawrence. He was an assistant basketball coach at his alma mater, as well as Coffeyville Community College, Brigham Young, and Stanford, and served as assistant athletics director and executive director of the Williams Educational Fund at KU. He also spent two years as AD at Illinois State.

Frederick left athletics and went back to the classroom fulltime in 2001, serving as assistant professor in the department of health, sport, and exercise science at KU. He also has worked as interim chair of the department.

He received all three of his degrees on Mount Oread, earning his bachelor of science degree in 1962, his master's degree in 1964, and his doctorate degree in 1984.

★   ★   ★

BECAUSE I GREW UP IN SUBURBAN ST. LOUIS in the '50s, my sports heroes were athletes like Bob Pettit of the St. Louis Hawks and Stan "the Man" Musial of the Cardinals. I believe it was around my senior year in high school when

Legendary North Carolina coach and KU alum Dean Smith, then an assistant at Air Force, steered Bob Frederick to KU to pursue a basketball career. When Frederick became AD and was looking for a basketball coach, it was Smith who suggested he consider an assistant on his staff by the name of Roy Williams.

Pettit scored 50 points against the Celtics and brought the first and only NBA title to St. Louis.

I have clear memories of warm summer nights and playing catch in my backyard with my dad while Harry Caray and Gabby Street described Cardinals games from the radio in our screened-in porch. Later, it was Jack Buck's voice that painted the picture for us. Both Caray and Buck are now in the Baseball Hall of Fame.

My dad was a major influence on my involvement in sports, particularly in baseball and basketball. He really enjoyed sports and took an interest in teaching me how to play. Dad was a pretty good basketball player, and I remember watching him shoot underhanded free throws with success.

Dad worked with me in baseball and made me a left-handed hitter and right-handed thrower with hopes it would contribute to a possible professional baseball career. I was a fairly good baseball player up until my freshman year in high school. At that point, I concentrated more on basketball and football.

Without question, the biggest influence on my life in sports was my high school coach, Denver Miller. He spent 43 years at Kirkwood High School and was an individual of great character and values. He placed an importance on education, and I can easily say that I never would have achieved the opportunity to be an athletics director had it not been for Denver Miller.

I was a good enough athlete to play both football and basketball. I was a tall, 6′4″ quarterback, and I could pass the ball down the field. There were about six of us being recruited to play at Missouri. As it turns out, the other five all ended up playing at Missouri. They backed off me by the time my senior season had ended.

Basketball turned out to be my best sport in high school. Early, during my senior season, Dean Smith started to recruit me to attend the Air Force Academy. Coach Smith was an assistant coach there and he came to St. Louis, visited with me and my family in our home, and took us to dinner.

I had not been serious about attending a military academy but decided to try that route. I did get accepted and was all set to play basketball and attend Air Force.

Then, about four weeks before I was scheduled to report, we received a telegram from the Surgeon General's office informing me that I was ruled physically unfit to enroll at the Academy. It had turned up during my physical examination that I had an astigmatism in one eye and that I would be nearsighted by the time I was in my mid-twenties. They had a rule in place at that time—which was changed just a few years later—that denied enrollment to students with this condition.

I think Coach Smith felt bad about the situation and placed a phone call to his old coach, Dick Harp, suggesting they take me as a walk-on in basketball at KU.

The Jayhawks had been on my radar screen as a possible college choice. I had been to the campus several times because my older sister, Susan, was a student there.

During my first year, I was a starter on the freshman team, and we often scrimmaged against the varsity. That was a good team that ended up being cochampion of the Big 8. Harp had a roster that included Wayne Hightower, Bill Bridges, and Jerry Gardner, among others.

It was obvious I would have to pay my dues to earn playing time as a sophomore. Hightower, Bridges, and Gardner were back, and we also had Nolen Ellison and Al Correll. The coaches affectionately referred to the backups on the bench as the "slugs" or "slug nuts." We ran the opponent's offense and defense in practice and always took a pretty good beating.

As it turned out, I got into one game—very briefly—during the first semester, and I believe it came against North Carolina. Little did I realize that would be the extent of my college basketball playing days. I was outside running during the semester break, stepped in a low place in the ground, and

74

severely twisted my knee. It required surgery in the spring, and my playing career was basically over.

I was considering transferring to Washington University in St. Louis, but Coach Harp encouraged me to stay involved with the program. I told him that I had interest in coaching, and he suggested that staying a part of the basketball program would be best for me in my future as a coach.

By the time I was a senior, I was working as a team manager. Coach Harp later brought me back as a graduate assistant coach, and that's how my 20-year coaching career got started. Coach Harp used to send me on the road to recruit, and I went to five of the seven Negro League State Tournaments around the country. I saw some great players.

Like any young assistant, I worked my way up the coaching ladder. I worked two years for Ted Owens, spent three years at Russell High School, and one season at Coffeyville Community College. I came back to KU for one season and then worked in the mid-1970s as an assistant at Brigham Young and later at Stanford.

I decided that I wanted to come back to Lawrence and start work on my doctorate degree at KU. I was hired as basketball coach and chemistry teacher at Lawrence High School.

During the spring of 1981, Tom Hedrick, who was broadcasting the KU games on radio, talked with me about taking over the Williams Educational Fund in the athletics department. He arranged a breakfast meeting for me with Bob Marcum, the new athletics director.

It was the three of us at Perkins Restaurant, and I'll never forget that Marcum told Tom to take care of the tab, and Tom had it in his hand as we approached the cash register. He leaned over and whispered in my ear that he had forgotten his wallet, and could I slip him enough to cover the charge? Of course, Tom promised to pay me back (I'm not sure he ever did). Thus I ended up paying for my meal at my own interview!

I worked four years as assistant athletics director in charge of the Williams Educational Fund under Bob Marcum and Monte Johnson. That experience opened the door for me to become athletics director at Illinois State [Normal, Illinois] in 1985.

After two years in Normal, then KU chancellor Gene Budig asked me to come back to KU and be athletics director. I had a decision to make because I had befriended the chancellor at a university in the Big Ten—whom I've never identified—and he told me that if I hung on for a few weeks longer he wanted to hire me as the athletics director.

But, coming back to the University of Kansas had more appeal. I took the job in 1987 for a salary of $74,000. My first year back at KU was a busy one. I made a difficult decision to change football coaches, and after early negotiations with Earle Bruce, the former Ohio State coach, broke down, we hired an up-and-coming coach from Kent State named Glen Mason. Midway through the basketball season, we were contemplating the possibility of hosting an NIT game. But the basketball team caught fire and won the 1988 NCAA national championship, and I found myself shaking hands with Ronald Reagan in the Rose Garden in early April. Immediately after the game, the whole episode of Larry Brown going to UCLA dominated our life, and keeping Larry continued to be an issue.

Meanwhile, Dick Harp was now on Dean Smith's staff at North Carolina, and he was already in my ear about a young assistant coach there by the name of Roy Williams. This was before we even had an opening.

Finally, Coach Brown decided to return to professional basketball. NCAA investigators were on the campus, and I had to find someone qualified to absorb the challenges of a storied basketball program, fresh from a national title, but under the dark cloud of serious NCAA sanctions. We went through a long search process, and the rest of the story, as they say, is history. We hired that unknown assistant from North Carolina whom Coach Harp was promoting to be our basketball coach and a short time later faced the jolt of the NCAA penalties.

It was certainly an eventful way to launch my 14-year tenure as athletics director.

I wouldn't trade those years at KU for anything. I've always been amazed at the emotional attachment that people have to the University of Kansas. I'm not sure there is another public university that has such a strong emotional attachment for alumni as this one seems to have. From my observation, it's tied to both the athletic and academic traditions. I believe they are unique and set us apart from most other public universities.

Walking down the hill for graduation is a memorable experience. Just like going to a basketball game in Allen Fieldhouse or seeing the fans wave the wheat at Memorial Stadium.

People don't forget about this place. It becomes part of their life forever. It certainly has for me.

CURTIS McCLINTON
FOOTBALL/TRACK
1959–1961

IT DOESN'T TAKE LONG TO DISCERN Curtis McClinton's deep and emotional appreciation for the opportunities the University of Kansas provided him. A three-time first-team All–Big 8 running back, he capped his career in 1961 with an All-America selection by *The Sporting News*. His 1,377 career rushing yards at the time of his graduation ranked fourth at KU behind Charlie Hoag, Homer Floyd, and Ray Evans. In addition, he was a three-time Big 8 high-hurdle champion, president of his Alpha Kappa Psi fraternity, an accomplished singer, and a member of the school's Fellowship of Christian Athletes chapter.

The Jayhawks tied for third in the Big 8 Conference in all three of McClinton's years of eligibility (1959–1961). Under Coach Jack Mitchell, Kansas was not afraid to take on all comers outside the league, either. In 1959, the team went 5–5, with losses to No. 7 TCU (14–7), eventual national champion Syracuse (35–21), and No. 18 Oklahoma (7–6). The 1960 edition of the Jayhawks went 7–2–1, finishing 11th nationally. The only losses were to No. 2 Syracuse (14–7), featuring All-American Ernie Davis, and No. 1 Iowa (21–7), while the tie was with Oklahoma (13–13). One of the greatest victories in Kansas football history came that year, a 23–7 win over No. 1 Missouri. That game would later be forfeited because it was determined that Jayhawk running back Bert Coan had received an extra benefit prior to his transfer from Texas Christian from alumnus Bud Adams. A football letter-man at Kansas and the son of Phillips Petroleum Co. executive K.S. "Boots"

Curtis McClinton ranks as one of the all-time great running backs in school history. He was a three-time all-conference selection and earned All-America honors as a senior in 1961. McClinton also excelled in the NFL and earned MVP honors for the league in 1962.

Adams, Bud Adams had provided Coan a flight to Chicago to watch an all-star game.

In 1961, Kansas was primed for a solid campaign. But the season began to unravel before it began. Coan broke his leg in spring drills and never did play. The team started 0–2–1 with one-point losses at No. 8 TCU (17–16) and Colorado (20–19) sandwiching a 6–6 tie with Wyoming. Six straight wins followed, moving KU to No. 10 nationally. A regular season–ending loss to

Missouri (10–7) ended any conference title hopes. The team went on to defeat Rice (33–7) December 16 in the Bluebonnet Bowl for the program's first-ever bowl victory. The Jayhawks finished 15th in the final UPI poll.

McClinton went on to a stellar career with the Dallas Texans/Kansas City Chiefs, earning MVP honors for the league in 1962 and the 1963 AFL All-Star Game. He was an AFL All-Star in 1962, 1966, and 1967, and played on the 1966 and 1969 Super Bowl teams. McClinton never lost his zeal for advancing himself, earning a master's degree from Central Michigan, a doctorate from Miles College in Birmingham, Alabama, and continued postgraduate studies at the Wharton School of Business at Pennsylvania and the Kennedy School of Government at Harvard. He was deputy mayor for Washington, D.C., before returning to Kansas City in 1992. He has been active in the community, founding the Black Economic Union and the Curtis McClinton Keys Youth Football League, and serves on the KU Alumni Board of Directors.

★   ★   ★

79

I HAVE BEEN BLESSED. There are many bricks with my name on them. I am proud of that. But that is not what I believe is most important. What is most important is the mortar that holds those bricks together. I was fortunate to grow up in a family of educators. I had many positive influences and many mentors. The University of Kansas is a major part of that mortar. [Head football coach] Jack Mitchell, [head track coach] Bill Easton, [chancellor] Franklin Murphy, the teammates that bonded together, the professors, my classmates—they are the mortar. They are what helped make me what I am today. The University of Kansas is a wonderful place. It challenges you. It provides you the opportunity to build relationships and to succeed. It proved to be a fertile soil for me.

I was recruited by the Big 7 schools and schools back east. Lynwood Sexton, my sixth-grade teacher and a person who played a pivotal role in my life, really brought my attention to those schools because of the academics. I attended Wichita University and played on the freshman team in 1957. I really was not mature enough at the time to leave home, to be very frank. I then went to the service as a reserve in the signal corps for six months in Fort Gordon, Georgia. Chuck Mather was the coach at KU when I was in high school. I did not have a particularly good feel for Mather when I was recruited, but he had some good people on the team. Most of them were from Ohio or they were Kansas boys.

After the service, I decided I wanted to get away from home. It was just a maturation process for me. I decided to go to KU because I knew Jack Mitchell, the head coach. He was the head coach at Wichita University [1953–1954], and my family had gotten to know him while I was in high school. I followed his career when he coached at Arkansas [1955–1957], so perhaps it was divine guidance that I ended up at KU. I had to sit out as a transfer [1958], and that helped me learn Mitchell's system and get established academically.

I was a high school All-American as an end. Mitchell loved to build teams with speed, so many of his linemen actually played fullback or running back in high school. I think he saw the speed and power I had as a hurdler and wanted to put it to use in the backfield. He ran that pigeon wing-T, where the halfbacks faced the quarterback at a 30-degree angle. He put me in at wingback, where the end would split out and I would be a lead blocker, go out for a pass, or carry the ball. My time was pretty evenly divided between running, blocking, and receiving. We really had some fine athletes in the backfield at the time, including John Hadl, Doyle Schick, Hugh Smith, Bert Coan, and others. We lined up against the best teams and showed we stacked up well against them.

I improved as a running back, but I never really became a complete one until I was under the tutelage of Hank Stram with the Chiefs. In fact, coach [Don] Fambrough lobbied hard to keep me on the line. He was an assistant at Wichita University for my freshman year, and he knew what I could do. He became an assistant to Mitchell and was a tremendous mentor. He'd often put me on the line during practice, but Mitchell didn't want that. To this day, I am sure Coach Fambrough thinks I was a better lineman than a running back.

My relationship with Jack Mitchell was superb. It was an honor to play for him. He knew my goal at Kansas was not only to play sports, but to graduate and be successful. He also knew I could be headstrong. But he allowed me to do what I needed to do to be successful. He knew how to read people. Mitchell was a great general. He was 60 percent people and 40 percent task. I think he knew how to read me because he knew my parents from our days in Wichita and he knew they were never really far away. My father was the first black state senator and spent much of his time in Topeka. My mother got her master's in education from KU the same time I was going to school. She spent her summers in Lawrence, so Coach Mitchell and she became friends, and knew that I could not act up too much.

It was a racially charged time in our nation, but I never felt the university discriminated against me. Most of the team was from Kansas, a free state, or from back East. We were close as a team. Our goal was to kick ass. Everyone took lessons from the same textbooks and had the same teachers. It wasn't quite the same in the community. Blacks could not sit in the same theaters as whites. We had to sit upstairs. Once Chancellor Murphy heard about this, he started bringing movies to campus and showing them to everyone. The businesspeople did not like that. They eventually changed.

I met Bill Easton my redshirt year. He was never one to extend himself overtly. I just went to him and told him I wanted to go out for track. In reality, I did it because I did not want to go out for spring football. More people got hurt then than in the regular season. He gave me this piece of paper, but I had no idea what it was. It was his training program. I had to run 10 sets of 120 highs [hurdles], then I had to run the 440 and 220 lows [hurdles]. I admired Bill Easton as a strong disciplinarian who had a sense of order. I took some of his classes. I learned more about myself and the accountability one had as an athlete to his body—training, stretching, relaxing. More than anything, Bill Easton taught me how to be a champion. Track was different than football. The hurdles were an individual event. I learned more about myself from Bill Easton than anyone else. He built great track champions. They had ability, but he embellished it with a sense of discipline, order, and conditioning that I had never seen in my whole endeavor of sports. He was truly dedicated to his craft and uncompromising to molding successful people. It was an honor and privilege to run under Bill Easton.

The great thing about being at the University of the Kansas is whom I was exposed to and what they did to help me become what I am. I learned that an athlete is a gifted, talented being, but more than anything, that person has to have a heart, a focus, and a passion to be successful. I saw this in my fraternity brother, the late Charlie Tidwell. He was a world-record holder. My heart and soul never went out to a person more than they did to Charlie Tidwell. Besides getting an academic education at a university, there is also the education in affiliation with an individual. There is something about Charlie Tidwell that we all have to learn as an athlete. You do not lose when you can win.

I watched Charlie Tidwell at the Olympic Trials. He jumped the start three straight times and got eliminated from the race. In following months, he had the opportunity to try out for the Denver Broncos. He got cut and then the ultimate tragedy is that he committed suicide. The reason I speak to this is that as a man and a sportsman, you learn that you must win, you can win, and you strive to win. And if you fail and stumble, there is another day. And that carries over to life. I cannot explain why Charlie Tidwell jumped the start or did not make the Broncos, but I learned that we must never lose that will to win. It really affected me.

Of all the experiences at the University of Kansas, the important thing is—whether it is academic or athletics—to walk away from that university a better person. We [classmates] were all trying to graduate from that damn university. I use that term because it was presented as a challenge. It was a litmus test. Was I going to be a loser or a winner? It [the university] would kick your ass if you were not prepared. Wilt Chamberlain was a fraternity brother of mine. I have great admiration for his ability. To this day, I do not appreciate that he did not graduate from the University of Kansas. I don't begrudge him from the standpoint of why he left, but he could have come back to finish what he started.

I am not saying I am any better than Wilt or anyone else. But graduating was what I was supposed to do, and anyone who looks like me can do it, too. And don't tell me that you cannot do it. The University of Kansas is a fantastic institution with wonderful opportunities to succeed and be a winner. The opportunity must not be wasted.

JOHN HADL

FOOTBALL

1959–1961

He was born in Lawrence in 1940 and raised just a few blocks down the road from Memorial Stadium. As a youngster, he didn't have enough money to buy a ticket, so Johnny Hadl and his buddies used to sneak into games for the opportunity to see the Jayhawks play football. Just a few years later, he was wearing a No. 21 KU jersey and on his way to becoming a legend for his exploits as a member of the Kansas football team. Today, his name and number are affixed at the top of the north bowl of Memorial Stadium in tribute to his playing career. Hadl became the school's first two-time All-American in football and helped KU to its first-ever bowl victory.

After 16 seasons of playing professional football, including 11 seasons with the San Diego Chargers, Hadl retired from the game in 1977. He is just one of 29 quarterbacks in NFL history who have thrown for more than 30,000 yards. He went on to serve two seasons as offensive coordinator with the Los Angeles Rams, was John Elway's first QB coach with the Denver Broncos, and was also head coach of the Los Angels Express of the United States Football League, where he coached Steve Young. Along the way, he also coached the likes of Vince Ferragamo, Bert Jones, and Steve DeBerg. He also served as an assistant coach at KU before moving to an administrative role as associate athletics director. Most recently, he played a significant role in helping raise outside funding for major improvements at Memorial Stadium, including a new office complex. He still owns KU football records for longest punt

(94 yards), longest kickoff-return average in a season (29.6 yards), and longest interception return (98 yards). He was recognized as NFL Man of the Year in 1971 and was inducted into the College Football Hall of Fame in 1994.

★   ★   ★

I lived on Forrest Avenue in Lawrence, not many blocks from Memorial Stadium. My dad was raised on a farm and had to quit school in the eighth grade and go to work. He and his brother ended up owning a garage on Massachusetts Street. In fact, my dad was a pretty good mechanic, and they had a successful business.

Our neighborhood was filled with other boys who played sports. There were some great KU people who lived around us, like Bill Easton and Bill Nieder.

On warm summer days, you could find most of us involved in pickup games on the playground at the old McAlister School, which is located just behind where Central Junior High School is now. At that time, it was Lawrence High School.

One of my best friends, Larry Hatfield, and I were in junior high when we started finding creative ways to sneak into KU football and basketball games. It wasn't very difficult because there wasn't much security in those days. Memorial Stadium had those massive wooden doors all around the stadium, and every Friday night before a home game, Larry and I would go there and take out the two-by-fours that locked those doors.

The next day, when the game was starting, we'd work our way around the stadium until we would find an open door. There were about 10 of us who would run through that door as fast as we could. If everything else failed, we would jump over the fence by the tennis courts and outrun the guards. We did that for about three years until they eventually caught on to what we were doing. When they caught us, they just escorted us out of the stadium. It wasn't a real big deal.

I can't remember how I did it, but one football game I actually worked my way down to the sideline and found myself standing side-by-side with Bud Wilkinson [head football coach at Oklahoma]. I was just standing there, looking around, and in awe of the situation. Coach Wilkinson kept looking down at me, and finally he said, "Hey, who is this guy?"

John Hadl became KU's first two-time All-American in football and helped the Jayhawks to the school's first-ever bowl victory. He enjoyed a 16-year career in the NFL.

We also found ways to sneak into Hoch Auditorium and Allen Fieldhouse for basketball games.

Larry and I used to get into Allen Fieldhouse through an open bathroom window. Once, I lowered myself down from the window into a bathroom stall, and a guy was in there using the facility. That was a memorable experience, probably for both of us!

I started playing football in junior high for Wilbur "Nanny" Duver. He went on to coach at Lawrence High School and had a positive influence on many Lawrence kids over the years. Nanny was the head football and basketball coach and the disciplinarian of Lawrence. He was really tough, and everyone was scared to death of the guy. I remember sitting in gym class while he took roll from his office, which had a cage around it. He'd mumble your name and you could hear a pin drop in there. We didn't have any youth discipline problems in those days.

I wasn't very big in the eighth and ninth grades. I weighed about 140 pounds, and Nanny said I'd never be big enough to play football in college. By the time I was a senior in high school, however, I was up to 195 pounds.

Nanny is the first one who got me into punting. We were at Haskell Stadium in Lawrence in junior high, and Nanny came over and asked me if I thought I could punt the ball. Now, this was during warmups before a game. I gave it a try, kicked it, and the ball took off. I couldn't believe it myself. From then on, I was a punter.

Charlie Hoag was a stud athlete in football and basketball when I was growing up and was my KU sports hero. As a matter of fact, that's why I selected No. 21 as my jersey number. That was Hoag's number when he played for KU. I was also a big fan of Mickey Mantle. He played high school ball in Oklahoma under Al Woolard, who later coached for many years at Lawrence High School.

One of my favorite memories of Mickey was a time after my playing career was over and I was playing in a charity golf tournament at the LaCosta Country Club in California. I was in the locker room, putting on my golf shoes. I looked up and in walked Mantle, Willie Mays, Jackie Robinson, and Joe DiMaggio. I couldn't believe it!

My first experience in organized sports was playing Little League baseball in the South Park League. I became a pretty good baseball player, and there was talk when I was in high school that maybe I should play baseball instead of football.

We had a pretty impressive American Legion team one year and actually won the state tournament. We moved on to the regional tournament in Oklahoma and played the host team and beat them. In the second game, we almost beat Missouri but lost when one of our outfielders dropped a routine fly ball.

It was a double-elimination tournament, and we had to face Oklahoma once again. This time they had a pitcher on the mound by the name of Von McDaniel. He and his older brother, Lindy, later played major league baseball for the St. Louis Cardinals. I'd never seen a fastball and curveball like the one he threw that day. I was the leadoff hitter, and I bunted four times.

That's when I decided I was going to be a football player.

The recruiting process for me began my junior year at Lawrence High School, when Chuck Mather was the head coach at KU. Chuck was a nice guy, but I had been watching that program firsthand, and I knew things were bad. I went to visit Oklahoma on a recruiting trip my senior year and actually committed to Bud Wilkinson. Mather had just been fired at the time, and Jack Mitchell was the new KU coach. I got back from Oklahoma about 10:00 PM, and there was a call waiting from Mitchell. He insisted on my coming over for a talk. By the time I left his house, around 2:00 AM, I didn't even remember having said I was going to Oklahoma.

I made up my mind that I was going to Kansas.

When I arrived at KU, I was a halfback. That's the only position on offense I had played in high school, and it's the only position I played at KU until my junior year. Mitchell moved me to quarterback my junior year, and it was a good decision. With Curtis McClinton, Bert Coan, and Doyle Schick along with myself in the backfield, it was a way to get us all in the game at the same time. I ran the option and didn't have to pass very often with that backfield.

We were ranked in the top 20 all year my junior season and ended up beating Missouri in Columbia [23–7] when they were ranked No. 1 in the nation. We later had to forfeit the victory after they ruled Coan was ineligible for accepting a free plane ride to the college all-star game from a KU booster.

We went 7–3–1 my senior year and beat Rice [33–7] in the Bluebonnet Bowl. It was the school's first-ever bowl win.

After the bowl game, McClinton and I signed our pro contracts right on the field. I signed with the Chargers, and he signed with the Dallas Texans. I think I got a $5,000 bonus and a car. Don Klosterman was there to sign me. My deal was a two-year contract for $17,500. I think Curtis got $10,000.

We got the checks as we were leaving the field. We were all in the locker room celebrating the victory. Curtis had that bonus check and he'd stuck it in his shirt pocket, hanging in the locker as he went to the shower. Some of the guys thought they'd have some fun with Curtis and took his check and stuck it in another player's pocket [Larry Allen].

So Curtis came back, dripping wet, and saw his check was missing. He started screaming and yelling about his check being gone. We all got down on the floor, looking all over the place for his check. He was about to go nuts with the worry that his check was lost. All of a sudden, Larry noticed it in his pocket and told Curtis. We had a great laugh.

I stayed in close contact with KU while I played pro football. I wanted to be a coach and would come back and help coach spring football during my offseason. I did that for Mitchell and also for Fambrough.

I played my final two pro seasons with Houston. I had a major back problem and it was really impacting my ability to play. I was tired of all the physical wear and tear. Al Davis called and wanted to see if I might want to try out for the Raiders. Al always liked to bring in those old guys. I told him thanks, but I had had enough. I wanted to get back and coach at KU.

The most fun I ever had was my time at the University of Kansas. We had a good bunch of guys, and Mitchell made it fun. We got it turned around a little bit. We won a bowl game and we won a league championship.

My experience at KU has served as the basic structure for my whole life. It allowed me to establish some great relationships with people, and that's what it's all about in life. It also helped open some doors from a business perspective.

I've always had a great respect for the university and I always will.

The
SIXTIES

GALE SAYERS
FOOTBALL/TRACK
1962–1964

GALE SAYERS HAS CARRIED THE BANNER of his alma mater to a level not many University of Kansas graduates achieve. He's recognized as one of the all-time great running backs in the history of pro football and, at the age of 34, became the youngest member of the Pro Football Hall of Fame.

In 1999, *The Sporting News* ranked him 21st in a listing of the all-time greatest NFL players. That ranking is even more impressive considering his pro career was limited to just 68 games due to two serious knee injuries. In 1994, his uniform number was retired at Soldier Field in Chicago. It also stands as one of just three jerseys retired in football at the University of Kansas.

He authored a book—*I Am Third*—which inspired the movie *Brian's Song*. The movie depicted the story of Sayers's close friendship with a teammate, Brian Piccolo. Sayers and Piccolo represented the first roommate pairing of a black man and white man in the NFL. The movie was made in the wake of racial tensions around the country and told of Sayers's devotion to Piccolo during his unsuccessful battle with cancer.

Sayers went on to serve as one of the first major-college African American athletic directors when he provided leadership for five years at Southern Illinois University. He later founded and continues to serve as CEO of a world-class computer technology company—Sayers 40—in Chicago.

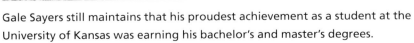

Gale Sayers still maintains that his proudest achievement as a student at the University of Kansas was earning his bachelor's and master's degrees.

The "Kansas Comet"—as he was known during his playing days with the Jayhawks—rushed for 2,675 career yards at KU.

Married, with six children and 13 grandchildren, Sayers is quick to point to his bachelor's degree and master's degree as achievements he's most proud of in his time at the University of Kansas. Recently, the University of Kansas established the Gale Sayers Microcomputer Center, in recognition of Gale's commitment to both education and technology.

★   ★   ★

I LIVED IN WICHITA AND A SMALL [north central] Kansas community called Speed during the early years of my childhood. There were minimal opportunities for me to be involved in youth football until the family moved to Nebraska when I was eight years old.

We moved to Omaha because of the job opportunities. My dad had a brother who lived there, and at that time, there were avenues for blacks to find work. It turned out to be a move that had a positive influence on my life because Omaha had a Pop Warner Football League, and I was able to participate in organized youth football as a result. That's what got me on the road to being a football player.

92

We lived on the poor side of town, and sports became an important part of my life as I got older. My dad had been a fairly good athlete, playing football and running track. I also had an older brother and younger brother who were outstanding athletes.

My older brother, Roger, was a world-class sprinter, and we played on football teams together while growing up in Omaha. Roger, in fact, went on to earn Little All-America honors at the University of Nebraska-Omaha. The same year I ran for an NCAA record 99-yard touchdown against Nebraska, he set a NAIA record with a 99-yard touchdown reception. He wasn't very big—about 155 pounds—but he was very fast.

People have often asked me how I developed my talents in football. I've always said it was not something that anyone taught me. I just went out and did it. I guess it was a natural ability I was blessed with.

By the time I finished my high school career at Omaha Central, I had received 125 scholarship offers. Notre Dame, many Big Ten schools, and most of the Big 8 schools recruited me to play football. The primary thing I wanted was a good football school close enough to allow my parents to watch me play.

Many people assumed that I would attend the University of Nebraska. But what you have to remember is that the Cornhuskers were not very good in football during that period of time. During my four years in high school, Nebraska went 1–9, 3–7, 4–6, and 4–6. Bob Devaney didn't become head coach there until my sophomore year at KU. He's the one who turned their football program around.

I had my eye on the University of Kansas because they were fairly close and had a good program. My junior year, I believe, they were cochampions of the Big 8 and had players like John Hadl, Curtis McClinton, and Bert Coan. I took a visit to Lawrence, and in those days, alumni were allowed to be somewhat involved in the recruiting process.

I met great people like Ray Evans and Roy Edwards, and they had a positive influence on my feelings about attending school at KU. I also got the opportunity to talk with Hadl and McClinton during my visit to campus. But the big reason I came to the university was head coach Jack Mitchell. He was a great salesman and did the best job recruiting me. I knew that it was just 150 miles from home and my parents would be able to see my games.

There weren't a lot of black students attending KU in those days, and I wasn't the best student in the world. I remember there was a black gentleman in town by the name of Jesse Milan who made himself available as a mentor to many of the black students on campus. He taught us how to study and about the importance of going to church. If you had a problem, you could go to Jesse for advice. He had a big impact on me during my college days.

Another individual who influenced me in a positive way was Bill Easton, the highly successful Jayhawk track coach. Of course, I also ran track and had a lot of respect for Easton. He had a little sign on his desk that read, "I Am Third."

I would always notice that sign when I was in his office but never fully understood its meaning. Finally, during my senior year, I finally asked coach, "What does that sign mean?"

He explained that in life we have priorities. "Our first priority is the Lord, our second is family and friends, and we are third," Easton explained. I thought it was great wisdom. That message stuck with me and has helped me navigate my way through life.

Later, I authored a book and called it *I Am Third* because I believed that concept best illustrates my approach to life. Those priorities are how I've structured my life throughout the years.

As I mentioned, I wasn't a very good student. Being one of just a few blacks on campus, combined with my student skills, I probably lacked some confidence in the classroom. I never lacked confidence playing football. But as I matured, I became determined to get my degree.

There were some people in Wichita who probably questioned if I would ever be a successful student at KU. That served as part of my incentive. As it turned out, I earned both my undergraduate and graduate degrees from the University of Kansas.

I learned that going to school and getting my degree was the most important thing I could do. I believe the average career for a football player is under four years. A college degree is something that will last you a lifetime. I've always tried to stress that to students, particularly football players, when I've had the opportunity to speak to them. They don't always understand the importance of having a degree to fall back on after their playing career is over.

94

One of my favorite sayings—something I use when I give speeches—is, "When you prepare to play, you must prepare to quit." You must have a plan for your life once your career is completed.

Without question, I'm most proud of the fact that I earned those two degrees at KU. It was my goal to take the walk down Campanile Hill on graduation day, and I was able to do that in 1974 and again in 1976. It was important for me to be a student-athlete and not an athlete-student.

I was drafted by the Chicago Bears and the Kansas City Chiefs. Although the Chiefs actually offered more money, I signed a four-year contract with the Bears for $25,000 a year. We didn't make much money in those days. At least, not compared to today's earning potential.

My first season with the Bears was 1965, and I was named Rookie of the Year in the NFL. I played eight years for Chicago and had a great experience. Of course, my career was cut short because of knee injuries in 1968 and again in 1970. While rehabilitating my knee in 1970, I took classes at New York University to become a stockbroker.

After my professional career with the Chicago Bears, I came back to KU and spent four years as an assistant athletics director. That helped open up an opportunity for me to serve as athletics director at Southern Illinois University in Carbondale for five years.

I was one of the first African American athletics directors at that time, but I was just 34 years old. It was not the best of times to be a black AD in college athletics, and I decided to pursue an opportunity in private business.

I went back to Chicago and in 1982 was able to start a computer business called, Sayers 40. I'm very proud of the fact that the business today is recognized as a world-class provider of technology services around the country.

Looking back on my life as a student, a football player, a businessman, and a father, I consider myself extremely blessed.

TED OWENS

MEN'S BASKETBALL COACH

1964–1983

TED OWENS'S APPRECIATION OF Kansas basketball began at an early age, so he did not think too long about leaving his job as head coach of a national junior-college power to become an assistant coach to Dick Harp in 1960. Owens lettered three years at Oklahoma, from 1949 to 1951, under Bruce Drake. He recorded a 94–23 mark in four years at Cameron (Oklahoma) Junior College from 1956 to 1959 before coming to Kansas as an assistant coach. When Harp retired, Owens was caught off guard, but was honored to be named the Jayhawks' head coach beginning in 1964. In 19 seasons, he would compile a 348–182 record, ranking third in wins behind Phog Allen and Roy Williams.

Owens won six Big 8 titles (1966, 1967, 1971, 1974, 1975, and 1978) and advanced to the NCAA Tournament seven times, including trips to the 1971 and 1974 NCAA Final Four. He was selected conference coach of the year five times and the national coach of the year in 1978. He mentored All-Americans Jo Jo White, Walt Wesley, Dave Robisch, Bud Stallworth, and Darnell Valentine.

Owens resides in Tulsa, Oklahoma.

★ ★ ★

When I arrived at Oklahoma as a freshman, it had been to the [NCAA] national finals the prior spring of 1947. A lot of those players were still in the program, so we were very good at the time. Freshmen were not eligible, but my sophomore and junior season we had to compete with World War II veterans for jobs. By the time I was a senior, all the veterans but one were gone. It was a difficult time to earn a job, but an exciting time to be with special guys who had served our country so well.

Kansas had assembled the great group that ultimately won the NCAA title in 1952—Clyde Lovellette, Bill Leinhard, Bill Hougland, Bob Kenney, and Charlie Hoag. Jerry Waugh was a class ahead of that group, and the Kelley boys [Dean and Al] and B.H. Born and crew followed shortly after. The first time I saw KU play was in the All-College Tournament in Oklahoma City [1946–1947 season] when I was a senior in high school. They were very good with Charlie "the Hawk" Black, Ray Evans, and Otto Schnellbacher, who were war veterans. We were always impressed with how hard the KU teams played under Dr. Allen and Dick Harp. When we played in Kansas City in the preseason tournament, we noticed the incredible noise when the Jayhawks played. One of my biggest thrills was beating KU in Hoch Auditorium my senior season with a last-second shot. Wins there didn't come very often.

My first coaching job was at Cameron College [now Cameron University] in Lawton, Oklahoma. We had very successful teams in my four years there, highlighted by the 1958 team, which was undefeated in the regular season and entered the National Junior College Athletics Association Tournament in Hutchinson ranked as No. 1 in the country. It was the first undefeated team to ever enter the national tournament. We made it to the NJCAA semifinals three straight years before losing. When KU asked me to visit the campus, I knew that Juco coaches rarely ever make the jump to head jobs at major universities, and those jobs usually go to major-college assistants.

I had a variety of feelings—joy at being named to be the head coach at such a great university, an awareness of the huge responsibility that went with that position, and confidence that we could continue the great tradition established by so many great coaches and players. I had attended OU when Bud Wilkinson had established such a great tradition in football. I knew how much it meant to the reputation of the institution, how much it meant in the lives of the students, faculty, and the graduates, and for that matter, the pride that it added to the state of Oklahoma. I realized that much the same was true

In 19 seasons as head basketball coach at KU, Owens compiled a 348–182 record and ranks third all-time in coaching wins behind Phog Allen and Roy Williams. Owens also won six Big 8 titles and went to the Final Four twice.

in Kansas. Dr. Naismith, Dr. Allen, Coach Harp, and so many had labored to build such a great tradition, unmatched by any other school in the country, that it was an enormous responsibility.

The challenges were awesome, but not overwhelming. I felt that we could restore KU to the prominence that it had achieved many times before. Coach Harp and I had recruited a nucleus of good players and, more important, great people. We simply had to add some quality players to that group to obtain success in a short period of time, and we were able to do that. I think that you always remember your first success. Our first team in 1964–1965 won the Big 8 Preseason Tournament, which was a great achievement in those days, and finished second in the conference during the regular season. Back then, you had to win the conference to make the NCAA playoffs. That group of Delvy Lewis, Riney Lochmann, Walt Wesley, Al Lopes, Ron Franz, Jim Gough, Kerry Bolton, Dave Schichtle, Fred Chana, etc., was joined the next year by Bob Wilson, Rodger Bohnenstiehl, and Jo Jo White, and formed what I believe to be one of KU's most powerful teams in 1965–1966.

That was the team that lost to the "Glory Road" team, Texas Western, in two overtimes [in the NCAA regional finals]. We definitely could have won the NCAA title. Even with heavy losses by graduation, we came back to win the conference in 1967 before losing to Houston, featuring Elvin Hayes and Don Chaney, in the regional. The 1971 team that won 21 straight games before losing to UCLA in the Final Four was a special team with Dave Robisch, Roger Brown, Bud Stallworth, Aubrey Nash, Bob Kivisto, Pierre Russell, Mark Mathews, Mark Williams, etc. That was the first time the finals were played in a dome and attracted the largest crowd in NCAA Tournament history to that point. After suffering through a dismal year in 1973, we added Roger Morningstar, Donnie Von Moore, and Norm Cook to a great nucleus of captain Tom Kivisto, Dale Greenlee, Danny Knight, Rick Suttle, Tommie Smith, etc., and made it all the way to the Final Four in 1974. The next year we lost only one player, Kivisto, and won the conference again before losing to Notre Dame with All-American Adrian Dantley in the NCAA Tournament. We could never recover from the loss of Tom, who was one of our greatest leaders.

The 1978 team was a team of great ability, good depth, and a team that was predicted to finish as low as fourth in the conference. It surprised everyone, however, with preseason and regular-season championships and was in position to make a run at the national championship with the first rounds in Wichita, the regionals in Allen Fieldhouse, and the finals in St. Louis. A defeat by Kansas State, whom we had beaten three times that year, in the postseason tournament sent us to the West Coast instead, where we lost to UCLA in a great game. That team of Paul Mokeski, Ken Koenigs, Donnie Von Moore, John Douglas, Clint Johnson, Darnell Valentine, Wilmore Fowler, etc. could play with any team in the country. Another team that improved dramatically and won the postseason Big 8 tournament against very strong Missouri and Kansas State with near perfect performances was the 1981 team of Darnell Valentine, Tony Guy, David Magley, Victor Mitchell, John Crawford, Booty Neal, Art Housey, etc. They defeated No. 2–ranked

Arizona State in the second round of the tournament. Arizona State fielded
a team of two NBA first-round choices. It was a nationally televised game,
and we were so far ahead at halftime that NBC cut away to broadcast another
game. Tony Guy had his greatest game, and Darnell had the satisfaction of
winning before his hometown crowd.

The games I remember most and made me the happiest would include the
win in the Big 8 tournament against Kansas State in my first year as head
coach in 1964. K-State had advanced to the Final Four the previous year, and
my first job was not to be the best in the conference, but the best in our own
state. Tex Winter was and is a personal friend and respected coach. That victory was a turning point in my tenure at KU. We went on to win the conference tournament that year and a total of eight times during my years at
KU. Some people downplay the significance of those championships, but
they were great achievements in some fierce competition. Maybe the greatest performance in Allen Fieldhouse history was in 1966 against top
10–ranked Nebraska. They had beaten us in Lincoln earlier, and we beat
them 110–73 in a near flawless performance. A road trip to Maryland and St.
John's in my first year as head coach resulted in victories over some great East-
ern powers. A win over Nebraska in 1971 against a very good Cornhusker
team set the stage for a conference title and the first team in conference history to go undefeated. An overtime win over Missouri in Columbia in 1971
in the closing of Brewer Fieldhouse and played before a capacity crowd that
included former Missouri players was very satisfying. A championship game
in Allen Fieldhouse in 1974 against K-State, Jack Hartman, and Lonnie
Kruger was a great game and allowed the team to advance to the NCAA,
where they battled their way to the Final Four in Greensboro. The greatest
comeback that I ever was associated with was in Lincoln in 1975 against a
very good Nebraska team. We trailed by 19 points in the first half but came
back to win in overtime. It was a difficult win against a very good team in a
hostile environment, and I think that the games you remember the best are
the ones played in the most difficult circumstances.

I still dream about losses from time to time. The controversial double-
overtime loss to Texas Western deprived us of a real shot at a national title.
The loss to Missouri at home [in 1968] when we had a one-point lead with
two seconds to go and we fouled on an in-bound play was heartbreaking.
Norm Stewart had his first win over KU on that night, and I would have
liked to delay that for a few more years. Maybe the hardest loss was losing to

a great Kentucky team in Rupp Arena in December of 1978, when we had a six-point lead with 40 seconds to play—maybe the most difficult loss to swallow. Our players had played a great game, and it took months to get over the loss. The loss to Wichita State in the 1981 NCAA Tournament was a tough one, but from a coach's standpoint, we made every correct play call, but we missed layups, free throws, and had a perfectly executed out-of-bounds play fail because an official didn't make the call. The games that bothered me the most were when I felt that there was something that I should or could have done to change the outcome. Bud Stallworth's game against Missouri in 1972 on national television with the 1952 team in the audience was a memorable game. What people forget is that Bud might have tied Wilt's record of 52 points had one of our players not stepped over the line on a free throw [Kansas won 93–80]. Most games that I remember were wins that led to championships. The beauty of growing older is that you tend to forget the disappointments and focus on the achievements.

Kansas State and Missouri are totally different rivalries. First of all, [K-State coaches] Tex Winter, Cotton Fitzsimmons, and Jack Hartman were my good friends, and I had great respect for them. I admired the volume of noise in old Ahearn Fieldhouse that was generated by their crowd. A victory there was a real achievement. Roy [Williams] and Bill [Self] need to be grateful that they didn't have to play there.

101

Missouri was a different story. As a history major, I had studied the history of the two territories [Kansas and Missouri], the border wars, the burning of Lawrence—which was the headquarters of the Free State movement—by Quantrill and his raiders, who were pro-slavery advocates. Kansans hid out along the borders, and when the raiders came across, they "bushwhacked" them. They called those bushwhackers "Jayhawkers." My first year at KU, I traveled with Coach Harp, who did the color analysis for the football games on radio and witnessed our victory over No. 1–ranked Missouri. We had a great backfield of John Hadl, Bert Coan, Doyle Schick, and Curtis McClinton, and our defense held Missouri without a first down for the first three quarters. On the way out, some of our band members were physically handled by a group of angry fans. When we went to Columbia to play Missouri on national television, our black players were spat on and later mobbed on the court by the Missouri fans. So my opinion of Missouri didn't get off to a great start. Norm Stewart and I had a bitter rivalry but in recent years have become good friends.

It was very difficult when I was let go. There is no question that we had two seasons that didn't meet the standards that are expected of KU basketball [1982 and 1983], but we had the finest freshmen I had ever had—Ron Kellogg, Cal Thompson, Kerry Boagni, Jeff Guiot—and I was redshirting Greg Dreiling, plus some very good veterans, Carl Henry, Kelly Knight, and Brian Martin. We knew that we were going to be back in the championship competition the next several years. I was very disappointed not to have had that opportunity, because I had always hoped to end my tenure at KU with a championship year. My last victory was in Norman against my alma mater, Oklahoma, and its great player, Wayman Tisdale. It was a great victory, and the players carried me off the court. As they carried me up that ramp to the dressing room, I looked up in the crowd, and there was my coach at Oklahoma, Bruce Drake, and his wonderful wife, Myrtle, smiling and waving at me. That made it an even more incredible night.

Coaching in Allen Fieldhouse is like no other experience I have ever encountered. Just running out on the court before the games—and the anticipation of a noise level unknown to most places—was electrifying. Our fans are pretty knowledgeable about basketball and pretty fair about recognizing the great plays of opponents. It isn't just a game, but an event—the "Rock Chalk Chant," the pep band, the pompon squad, and the cheerleaders all add significantly to the game. When I go back to games, I can still sing the same songs and chant the same chants as if it were yesterday. That is tradition.

It is something that stays with you forever. You can walk into a sports apparel store in almost any city and buy a Jayhawk cap. There aren't any other Jayhawks. It is a unique name with a unique history. I live in Tulsa, and I see people wearing Jayhawk caps and shirts all the time. You can be proud of being a Jayhawk because it represents more than athletic victories. It represents great academics, great tradition, from Dr. Naismith and Dr. Allen and so many great achievements in politics, aerospace, and other professional areas. Being a Jayhawk fills you with pride.

I stay as close [to the program] as I can while living in Tulsa. I think that Bill Self and his staff have done a great job. Having a consistent winner is not easy, but as long as he is there, I feel confident that KU basketball will remain at a very high level. He is one of the finest communicators I have ever known. I love to come back every time I can and see my former players and coaches. It is one of the great joys of my life.

BOB TIMMONS

TRACK COACH

1965–1988

THE PLAN WAS ESTABLISHED well before Bob Timmons set foot on the University of Kansas campus. He would earn an education and return to his Pittsburg, Kansas, hometown to run the family business. But not everything always goes according to plan. After his freshman year, the Marines came calling, interrupting his education for three years. He returned to KU to finish his degree, joining a Beta Theta Pi pledge class that included basketball standout Jerry Waugh, future broadcaster Max Falkenstein, and eventual Kansas governor Robert Docking.

Timmons, who is known to one and all as "Timmie," graduated in 1950 but never made it back to Pittsburg to become a businessman. Instead, he went on to be a successful coach at Kansas high schools in Caldwell, Emporia, and Wichita (East and West). Over his career, he coached tennis, football, swimming, basketball, track, cross country, and volleyball. In 1964, he accepted an assistant track coach position at Kansas under legendary coach Bill Easton. He would become the head coach one year later and go on to compile an amazing record over 24 years.

With the Jayhawks, Timmons led the school to four NCAA team titles, 12 top-five finishes, 11 consecutive conference titles, and 11 NCAA individual championships. During his career, Timmons coached seven Olympians, 16 world-record holders, 77 NCAA All-Americans, and 24 NCAA champions. The list of athletes who competed under Timmons includes Jim Ryun, Cliff

Wiley, Karl Salb, Randy Smith, Jeff Buckingham, Deon Hogan, Archie San Romani Jr., and Jeff Farrell. Other students include CIA chief Robert Gates and Stanford swimming coach Richard Quick. He was elected the 1975 National Coach of the Year by the U.S. Track and Field Coaches Association, and is a hall of fame member of the University of Kansas Athletics Department, Kansas State High School Activities Association, and State of Kansas.

★   ★   ★

"One of our close family friends was George Nettles," Timmons said. "George was a captain of the Kansas football team the year Doc [Phog] Allen coached [1920]. He loved Doc and he loved KU. So he would take his son, me, and other kids to football games at KU. We'd come driving down the hill south of town, and he would start singing the fight songs. He had great enthusiasm, but he could not carry a tune. He taught us all to sing. It was great fun, all of us singing at the top of our lungs. We really looked forward to the games.

"I was the oldest grandson, so the plan was to go to school and come back to run my grandfather's bank. But I was sold on coaching. I was not a great athlete in high school. I was only 5′2″ and weighed 95 pounds. I played foot-ball for one year, tennis, and ran the hurdles. I had great coaches in high school, especially Fritz Snodgrass, who was successful at Wichita East High School and then at Wichita State. Being around Jerry [Waugh], I got to know Doc Allen and the other coaches in the athletic department. I took classes under Doc and Bill Easton. The instructors in the physical education depart-ment, especially Henry Shenk and Doc [Ed] Elbel, were wonderful. I remember taking a square dancing class, where my partner was Clyde Lovel-lette. That was quite a sight, Clyde at 6′9″ or so and me at 5′2″. My first love was basketball, even though I could not make my YMCA team. I wanted to coach basketball because of Doc Allen. He was an amazing person. I had so many great, positive influences at KU. I was very fortunate."

"Timmie was ahead of his time as a student learning to be a coach," said Waugh, who to this day remains close to Timmons and his wife, Pat. "He would check out books on coaching, research sports organizations, and observe coaches closely. No one has ever been more prepared than he. And that did not stop when he became a coach or when he retired. He still keeps up on coaching. I marveled at him because he put a road map together on

In his 24 seasons as head cross-country and track and field coach at KU, Bob Timmons (middle) led the school to four NCAA team titles, 12 top-five finishes, 10 consecutive conference championships, and had 11 NCAA individual champions. He also coached seven Olympians, 16 world record holders, and 24 NCAA champions.

how to become a coach. The rest of us had no clue, but Timmie had a focus. I remember when he went home to tell his parents that he was not going to run the family business. It was very traumatic. Not so much for him, but more for his parents."

Timmons had brought many of his track teams to the Kansas Relays and had gotten to know Easton well, so going to Kansas as an assistant was enticing. However, the move meant that he would have to leave his star pupil, Jim Ryun, for his senior season at Wichita East High School. In the spring of 1965, opportunity knocked again for Timmons as Oregon State offered him its head coaching position. Timmons would leave for Corvallis after the Kansas Relays.

"I remember packing up the car and driving out to Oregon immediately after the relays," said Timmons. "Oregon State was not Oregon when it came to track, but I was looking forward to building a program and competing against the best. I had just crossed into Oregon and I called back home to my wife. She told me that Bill [Easton] had been fired. I was shocked. It was all because Bill had purchased a fiberglass pole-vaulting box without the approval of Wade Stinson, who was the athletics director. Bill and Wade had butted heads for quite a while. Both had powerful personalities and both were hard-headed. I was caught in the middle. Before the Kansas Relays, Wade told me to send it back to the company. Bill found out and was upset with me. He sent me down to the post office to pick it up before it had been sent back to the manufacturer. So I went to get it and reinstalled it for the relays.

"As I remember, I did not coach one day of track at Oregon State. It seemed like I was on the phone the whole time. Wade had called me and asked me to come back to be head coach. I pleaded with him. I told him nobody should be fired over a vaulting box. But Wade wasn't going to change his mind. Finally, I told the Oregon State athletics director, Slats Gill, that I was going back to Kansas. He was upset, but I think he understood my situation. He knew that it was my school, and he knew how much I loved it. I really think they were more upset because it meant Jim Ryun was not going to go to Oregon State. It was just assumed he would go to school there with me as the coach. What's ironic is, several years later they dropped track.

"I didn't know who Jim Ryun was when he came out for track at Wichita East. We had 150 kids who came out for track. I don't even think he lettered in junior high school. But, my, did he ever develop. I soon found out that I had a kid who was really going to be something. What was wonderful about him was he was genuinely grounded. Success never turned him. As a runner, he had a tremendous kick. I am not sure where it came from, but probably from the intense training. He was in such great shape. There were so many great races for Jim, but I remember the build-up for the 1972 Kansas Relays, which many Olympians were using as part of their preparation for Munich. Jim had graduated, so he was running in the open division. There was a lot of interest and excitement. The west side of the stands was closed, but the crowd was so big they just broke through the chains on the gates. I don't know for sure, but we had to have more than 30,000 people there."

Despite his 5′2″ stature, Timmons was known as a man of discipline. He and others in authoritarian positions were put to the test in the late 1960s and early 1970s, as the Vietnam War caused much unrest on campuses across the nation. He was also beginning his own personal battle versus the National Collegiate Athletic Association. Timmons thought that many of the policies of the NCAA put the well-being of the student-athlete in jeopardy. He carried his crusade to his coaching peers, the media, the NCAA, and Congress. Timmons eventually published a 65-page document on June 25, 2002, which was a nearly 40-year compilation of his thoughts regarding the NCAA and its treatment of student-athletes. Entitled "The NCAA: Who Protects the Student-Athletes?" it was his proposal for a student-athlete bill of rights. The document was discussed in many circles, and though not adopted, many of his principles have been incorporated by the rule-making body in some form or fashion. It also earned him the respect of administrators, coaches, and student-athletes for his commitment to the cause.

"It was a tough time on campus," recalled Timmons, referring to the late 1960s. "People in authority were being challenged. In one particular case, we had a student-athlete, Sam Goldberg, who showed up to the bus wearing sandals. We had a rule that they had to wear street shoes when we traveled. He said he did not have any money. So I gave him $10 and told him to go buy some shoes. He did some other things, and finally we dismissed him from the team. He then spread lies about the program. We would go on NCAA probation. The only thing we did wrong was pay for his shoes, but we never had due process to address the other allegations. After numerous requests, we finally got a chance to present our information before the infractions committee, and the ban was lifted. You had the student-athletes being punished for things they had not done. I did not think that was fair. I thought there were many things that the NCAA did that were not best for the student-athlete.

"Clifford Wiley was a great sprinter for us, an Olympic qualifier. His parents were divorced when he was young, and his mother cared for nine children. I remember when I visited his house for recruiting, there was hardly any furniture. Clifford had a scholarship but also qualified for a BEOG [Basic Education Opportunity Grant] beyond that. He needed that money to cover travel expenses to get to and from school. That money was given out through the financial aid office, so we had no control over his receiving it. We [the Kansas athletics department] ruled that it was not within the rules and had to suspend him. So Clifford went to court, sued the NCAA, and won. We were required to let him participate. The NCAA appealed, which was heard after the season. If Clifford earned points, we would lose them if the NCAA won the appeal. The NCAA won, and we lost the Big 8 and NCAA championships because we had to forfeit his points. We had to run him because our attorney said we had to do so. We could not disobey the ruling. We were caught in the middle. I did not think the NCAA should have more power than our court system. It was not fair to the team, and I felt sorry for Clifford."

In the document submitted to presidents and chancellors, Timmons wrote: "My goal is to somehow change NCAA rules and policies that adversely affect the lives of student-athletes. You are their protectors."

One of Timmons's last team titles, the 1982 Big 8 Indoor, came under the most unusual circumstances. Kansas was favored to win, but that was based on high-jumping phenom Tyke Peacock's performing. The rub came because Peacock was also a member of the Jayhawk basketball team, which just so happened to be playing Iowa State in Lawrence the same day as the track championship, February 27, 1982. The plan was to have Peacock play in the basketball game, then board a charter flight to Lincoln, Nebraska, to compete in the high jump. The league coaches had originally ruled that, if the high-jump competition began before Peacock arrived, he would be disqualified. But the decision was later reversed, and Peacock would be allowed to pass on heights if he was not in attendance. The game's tip was moved up one hour to 1:00 PM and ended at 2:50 PM. He was on a flight by 3:00 PM and landed at 3:32 PM. The competition began while he was in the air at a height of 6′5″. Though in the arena, he also passed at 6′8″. Later, he cleared 6′11″ on his first attempt, 7′1″ on his third, and set the league record at 7′7¾″ to secure the Jayhawk championship.

"Man, I was a nervous wreck," Timmons said. "We were following the game in Lawrence, so we knew it would be tight for him getting to Lincoln. We got news that the plane had landed, but the competition had already begun. I was sweating bullets. All of a sudden, I saw him kind of saunter in. He was dressed, but he had his shoes off and was just swinging them by the laces. He was smiling. He was a California kid, so he was laid back. I was really dying now. I had to pass him on a second height. Well, he jumped and made his first attempt. I don't think he warmed up at all. He went on to win and set a league record. We won the meet with his points."

Nobody packs more in 24 hours than Bob Timmons. Not one to sit still after retirement, he spent several years coaching high school track and junior high volleyball in nearby Baldwin, Kansas. Though volleyball was new to him, he became proficient in coaching the sport by reading books, attending clinics, and watching games. Once a coach, always a coach. Timmons is also a self-made artist, having created statues that fill his home, the track office at KU, and other venues. His summers have often included missionary work all over the world.

For numerous years, Timmons maintained Kansas's home cross-country course, located at his very own Rim Rock Farm, just north of Lawrence. Purchased in the early 1970s, Timmons, along with his coaches, administrators, student-athletes, and friends cleared the land. This labor of love afforded him and the program with eight different course configurations. He even made life-sized, steel silhouette cutouts of former KU greats such as Jim Ryun, Billy Mills, Johnny Lawson, Wes Santee, Herb Semper, and Al Frame to dot the course and serve as inspiration to the runners. Respected as one of the top cross-country venues in the nation, it has been host to numerous high school, collegiate, conference, and NCAA championship events. As a demonstration of his love for KU, Timmons donated the land to the KU Endowment Association in 2005, ensuring a long-term home for the Jayhawk cross-country program.

BOBBY DOUGLASS

FOOTBALL

1966–1968

As an assistant football coach at the University of Kansas, Don Fambrough considered it an honor to watch Bobby Douglass quarterback the Jayhawks. To be honest, though, there were times when he could not watch the El Dorado, Kansas, product play. "The best part of watching Bobby Douglass play foot-bawl," says Fambrough in his Texan dialect, "was to watch the eyes of defensive backs get real, real wide when Bobby came rolling out around the end. Those poor guys did not know what to do. They had this physical specimen coming at them, and they either had to tackle him or defend that rocket arm. I tell ya', I felt sorry for some of those poor guys. Sometimes I had to turn my head so as not to see them get hurt."

Long before there was Tim Tebow, the 2007 Heisman Trophy winner from the University of Florida, there was Bobby Douglass. At a fraction under 6′5″ and weighing 225 pounds, Douglass was the first of his kind. He could run around or through defenders. He could thread the needle or throw deep. A 1968 first-team All-American, he finished seventh in the Heisman Trophy balloting, won by USC's O.J. Simpson. That year, he and his Kansas teammates tied for the Big 8 title and advanced to the Orange Bowl, losing a hard-fought 15–14 battle to Penn State. As a senior, he passed for 1,316 yards and 12 touchdowns. He was selected to play in the Senior Bowl, College All-Star Game, and the American Bowl (where he would win MVP honors).

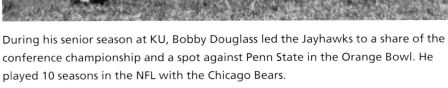

During his senior season at KU, Bobby Douglass led the Jayhawks to a share of the conference championship and a spot against Penn State in the Orange Bowl. He played 10 seasons in the NFL with the Chicago Bears.

Douglass would go on to be drafted in the second round (41st overall) of the NFL Draft by the Chicago Bears. He would play 10 years and set the record for rushing yards by a quarterback with 968 yards in a 14-game season in 1972. It would stand for 34 years until Atlanta's Michael Vick ran for 1,039 yards in 16 games during 2006. Douglass would play one year (1979) in the minor leagues as a pitcher for the Chicago White Sox after retiring from football.

The son of a football coach, Douglass spent every moment by his father's side. There really was never much question that he would be an outstanding athlete, going on to letter in football, basketball, baseball, and track in high school. A dyed-in-the-wool Jayhawk, Douglass was actually born in Manhattan, Kansas, but moved when he was two years old after his father Robert was appointed head coach at El Dorado Junior College (now known as Butler County Community College).

★　★　★

EVEN THOUGH MY DAD PLAYED FOOTBALL at Kansas State, he never tried to steer me that way. Kansas was the better program and really competitive against the powers in the Big 8. They had John Hadl, Bert Coan, Gale Sayers, and others. Jack Mitchell was the football coach, and he recruited me very hard. Back then, you signed your letter of intent in May. He came to my house every weekend in January, February, March, and April. My dad had sent some of his players to KU and was comfortable with Jack, as was I. I got letters from a lot of schools. My brother played at Arkansas, which was a top-five program at the time. Frank Broyles thought they could get me, too. But they didn't have a chance against Jack. I've known a lot of college football coaches in my time, and none had the personality of Jack Mitchell.

I was actually a better baseball player than football player. My dad loved baseball, but he wanted me to go to college. I was a pitcher and had a great arm. I may have had the best arm of any high school athlete in the state as a senior in high school. I later found out that I had several major league teams who wanted to offer me a contact out of high school. My dad didn't tell me that because he wanted me to get a college education. I almost contacted some teams following my sophomore year in college. My dad died during my freshman year, and I had a real tough sophomore year in college. But I know he would have never approved of my dropping out of school.

I could have played baseball in college if Jack Mitchell had remained coach. But he was fired in December of my sophomore year, and Pepper Rodgers came in and said he needed me full-time to install the new offense. Others could play baseball, but not the quarterbacks. People told me I was the best pitcher on campus, but I don't now if that was true.

I really admired what Jack Mitchell was able to do at Kansas. He was a great administrator and communicator. Toward the end of his career, he got caught up competing against other programs, especially in the South, that were making major investments in their football infrastructure. Other programs were building new stadiums or adding on to existing ones. They built athletic dorms and training tables, and they had big coaching staffs. Jack was so good that he could compete with what he had. I was upset when he was fired by Wade Stinson. Stinson was a good athletics director, but they were both very strong-willed. I had become close to Jack and I was hurt.

I am not sure if we could have found a better person to replace Jack than Pepper Rodgers. He was an outstanding football guy and, like Jack, had a great personality. Pepper had trained under Tommy Prothro at UCLA. Prothro was a bright, cerebral guy, and Pepper was that way, too. The system he brought in from UCLA was great for us. We were unstoppable. Pepper was smart. He went out and got a lot of bright, young assistants to help. I am not sure if any school has ever had a staff as good as ours. We had several guys who went on to become head coaches or athletics directors (John Cooper, Terry Donahue, Dave McClain, Dick Tomey, Don Fambrough, Larry Travis, and Doug Weaver). People still talk about that staff today.

113

Pepper was at a younger point in his career than Jack. Jack would have stayed forever. This was the era when coaches started to move around a bit. Pepper was gone in four years. The people at Kansas knew he would eventually leave, but not that quick. I think if Pepper would have stayed, we could have built something. He left UCLA, too, after being there a short while. I think he wanted to get back to the South where he was from. That is not a negative. He was always on the go. If his focus had strictly been on Kansas for a long time, then I don't think there was any doubt we would have had a great program. But I know he still loves Kansas and the people at the university. He would do anything for them.

It was a great time to be at KU. We had a great athletics program. Football was doing well, basketball was dominating the league and had some All-

Americans. Our track program was the best in the nation. Hell, we even had a good gymnastics program. I remember someone in the art department did a painting of Jo Jo White, Jim Ryun, and me as All-Americans. As athletes, we hung around those from the other sports. The school was not as big as it is now. There were some great people there. We may have had as many All-Americans during that four-year period as any time in school history.

The Orange Bowl team had great camaraderie. The seniors provided great leadership. We were so good on offense that we rotated a lot of players, which was unusual at that time. We had a lot of great athletes, so nobody had the huge statistics that other teams had. Jack's strategy was to go out and get the best Kansas kids and then complement them with athletes, predominantly from the South. Donnie Shanklin was one of them. He was from Amarillo, Texas, and was the star of our freshman team. He was one of the best running backs I have ever seen. But we were so deep that he was moved to flanker. He was dominant in a time when the field was not as spread out as it is today. We used him as a runner, receiver, punt returner, and kick returner. I wish he could have played with today's rules. Our speed was amazing. We had Shanklin, John Jackson, Ron Jessie, and Thermus Butler—man, they were fast. Jessie was a wide receiver who also competed in track as a hurdler and long jumper. He was a fantastic athlete, maybe the best I had ever I seen at KU. He could high jump 6′10″. I think he could have been a great decathlete.

114

I would say the whole season was the highlight of my college career. There really wasn't one game that stood out. We knew we would be good. We were 5–5 as juniors and lost some close games [four games by a total of 12 points]. It was just a matter of our gaining confidence early in the season and building on that. That is so important in college. You saw that with this year's team. They lost a lot of close games last year. This year, they built confidence by winning early, and it just grew each game. We felt we were just as good as Penn State, maybe even better. I am sure if Pepper had to do it over again, we would have kicked a field goal to go up 17–7. But we went for it on fourth and 1 and missed at the Penn State 5-yard line in the fourth quarter. I don't think we were stopped on fourth and 1 in two years. That allowed them to change the momentum.

I think one reason we did so well is the pride the Kansas kids had in the school. We had a great number of kids from the state, and the non-Kansans fed off that. John Zook was my roommate my whole college career. He was a big kid from western Kansas [Larned] who was also an All-American at defensive end. We had a lot of fun together—maybe too much fun. I don't say that proudly, but that was kind of what you did back then. We didn't get into big trouble, though. We just liked to have fun. I remember my senior year I decided to try to make a little money on the side. It was probably illegal from an NCAA perspective. Since my brother played at Arkansas, I remember going to the Cotton Bowl and seeing all of those fans wearing hats with logos on them. I hooked up with Mike "Toobie" Miller, a friend of mine whose mother worked in a department store and was able to get some hats for us. We put logos on them and sold them around campus and Lawrence. I wasn't dumb. I got a bunch of pretty girls to sell them for us. My lead salesperson would go on to be John Riggins's wife.

KU was such a great experience for me. The one thing I notice is how much the alumni love the school. I love the campus and the town. I guess you could say I'm just a big fan. The school means a lot to me. I met some life-long friends there. I have a great time coming back to football games and going to the NCAA Tournament games. Kansas fans really support their school. I think you saw that in football this year. We've been down so long. Give them some hope, and they'll come out in droves.

JOHN RIGGINS

FOOTBALL

1968–1970

JOHN RIGGINS MIGHT HAVE BEEN one of the most colorful student-athletes ever to attend the University of Kansas. Ask anyone about him, and you get a quick smile and a head shake. Riggins kept the atmosphere lively. But make no mistake—Riggins was a competitor and a producer. As a sophomore, he was a huge reason the 1968 team went 9–2, tied for first in the Big 8 Conference, and earned a berth in the Orange Bowl. Riggins called it a special team, made even more so by the fact that 17 of the 22 starters were Kansas high school graduates. The only losses that year were to Oklahoma (27–23) and the 15–14 heartbreaker to Penn State in the Orange Bowl. The Jayhawks were ranked as high as No. 3 and finished No. 6 in the UPI rankings and No. 7 in the AP poll.

While at Kansas, Riggins rushed for 2,659 yards, which at the time was second only to fellow NFL Hall of Famer Gale Sayers. He ranks sixth in career rushing yardage, and his 1,131 yards in 1970 is the fifth-best season mark. He was a two-time first-team All–Big 8 selection and was a first-round draft pick (sixth overall) by the New York Jets in 1971. In his 14 NFL seasons with the Jets and the Washington Redskins, he rushed for 11,352 yards. He was the MVP of the 1983 Super Bowl, a member of the NFL 1980s all-decade team, and was elected to the Pro Football Hall of Fame in 1992. On October 13, 2007, Riggins returned to Lawrence to be inducted into the Jayhawks' Ring of Honor at Memorial Stadium.

A native of tiny Centralia, Kansas, located 50 miles northwest of Topeka, Riggins combined a bruising running style with great speed. The town honored him by naming the street where the high school is located as John Riggins Avenue. A quarterback in high school, he was a state track champion in the 100-yard dash and even played the tuba in the band.

A resident of New York City, Riggins has remained in the public eye since his retirement, parlaying a local television commercial into an acting and broadcasting career. He has done both simultaneously, keeping him as busy as he was when he played in the NFL. His performances in various off-Broadway shows have been positively reviewed, prompting producer Peter Dobbins to predict that people will ask, "What did John Riggins do before he was an actor?" Radio has become Riggins's focus today. He is currently hosting *The John Riggins Show*, airing Monday through Friday, from 4:00 to 7:00 PM (ET) on the ESPN Radio affiliate in Washington, D.C. He has also been a part of various Redskin radio and television productions and served as pregame, halftime, and postgame analyst on Fox television for the Kansas–Virginia Tech 2008 FedEx Orange Bowl BCS game.

★   ★   ★

THERE ARE A LOT OF STORIES ABOUT ME out there. I've done a lot of things in my life. I'm not one to sit still too long. I played football, have done some acting, and now I'm into broadcasting. I've never really pursued anything—things just seemed to find me. I will tell you, however, the stories involving me are generally told for effect. They sound better than what really happened. Well, there was some truth to them, but what has been said really doesn't bother me too much. You can't take yourself too seriously. I think that is why the fans have embraced me in whatever I have done and wherever I have been. They know I like to have fun, but they also know that I am not going to cheat them.

Recruiting back then was nothing like it is now. It was always a foregone conclusion that I was going to KU. We had a doctor in town who was a KU grad whom my parents were friends with. I know he was an influence on us. My older brother, Junior, played at KU from '66 to '68, and my younger brother, Billy, from '71 to '73. We were a KU family. That is why I said my induction into the Ring of Honor at KU would probably have meant more to my parents than any of the other awards I had received. They were proud to have three sons who attended the University of Kansas.

John Riggins ended his KU career with 2,659 rushing yards to rank second all-time in school history behind NFL Hall of Famer Gale Sayers at that time. He was the MVP of the 1983 Super Bowl as a member of the Washington Redskins.

I received letters from a lot of schools, however. I remember talking on the phone with Duffy Daugherty at Michigan State, coaches at Oklahoma and other schools. Heck, Dartmouth even contacted me. A few years ago, I took my daughter to Hanover, New Hampshire, to visit Dartmouth. I saw moose and black bear, and said to myself, "I probably would have liked it up here." It's a little different than the barbed-wire fences in Kansas, but I could have gotten used to it.

I took visits to Colorado and Missouri. But I had already known Jack Mitchell and the other coaches at Kansas when I was in high school and was comfortable with them. Of course, Mitchell moved on and Pepper Rodgers would be my coach, but that did not change anything. It was kind of like a prearranged marriage. Pepper was quite a character. He was very personable and kept things lively. I actually played quarterback in high school, but only Oklahoma recruited me to play that position. I looked more like a running back at 6'2", 230 pounds. Looking back on it, I wish I would have given it a try in college. I think Pepper's offense, where the quarterback rolled out and had the run/pass option, would have suited me. It was made for Bobby Douglass. He ran it to perfection in 1968, but when he graduated after that year, there was nobody who could run it like he did. I should have asked the coaches to let me try it. Not a lot worked that next year, so it probably wouldn't have hurt anything to try.

I also played baseball at KU. Like a lot of guys, if you were good enough to play another sport, you did so to get out of spring football. Spring football was physical in those days. Coming off the Orange Bowl, there was never an issue with my playing baseball. But after going 1–9 the next year, the staff made me participate in spring drills. I still played baseball, but I remember taking batting practice and doing my outfield drills in my football cleats and pants. I would then put on my shoulder pads and helmets and head over to football. Track was one of those "could've, would've, should've" things. I was a state high school champion in the 100 [yard dash], but with football and baseball, there just was not enough time.

The 1968 team that went to the Orange Bowl was great. We had strong senior leadership. It was also primarily a team of Kansans. You had Bobby Douglass, Ken Wertzberger, Mickey Doyle, John Zook, and others. You also had a heck of a coaching staff with Dick Tomey, Larry Travis, John Cooper, Doug Weaver, Don Fambrough, and Dave McClain. I don't know if we were the best team in the nation, but we felt we could beat anyone. We had a good

119

defense, and Bobby really ran the offense well. If he would have went down, we would have been toast. I really don't think he gets the credit he deserves for being a good quarterback and a good leader. The Orange Bowl against Penn State was a tough loss. As time goes by, the hurt goes away. I remember it more for the great group of guys we had and the coaching staff.

KU was good for me. I liked the people there and my teammates. I probably was not the most conscientious student. That was a time in your life where you did not have the responsibility you do as an adult with a job and a family. You were kind of fun and fancy free. Lawrence was really my home from 1967 to 1983. I lived there in the offseason when I played in the pros. In fact, when Joe Gibbs came to lure me out of retirement, he came to my place on Folks Road to talk to me. I don't get back as much as I would like to. I am pretty busy in my work. I still have my farm back in Centralia. It is a great place to hunt. But, yeah, if I had to do it again, KU would be the place—no doubt.

Being from Centralia, I always thought Topeka was a big city. Then I went to Kansas City and thought I knew what big was. My senior year, I went to Chicago for a photo shoot for the All-America team, and suddenly Kansas City didn't seem so big. So you can imagine my reaction to New York City when I was drafted by the Jets. I remember flying alone in to LaGuardia [Airport] and just looking down at all the buildings. I took a cab to my hotel and remember the trains that ran along the Garden State Parkway. My dad worked for the railroad, and I remember thinking I had never seen anything like that. After I checked in, I went for a walk to Times Square. I think I had a sore neck for a week after looking up at all of the buildings. I liked a lot of things about the city, but by the end of the season, I had to get the hell out of there and get back to Kansas to get away from the rat race.

You could say I was a bit of a free spirit as a player. I liked to have fun, but I didn't let it get in the way of team success. I am not sure what people thought of this boy from Kansas. I may have been a bit different than they expected. Things with the Redskins did not start off great. I came in as a free agent for [coach] George Allen, and I was seen by some as one of his boys when Joe Gibbs was hired. I sat out the 1980 season due to a contract dispute. Gibbs came to Lawrence to see me, and that is when the story got a bit exaggerated. I was quoted as telling Gibbs that he needed me to make him a good coach. That is not what I said. I told him he would be a good coach with or without John Riggins. And he would have. He was tremendous with people and utilizing their skills. I enjoyed playing for him and the Redskins.

I got my start in broadcasting when I was playing for the Redskins. I did a few commercials for a Washington Ford dealership in 1983. Then after I retired, I started doing some radio and television for the Redskins. I was even a radio disc jockey for a while. That led to an analyst position for ESPN Radio's *Sunday Night Football* broadcasts. A few years after I retired, I got an agent, and all of a sudden I was appearing in some off-Broadway musicals, some episodes of *The Guiding Light* soap opera, and then on the television series *Law & Order*. I am not really pursuing much of that anymore because I am so busy, but I did audition for the show *Chicago* recently. I don't know how good of an actor I am, but I have received good reviews. I could probably get more parts, but I can't sing worth a darn. You have to be able to sing to go far in that business.

I've done my radio show for a year now. It is kind of new for me in that I am the host. In the past, I was the analyst or the sidekick. Now I am the one to stick my neck out. It's a good show. We talk about a lot of different things. We do some things with culture—we did some wine-tasting. But we always have fun. I always felt I had a pretty good relationship with the media as a player. Oh, there were some disagreements, but I tried to make myself available as much as possible, especially after games. But the New York and Washington media are a bit different than being back in Kansas. There's just so much of it. Believe it or not, I was a journalism major at KU. I really did not know what I wanted to major in, but I know what I didn't want to do. Everyone else on the team was majoring in P.E., and I wanted to be different. I asked them, "What else is fun?" They said, "Try journalism." So now I am putting my education to use.

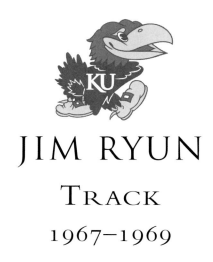

JIM RYUN

TRACK
1967–1969

IN THIS AGE OF UNLIMITED CABLE CHANNELS, MySpace, YouTube, Internet message boards, blogs, and personal websites, it is not unusual for high school athletes to arrive at college campuses already known as household names. Such was not the case nearly half a century ago, unless of course your name is Jim Ryun.

A skinny, bespectacled kid from Wichita East High School, Ryun appeared on Mount Oread in the fall of 1965 having become the first high school athlete to eclipse the four-minute mile (his high school record in the mile would stand for 36 years) and owning world records in the half-mile and mile run. A member of the 1964 U.S. Olympic Team, Ryun had been interviewed by media on every continent and was in constant demand by reporters in the United States. All of this is pretty heady stuff for a person who had failed in nearly every sport he had ever tried and who was a virtual unknown to his high school track coach until the latter part of his sophomore cross-country campaign. In fact, the coach kept on misspelling his last name during his first year on the team. All that quickly changed, however. In his sophomore outdoor season, he lost his first mile race by a whisker to the defending state champion. It would be the last mile competition he ever lost in high school. He was so dominant as a prepster that ESPN would later name him the top high school athlete of all time.

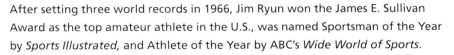

After setting three world records in 1966, Jim Ryun won the James E. Sullivan Award as the top amateur athlete in the U.S., was named Sportsman of the Year by *Sports Illustrated,* and Athlete of the Year by ABC's *Wide World of Sports.*

At Kansas, the legend of Jim Ryun continued to grow exponentially. He would continue to set world records. He would win individual, relay, and team NCAA national championships. In 1966, *Sports Illustrated* named him Sportsman of the Year, ABC's *Wide World of Sports* selected him Athlete of the Year, and he won the James E. Sullivan Award in honor of his selection as the top amateur athlete in the U.S. From 1965 to 1967, Ryun was the AAU outdoor mile champ and the 1967 NCAA mile champion. He established three world records in 1966 in the 880-yard run, the 1500-meter run, and the mile at 3:51.3 on June 16, 1966, in Berkeley, California. One year later, June 23, 1967, in Bakersfield, California, he lowered that to 3:51.1. That mark remained a world best for eight years. All told, Kansas won the Big 8 Indoor and Outdoor Track and Field team titles in each of Ryun's three seasons, and the Jayhawks won the NCAA indoor title and finished second in the outdoor in 1969.

"Jim was such a quiet and shy person," says his former coach, Bob Timmons. "If you did not know him, you would have thought he might have a big ego. That was not the case. He was just very uncomfortable talking about himself and what he had done. This was from a guy who had set a couple of world records and had been to the Olympics as a high schooler. But he was very much a team-oriented person. I know his teammates appreciated that about him. He was certainly not a prima donna, and his teammates didn't treat him like one. I was just honored to coach him and to be his friend. He was a rare breed as an athlete. He was just a great person and a very focused student."

A three-time Olympian, Ryun returned from California to rural Lawrence in 1981 to raise his family and later enter politics as a U.S. representative. He is a member of the State of Kansas, University of Kansas, National Track and Field, and Distance Running Halls of Fame. He continues to conduct the Jim Ryun Running Camps, speak publicly, write books, and assist the hearing impaired.

★   ★   ★

THE HIGHLIGHT OF THE YEAR FOR ME as a high school athlete was to run in the Kansas Relays. In regular meets and state championships, you ran against runners in your own class. But at the relays you ran against competitors from all classes and some from other states. It was always our best competition of the year, and of course running in Memorial Stadium was a treat. So I was fond of KU and Lawrence at an early age. But I was recruited by just about everyone. I think I even got a letter from Hawaii. I did very little visiting of schools because all of the travel would serve as an interruption to my training. I had always wanted to go to KU because I felt comfortable there. Plus, it would allow my family to see me compete. You also have to remember that Kansas was the top program in the nation. You had some of the best track and field athletes in the world, such as Glenn Cunningham, Wes Santee, Al Oerter, and many others. I considered it an honor to be a part of that. There was a time that I thought it may not happen for me, however. My high school coach, Bob Timmons, took a job as an assistant coach at KU after my junior year, and I looked forward to being reunited with him the next year. But during the spring semester of my senior year, Coach Timmons was offered the head job at Oregon State, and I was faced with a tough decision. As it would happen, there was a coaching change at KU a few days after he left, and Coach Timmons returned to Lawrence. I think we were both happy with the result. But for a time, yes, I was in a quandary. Thankfully I did not have to make a choice.

Freshmen weren't eligible at the time I was in school, but you still had the opportunity to run in non-collegiate events if you were invited. Track and field was popular at that time, and promoters and organizers would travel all over the country to sign up participants. Both Coach Timmons and I would get organizers and promoters calling us all the time. Some would even show up in Lawrence unannounced. I am glad we did not have cell phones at the time. I lived in Templin Hall with the rest of the track team, so to avoid these people, I would often go study elsewhere on campus. I would go find empty classrooms and study there. Nobody would know where I was. It made it quite a challenge to get my training and school work done. It was quite a distraction.

We didn't have a training table at Kansas, and there were no athletic dorms. We were integrated with the other students. I remember vividly that we had an indoor meet one afternoon, so before that we went down to the cafeteria and had what the other students had to eat. I enjoyed a meal of sauerkraut, hot dogs, and onion soup. At that time, the track at Allen Fieldhouse was dirt, and the inside lanes got pretty chopped up. You wouldn't call that a prescription for a fast time. I ended up setting a world indoor record in the 880-yard run [1:48.3 in a dual meet versus Oklahoma State, February

125

23, 1967]. Leading up to the race, the coaches and I felt the record was in reach, but I must admit my stomach wasn't feeling too good after that meal. I ran on adrenaline.

I've been asked about what stands out for me as an athlete. I would say it was being part of the KU team. We lived together in the dorm, we studied together, we trained together, and we competed together. My fondest memories are the activities we did together as a team. KU was a top-ranked basketball team, so we would hurry to get our studies done, then run over to Allen Fieldhouse to watch the games. Another thing we often did was, after we had finished our studies late at night, we would run down to Joe's Bakery and get some doughnuts. We burned so much energy in training that we'd have no problem putting down half a dozen doughnuts before we went to bed. We were close as a team. I remember that we would drive station wagons down to Austin to compete in the Texas Relays, then go over to Lafayette, Louisiana, to compete in the Southwest Relays. At night, we'd go to the drive-in theater, take folding chairs, set them up in a couple of rows, sit down, and watch the movie. Those were great times with some great people.

One of the unknown stories during my time at KU was the fact that I almost had to spend time in a full-body cast. We were running on a cross-country course that Coach Timmons had laid out on west campus in hopes of getting to host an NCAA meet. I had stepped in a hole that caused some back pain, so they sent me to the KU Medical Center. I drove over to the Med Center with Bobby Skahan, who would become a good friend of mine. He was our quarterback and had just hurt his knee against Oklahoma. I ended up wheeling Bobby all over the Med Center and finally into surgery. When I got into an examination room, the doctor looked at me and suggested that I wear a cast for a while that would stretch from my hips to my chest. That would allow my back to align. I wasn't going to do that because I was in training. So I went back to Lawrence and decided to see a chiropractor that Timmie [Timmons] had suggested to me. After examining me, the doctor told me he had seen the same thing in several basketball players, so he knew just what to do. Well, I went to him about a half dozen times and never had back pain again. The chiropractor was Dr. Phog Allen, our former basketball coach. He was certainly a talented man, and quite a character at that.

I was a photojournalism major at KU. I got into it by chance. When I was a high school student, Rich Clarkson of the *Topeka Capital Journal* gave me a camera and asked me to take photos during a trip I was taking as part of a United States Track and Field team traveling to Europe and Russia. The newspaper ended up publishing some of them. In college, they asked me to take some photos at KU sporting events. In fact, I would become a staff photographer for the *Capital Journal* after graduating from KU in 1970. Later, I was offered a job by *Sports Illustrated* to become a staff photographer. This was in 1972. The International Olympic Committee got wind of this and said that being a photographer for *Sports Illustrated* would make me a professional and thus make me ineligible to compete in the 1972 Munich Games. Obviously, I decided to give up my pursuit of being a photographer.

My time at KU was rewarding. I had a great coach and great teammates. The fans were also very supportive. For that reason, two races really stand out. First, as a freshman I could not compete with the varsity, so I ran in the open mile at the Kansas Relays. I set an American record, but could not have done it without my teammate Tom Yergovich. He went out and set the pace for me. It was totally unselfish on his part. That was the kind of person he was. The other race that stands out was my final race in Memorial Stadium in 1972. I had come out of retirement to train for the Olympics. I came back to run in the Kansas Relays as a thank-you to the great fans. It was a great rush to run before all of those people. I was told that they ran out of tickets after 36,000 had been handed out. The stadium was buzzing with excitement.

127

The best race of my life came in the summer of my freshman year. It was a meet in Berkeley, California, when I set my mile world record. I ended up meeting my wife, Anne, although I really didn't remember it at the time. She was actually a Kansas State student, and she came up and congratulated me after the race. But I was tired and upset because someone had stolen my bag and warmup clothes. I really didn't have time for her right then or the autograph she was seeking. Later on, I would meet her on a blind date in Wichita on Thanksgiving Day and marry her two and a half years later.

As I reflect on my years at KU, I am in awe of how the Lord blessed me with a superb coach, sacrificial teammates, and fantastic fans. I am grateful to God for the talent he blessed me with and the grace to use it so well.

JO JO WHITE

BASKETBALL

1966–1968

Jo Jo White easily qualifies as one of the greatest players to ever suit up and represent the University of Kansas. A three-time All–Big 8 and two-time All-America selection for the Jayhawks, White was a member of the 1968 U.S.A. Olympic team and enjoyed an 12-year career in the NBA.

White's jersey was retired and now hangs in Allen Fieldhouse. In addition, his No. 10 jersey has been retired by the Boston Celtics.

During his years as a member of the Jayhawk basketball team under head coach Ted Owens, he scored a combined 1,286 points. He led KU in scoring in 1968, averaging 15.3 points a game.

White was a catalyst in KU's run in the NCAA Tournament in 1966 and 1967. He guided the Jayhawks to the NIT finals in 1968. In addition, he served as an assistant coach at KU in 1982–1983.

★   ★   ★

I grew up in St. Louis and was the youngest of seven children. I played basketball throughout St. Louis, so I was fortunate. Each year I got better as I was developing and growing. I ended up getting about 250 offers to go to college, and I knew nothing about KU. My high school coach, Jody Bailey, chose KU as one of the five schools I would visit.

128

During his recruiting visit to KU, Jo Jo White attended a Jayhawk football game and saw Gale Sayers play at Memorial Stadium. He credits that experience as one of the major selling points in convincing him to sign with Kansas. White was also a member of the 1968 U.S. Olympic team.

When I got the opportunity to come and visit the campus, I had the greatest experience I could imagine. And, I got to see one of the greatest players ever to run a football in Gale Sayers. This was one of the selling points on my coming back to school in the fall.

Sam Miranda was the guy who recruited me at KU. I didn't know Ted Owens until I arrived at KU. I knew all about Sam, and I have a lot of admiration for him. He brought a lot of the Marine tactics to the table in training us for the season. I remember we were out running in a field, and I asked Sam if doing this had anything to do with basketball. We were running in the trees and seeing cows and stuff as we trained. We ran up hills and we ran at the football stadium. At the time, we didn't understand what this had to do with playing basketball. We soon learned that the training Sam took us through turned out to be the most important thing in terms of basketball and our success.

I started my high school career coming in and playing half a season, starting at midterm. So I had to follow up with another half, which made it a full season. I was able to graduate at midterm, and Kansas wanted me to come to school then. Of course, freshmen at that time had to play one year on the freshman team before they could play varsity.

So, by coming in half a year ahead of time, I played the second half of the season on the freshman team and the first half the following year. Then, at mid-season, I had the choice of either going up to the varsity squad or waiting until the following season. The varsity team was really good that year, and Coach Owens decided, since I was kind of killing their backcourt players on the varsity squad, it would be best for the team if I started playing at mid-year.

130

I replaced Riney Lochmann in the starting lineup. Riney was a terrific individual. He told Coach Owens that he would step down out of his starting position and allow me the opportunity of starting in the backcourt because he felt that it would add to our opportunity for success. I have a lot of admiration for him. He was an outstanding player who took an unselfish position to become the sixth man so I could be a starter.

We went from beating teams by a margin of 10 points to about 22 points a game. It upped the tempo when I moved into the lineup, and I have Riney Lochmann to thank for stepping down and allowing me to start.

Ted Owens was more than just a coach to me. He was like a father figure, and he intrigued me. He was fundamentally sound. He really instilled in us the importance of not being tricky, but being efficient on the floor. He taught us why it was important for your teammates to know exactly what you were going to do out on the floor. He was one of the true fundamentalists in the game, as far as coaches go. I believe that, right now in our game, we're lacking what Coach Owens was teaching. Rules have changed now, and they don't allow our young players to get all of what this great man and coach gave us in terms of the basics of the game.

Walt Wesley was one of my teammates at KU, and he was the first big man I ever played with in a game. Here's a guy who was 6′11″, and I had never played with or against a guy his size with that talent. As the years went on, he got better and better. He had a great work ethic. Walt had a turnaround jump shot that was deadly and a rolling hook shot across the middle. When I first came to KU, I was told to get Walt Wesley the ball.

I was saying to myself, *Well, I can shoot it, too. I mean, why am I getting it to him?* But as I worked with him, game in and game out, I soon understood why our coaches wanted us to get him the ball in the low box. Every day, he was out working on his shot, to the point where he was pretty automatic inside.

The opportunity to play in Allen Fieldhouse was second to none. I thought I had died and gone to heaven when I came to school at KU. I had visited five schools, and getting to see a game in Allen Fieldhouse and experiencing the atmosphere was a selling point. It was a pleasure and honor for me to play there for four years. I tried to give the fans everything I had each and every time I played on the floor. I felt that I had a good relationship with the KU fans, and it's one that still goes on. Every time I walk into Allen Fieldhouse, I feel that same kind of uplifting feeling, because the fans haven't changed. They're even better.

131

I suppose the game everyone always remembers from my playing career at KU was the 1966 NCAA Tournament game against Texas Western. We felt, as a team that year, we had a great chance to win it all. Texas Western, in my opinion, was the most athletic team that we had faced all year.

It was a game that went back and forth in terms of both teams leading by as many as five or six points. It was about the biggest lead one team or the other had throughout the game. Both teams competed at a high level. I felt, personally, that I had the handle of the game. If we went down three or four points, I was able to come up with steals or hit shots at the right time to keep us in the game.

I'll never forget, we were down one point and they had the ball. Time was running down, and they missed a shot. We got the rebound and called a timeout with seven seconds left on the clock. We went into the huddle, and I said, as a freshman, "Let me have the ball." I mean, how much could we do in seven seconds? The coaches agreed.

I started down the middle once the play started, and they closed the middle up. I reversed my dribble and went down the left side of the floor. I glanced at the clock at the same time and saw three seconds left on the clock. I put up the shot, and as I let the ball go, I hit the floor, bounced up, and ended up on this lady's lap. I'll never forget, she had her arms around me and she was hugging me. Everyone was screaming. I looked across the floor, and the coaches were hugging each other, jumping up and down. Then the official came out of the backcourt and said my foot was on the out-of-bounds line. I couldn't believe that.

I've watched that game until there were only silhouettes on the screen, and it never showed my foot on the out-of-bounds line.

The official made the call, and for me to get upset and rant and rave was not going to change the call. I've seen it 500 times. You can question a call once the official has made it, but nine out of 10 times they are not going to change it. It's someone else's opinion whether or not the basket is good or you're out of bounds. He chose to say my foot was out of bounds.

So I had to accept that. The next morning, I thought the sun was shining brighter than ever outside. I didn't have any ill feelings other than that was an opportunity for us to win the whole thing. In our minds, we had the best team and one controversial call made the difference in winning versus losing.

I will say that my four years at Kansas was, perhaps, the greatest experience in my young life. I wouldn't trade those years for anything in the world. Even now, with the rule changes and players able to come out early, I think our young athletes are really missing the most important growth period in their life by not staying in college all four years.

The SEVENTIES

NOLAN CROMWELL
FOOTBALL/TRACK
1973–1976

KANSAS FOOTBALL COACH Don Fambrough looked like he had swallowed a canary as he conducted the weekly staff meeting with his assistants to review their recruiting assignments. After each coach had provided his update, Fambrough leaped to his feet to proclaim, "Men, I have discovered the best athlete in the state of Kansas, maybe the whole world. And you know what? His sister might be the second best."

Nolan Neil Cromwell (born January 30, 1955, in Smith Center, Kansas) is arguably one of the best athletes ever produced by the state of Kansas. All-state in football and basketball, he was an AAU junior champion in the decathlon, a three-time state champion in track, and a standout baseball player. Cromwell grew up in western Kansas, attending Logan High School as a freshman and sophomore, then moving to Ransom, where he completed his high school eligibility. He would go on to star at the University of Kansas in both football and track. On the gridiron, he was the 1975 Big 8 Conference Offensive Player of the Year and an honorable mention All-American. He set an NCAA record for rushing yards for a quarterback with 294 yards versus Oregon State on September 27, 1975, and engineered a 23–3 upset at No. 12 Oklahoma on November 8 that same year, breaking the Sooners' 28-game winning streak. On the track, he was an All-American in 1975 and set KU records in the 400-meter hurdles, 600-yard dash, and decathlon. He was inducted into the State of Kansas Hall of Fame in 1996 and the University of

Kansas Football Ring of Honor in 2005. The Kansas football program pres-
ents an award annually in his name to a member of the team, recognizing
leadership skills. And, yes, Cromwell's sister was good in her own right, setting state track records as a freshman in high school.

★   ★   ★

"I first started getting attention from schools after my sophomore year in
high school, when I had done fairly well at the state track meet in Wichita,"
Cromwell said. "I was getting questionnaires from schools that had interest
in me for track. But I was upfront with everyone that I wanted to play football and run track in college, and that I wanted to stay fairly close to home so
my parents could drive to the games. So I narrowed it down to Nebraska,
Oklahoma, Kansas State, and Kansas. The deciding factor for me was primarily Don Fambrough. He was so genuine, yet so passionate. You just felt comfortable around him. He was a very positive man. That, combined with the
tradition of the track program, made my decision easier. I love Don Fambrough. He's just an honest guy and a great ambassador for KU. I've got a
warm place in my heart for him. He gave me a fair opportunity, and I got to
achieve everything I wanted to in college, and that all stems from his taking
a shot on me as a small-town kid from western Kansas."

135

"Man, everybody wanted him," Fambrough said. "His mother worked at
the hospital, and I made so many recruiting trips to Ransom that I knew all
the patients by name. Heck, Ransom was so small [population 450] it could
fit it in my living room. [Head coach] Vince Gibson of Kansas State was a
hell of a recruiter, and when I went out there, I would see his car parked
around the corner, just waiting for me to leave so he could talk to Nolan. I
would leave, but circle around and wait for Gibson to leave so I would get in
the last word. But even when Nolan said he was coming to Kansas, baseball
came after him. He could have made a heck of a lot of money playing professional baseball. I was sweating bullets until he showed up. Nolan Cromwell
had it all. He was talented, he worked hard, he was competitive, and he was
smart. He was a true student-athlete. I coached many fine people, but none
finer than Nolan Cromwell."

"Coming from a small town," Cromwell said, "I was a bit concerned at
first that I might be in awe of the campus and competing with the other athletes. But I played in the high school all-star game in Wichita just before I

went to school, and I did fairly well. It was the first year they had the game. So I was confident that I belonged, despite being from a small town. When we first reported, all freshmen were tried out on offense and defense. I was a high school quarterback and linebacker, but I played defensive back in the all-star game. I was recruited as a wide receiver. We had good receivers, so my best opportunity came at free safety. They said I had a better chance to make the traveling squad, so I jumped at that opportunity. That was the first year freshmen could play [1973], but I was playing behind Jimmy David. He broke his arm against Iowa State, so I got my opportunity to play then."

The 1973 squad went 7–4–1 overall and finished in a tie for second in the Big 8 at 4–2–1. It finished the season ranked 18th in the Associated Press poll, falling to Lou Holtz's North Carolina State Wolfpack in the Liberty Bowl, 31–18. The next year, Kansas slipped to 4–7 overall and 1–6 in the Big 8. Bud Moore came from Alabama to replace Fambrough for the 1975 campaign, and with him came the wishbone offense.

"The plan was for me to participate in track in the spring, which I did as a freshman," Cromwell said. "But when Bud came in the spring of my sophomore year, the staff asked me to try out at quarterback. I would do my track drills, then go to spring football practice. We played a bit of option football in high school, but it was not as sophisticated as what we were doing under Bud. In my junior year, we got off to a slow start, losing our first game [18–14 versus Washington State]. The next week, I came off the bench and we won [14–10 at Kentucky]. I started the rest of the year, beginning with the Oregon State game."

Cromwell may have been green as a college quarterback, but he played like he was born into the position. He combined tremendous speed with great strength and intelligence, making him a threat with every snap. That playmaking ability earned him the moniker "the Ransom Rambler" from Jayhawk broadcaster Tom Hedrick.

"What is interesting about that game," said Cromwell, "was our former defensive coordinator, Ken Blue, had been the defensive coordinator for Oregon State. We had such great running backs in Laverne Smith and Billy Campfield, that they assigned two defenders to the pitchman for the option. They did not think I was any threat at all, and they didn't have a reason to believe so up to that point. All I had to do was hit the hole. I didn't have any idea I was on my way to setting an NCAA record. It was hot on the artificial surface, and I was cramping up, so I knew I had run for quite a bit of

Nolan Cromwell, nicknamed "the Ransom Rambler" in honor of his small Kansas hometown, brought a combination of speed, strength, and intelligence as an option quarterback at KU. He set an NCAA single-game rushing record for a quarterback with 294 yards versus Oregon State in 1975.

yardage. But I had no clue how many yards I had. I really did not play much of the fourth quarter, but that was okay, because we needed to give younger players some time.

"We really had a good young defense, and our offense was starting to jell [5–3 heading into the Oklahoma game]. Oklahoma was highly-ranked [12th nationally] and had not lost in 37 games. We were a huge underdog and were not expected to do well, but we didn't know any better. By keeping it close in the first half against Oklahoma, we built some confidence. They went up 3–0, but we scored right before halftime to go up 7–3, and that put a bit of pressure on them. It then snowballed a bit on Oklahoma as they began to turn the ball over, and we capitalized a few times. The defense played great, and the offense didn't turn the ball over. It was a big win for our program. We went on to the Sun Bowl and lost to a great Pitt team featuring Tony Dorsett [33–19] that won the national championship the next year. But we had a lot of players coming back for the next season, too, and we had high hopes, ourselves."

Cromwell was back to lead the squad in his final season [1976] after rushing for 1,124 yards as a junior. Kansas reeled off four wins in five games as Oklahoma visited Lawrence for homecoming in a matchup between the No. 15 Jayhawks and No. 6 Sooners. Oklahoma keyed on Cromwell from the opening kickoff and eventually knocked him out with a torn medial collateral ligament in his knee, with the Jayhawks owning the lead. Kansas eventually fell to Oklahoma 28–10, and with Cromwell out for the season, the team limped to a 6–5 record.

"Oklahoma was still smarting a bit from the previous year when we beat them," Cromwell said. "We fought them even, but they were putting a hit on me every play. Eventually, I went out with a knee injury that ended my season and my [college] career. It kind of took the wind out of our sails for that game and the rest of the year.

"Competing in both track and football on the collegiate level was not easy. But both programs worked well together because they saw the advantage of the dual training regimen. It really helped our speed. The challenge for me was that I participated in events [hurdles and decathlon] that required a considerable emphasis on technique. Technique was never my strong point because I just did not have enough time to train. I had to rely on my speed and strength." Cromwell was up to the challenge, setting school records in the 400-meter hurdles, 600-yard dash, and the decathlon en route to earning All-America honors in 1975.

"It was beautiful watching Nolan compete," Kansas track coach Bob Timmons said. "He was so fast and powerful. You marveled at him because he could do everything with such grace. And he was wonderful to have on the team. He was such a leader. Competing in both sports was not easy. Oftentimes, he would go right from one practice to another with no break."

"I would say my greatest experience in college was running against Ralph Mann in 1975 at the Drake Relays," Cromwell said. "It was the first time I had the opportunity to run against a world-class athlete. He was the world record holder in the 400 hurdles at the time. The stadium was packed because the Olympics were a year away. I was neck and neck with him, but after I hit the hurdle, I messed up on my footwork a bit and lost by two-tenths of a second. It killed me. I knew in my mind that I could run with those guys. I just remember how excited everyone was to have the Olympians there, and I was competing against them.

"That next spring we had the Olympic Trials in Eugene, Oregon, and I was matched up against Edwin Moses in my heat. Of course, he went on to win all of those gold medals. I was running a good race, but nicked a hurdle and missed the finals. I really did not have great technique compared to those guys who were full-time, Olympic-caliber track athletes. When I hit the hurdle, it cost me. Moses just blew right past me. It was disappointing because my best time that year would have qualified me for the U.S. team.

"I have been told by a lot of people that I was the person responsible for the [NFL] Combine. I don't know about that. But I do know that I wanted to play, and the only way to prove I was okay was to go to them. Teams were reluctant to take a chance on a knee injury. I have a seven- or eight-inch scar on my leg from the surgery. Today, the way medicine has improved, I might not have needed surgery or it would have been done with less down time, as they might have gone in there cleaned things out a bit. But I remember going on my own to 13 teams with my X-rays and working out for them. On my last trip, which was to Dallas, I ran into general manager Tex Schramm and player personal director Gil Brandt. They told me that a person should not have to go through what I did. The next year, the NFL Combine was started."

The Los Angeles Rams were convinced Cromwell was worth the risk, taking him in the second round. He would play 11 years as a free safety, earning

NFC Defensive Player of the Year in 1980. He was selected to the Pro Bowl four times and was named to the NFL's all-decade team for the 1980s. It is no surprise that Cromwell's leadership and talent were put to work in the NFL after his retirement. He coached one year with the Los Angeles Rams under John Robinson as a defense/special-teams assistant (1991), then began his association with Mike Holmgren, first with the Green Bay Packers (1992–1998) and then with the Seattle Seahawks as the wide receivers coach (1999–2007). He retuned to the college ranks with his appointment in January 2008 as the offensive coordinator at Texas A&M.

"The university gave me every opportunity to be successful academically and athletically," said Cromwell. "I could not have imagined going anywhere else, looking back on it. My parents had a chance to go to every game, and that was important. It was a beautiful campus, and everyone was so good to me. The people were tremendous. I owe so much of what I have accomplished to my days at the University of Kansas and the people there."

Cromwell was a world-class track athlete in the decathlon and high hurdles.

GARY KEMPF

SWIMMING ★ HEAD COACH ★
ASSISTANT ATHLETICS DIRECTOR
1973–1976 ★ 1976–2000 ★ 2000–2005

GROWING UP IN BARTLESVILLE, OKLAHOMA, in the shadows of Oklahoma and Oklahoma State, one would have expected Gary Kempf to become a Sooner or a Cowboy. Kempf's father worked for the Phillips 66 Corporation, thus he had the opportunity to swim for the nationally renowned Phillips 66 Splash Club. A top junior, he was recruited by many of the top collegiate programs. But you could say Kansas had an ace in the hole. Phillips 66 president William Douce came from KU, and Kempf tended to his yard. In addition, Kansas swimming coach Dick Reamon had successfully recruited Kempf's older brother, Tom. As they say, the rest is history. For 33 years, Gary Kempf called the University of Kansas home. He competed for the swim team from 1973 to 1976, winning eight individual league titles and earning Big 8 Swimmer of the Year status as a freshman. He coached the women's team beginning in 1977, added the men's program to his duties in 1982, and then moved into athletic administration in 2000. On July 1, 2005, Kempf was named athletics director at Asbury College in Wilmore, Kentucky.

★   ★   ★

"We were unbelievably blessed to participate in the Phillips 66 Splash Club program," Kempf said. "Since my dad worked at Phillips 66, the program was free. We traveled all over the nation. By the time I was 16 years old, I bet I had traveled to 40 of the 50 states. This was one of the tools Phillips 66 used to spread its name. We loaded up in a bus with the Phillips 66 logo all over it. They also had a basketball team that I watched growing up. They had some great players—Kendall Rhine, Jim Currier, all those guys were great people. I remember watching Larry Brown, who was playing for Dayton, come to the Phillips gymnasium.

"I visited Oklahoma, Oklahoma State, BYU, and Florida State, but looking back, I really didn't have a choice," Kempf chuckled. "The engineering department at KU was so strong and Phillips 66 had a close relationship with the university. The president of Phillips 66 was William Douce, and he came from KU. I was his yard boy. Every time he saw me between the ages of 14 and 17, he would tell me that I would be going to KU. When Dick Reamon came down to recruit my brother [Tom], I would have signed that day, too. Dick was from Topeka and swam for KU. Dick was a different breed. He could have offered you a scholarship for three pencils and you would have thought you had signed to save the world. I really knew KU was the place when I went to visit Tommy in school. I knew KU was a special place.

142

"My greatest memory as an athlete came my freshman year at the Big 8 meet when I swam the preliminaries of the 500 freestyle with my brother in the lane next to me. I can remember that I had never been so scared going to the blocks because I had not swum the 500 freestyle very much. He just told me, 'Stay with me.' And that is all I did. I moved over by the lane rope and just followed him. He finished first, and I finished second. He was a junior, one of the country's premier distance swimmers, and an All-American in 1971. But he knew this was his last year. He was going to join the Navy in March. At the finals that night, I was even more scared. I went over to him and asked for some encouragement, and he said, 'Stay with me, then take off.' So I stayed with him, and the first 200 he took me out very, very fast—faster than what I had wanted to. Then he eased back, and I took off and won the race. He set me up to win. He knew he was done with college. He won't admit it, but I would never have gone out that fast. That meant so much to me that he would do that and be so selfless.

"We won three titles [1973, 1974, and 1975], and it should have been four, but it was probably my fault. I was having the best year I could have ever

Gary Kempf spent 33 years at the University of Kansas, first as a student-athlete and later as head swimming coach for Jayhawk women's and men's teams.

imagined. I was going home for Thanksgiving, and Dick pulled me aside and told me not to do what I wanted to do—play football. So, I told him I wouldn't. Well, I got a call on Wednesday night to play, and I said, 'No, not going to do it.' Thursday, no again. Friday, no. Saturday, no. And then Sunday I was ready to go back to school, and they asked me to play. I figured I could play all-time quarterback. On the last play, the score was tied. My coach at Phillips 66 suggested I play receiver and go long. It was the last play, so I thought there was no harm. I went long and the pass came to me. I went up for it and came down on my left leg and tore every ligament in my knee.

"They gave me the choice to swim on the injury or have surgery and be done for the year. That was a no-brainer. I tried to swim on it. I sat out until the first of the year. My best event was the individual medley, but I could not kick. I was limited in what I could do. I ended up having 14 knee surgeries in total. I felt like I let down the entire program, but most of all, I felt I let down Dick. I was devastated. He was probably the biggest influence in my life as a coach. He had put me in a position where I knew what I needed to do, and I felt like I let him down.

"I was a biology major and had every intention of going to medical school at first. But I had just graduated and really wasn't ready to go to graduate school. I was tired of school. But after the school year, the women's swimming coach had resigned, and they opened up the search. I talked to Marian Washington, who was the women's athletics director and the basketball coach at the time. I got the job, probably because I was a known quantity. I thought I would do it for a few years. I thought it would be better than getting a real job. I thought it would be something to do for one or two years. I really liked it after the first year, so I thought I would do it a few more years. Obviously, that few years stretched on a little bit.

"I think the 1982–1983 women's team that finished seventh in the nation might be the most memorable for me. We had some great swimmers. People like Tammy Thomas [world-record holder], Jenny Wagstaff, Celine Cerny, and others. It was so much fun to coach that team. They were great swimmers and great kids. They were very individualistic and loved to live life."

"We kid Gary a lot now that we are gone," said Jayhawk All-American swimmer Glenn Trammel. "We could all do the famous Gary Kempf pose. He would sit in a chair and cross his gargantuan knees—he had so many knee surgeries that they were bigger than his thighs. He'd rest an elbow on a knee and place his index finger next to his nose. His temple would start bouncing. He was restraining himself so he would not jump out of his chair. He was a tremendous coach and a tremendous person. He laid out his expectations and your accountabilities. Then he empowered you to meet them. His passion was to get you to maximize your efforts and help you reach heights you had not reached before. He was so proud of the university and demanded that

144

you represent it in a first-class manner. His coaching was focused on not only making you a better swimmer, but also a better person. There were no professional contracts out there, so he was preparing you for life after school. If you look at our program and the people who have come out of it, the level of success is amazing.

For all of the success Kempf enjoyed, two events left indelible marks on his heart and the program. In November of 1985, three members of the team were returning from Thanksgiving break in Bartlesville, Oklahoma, when their car hit an ice patch and crashed. Killed was Tammy Pease, while Karen Dionne suffered a severe head injury, and Dan Mendenhall was severely bruised. In January of 1996, swimmer Seth Dunscombe passed away due to complications from an enlarged heart.

"It changes your life," said Kempf. "Tammy and Seth are with me in my office today and they always will be. The accident happened just outside of Independence, Kansas. It was a route I had taken many times myself over the years. It took me four years before I could go that way again. I was put in a role that I was not prepared for. When you see people hurting, you needed to lead. You had to be strong. With Seth—one is bad enough, two shortens your career. I know that is what it did for me. I probably went too long, but I loved the program, I loved the kids, and I loved KU.

"I would never, ever trade my time at KU for anything. It was the greatest time of my life. It is a great institution. I retain my friendships with the coaches whom I worked with. I love them a lot. That was the heart and soul of my life. I could walk into any office of any coach and talk to them. They always had time for you. I learned so much from those guys. I have a picture on my wall. It has Dick Reamon, Jerry Waugh, Bob Lockwood, Bob Timmons, Don Fambrough, and Floyd Temple. Of all the things, that is what I cherish the most, the relationships. These are some of the classiest guys ever at KU.

"It was a difficult decision to leave KU. But we did take a piece of KU with us. I have a coffee table made from a piece of the original floor of Allen Fieldhouse from 1955. It came from an old dairy barn south of Lawrence. We went out there one day for an open house. It was on a Sunday, and I didn't want to go because football was on television. It was being remodeled into a house. I walked in and saw the original Allen Fieldhouse floor and knew we had to have it. We enjoyed living there, knowing a special part of KU history was under our feet.

DARNELL VALENTINE

BASKETBALL

1978–1981

IT WAS A PERFECT MARRIAGE. Kansas was looking for a floor general to mesh with a talented group of returning veterans. Darnell Valentine wanted to improve his basketball skills, develop into a well-rounded person, and receive a quality education. There were many suitors for Valentine, but in the end the allure of playing in his home state was too much to resist. Spurning the full-court press of North Carolina, Valentine would become a Jayhawk.

During his four-year career, Valentine recorded 1,821 points, which was second only to Clyde Lovellette at the time, and now stands fifth on the school's all-time list. He is the career record holder with 336 steals and fifth in assists with 609. He was a four-time first-team All–Big 8 selection (the first time a Kansas player earned all-league honors four times since 1947), a 1981 All-American, a three-time Academic All-American (1979–1981), and a member of the 1980 Olympic team that eventually boycotted the competition. He was drafted in the first round of the 1981 NBA Draft by the Portland Trail Blazers and would play nine years in the league, including stints with the Cleveland Cavaliers and the Los Angeles Clippers.

Valentine was a model of consistency, averaging in double figures in each of his four seasons at Kansas, playing relentless defense, and directing the offense in starting 114 of 118 games played. His coach, Ted Owens, said of the Wichita, Kansas, product, "He was an enormous worker who was always prepared and focused. He was so disruptive on defense." His No. 14 uniform was retired January 1, 2005, at halftime of the Jayhawks' thrilling 70–68 overtime win against Georgia Tech.

Valentine's inaugural season (1977–1978) was a hit. He led a balanced scoring attack with 13.5 points per game, as Kansas won the Big 8 title and advanced to the NCAA Tournament. The No. 10 Jayhawks were sent to Eugene, Oregon, to face No. 2 UCLA. A late Bruins charge pinned an 83–76 loss on Kansas and ended its season with a 24–5 record. Valentine would end his career at Kansas in grand fashion as the Jayhawks finished 24–8 in 1980–1981, winning the Big 8 postseason tournament and advancing to the NCAA Sweet 16. The season included a 56–55 win over No. 6 North Carolina in Kansas City's Kemper Arena in Tar Heels head coach Dean Smith's first game against his alma mater. In the 80–68 Big 8 tourney title game win over Kansas State, Valentine and his four other starting mates played the entire 40 minutes.

Today, Valentine and his wife, Cindy, and daughter, Tierra, live in Portland. He is an executive with Precision Castparts Corp.

★   ★   ★

I was born in Chicago and would visit relatives in Wichita each year. One summer, I asked my mom and dad if I could stay for the rest of the summer with my uncle and aunt. They said that would be fine. Then they decided to move the rest of the family down about a year later. I was the youngest of four siblings. I was about seven or eight at the time and always had a good time when I would go to Wichita.

Our neighborhood was at Kansas and Green Streets in north Wichita. It seems like there was always some activity going on. One day a person who would later become a friend of mine drove by and asked us if we wanted to play in an organized program. That would be unheard-of today to have a stranger drive down the street stopping to talk to a bunch of kids about coming with him to play basketball. But that was a different time. That person was Jamie Coulter, who worked for Pizza Hut at the time and was involved in the community. He asked my uncle if it would be okay for me and some of the others to play for his team. So we got in the car and went to play basketball. It was the local Biddy Basketball program. Afterward, we would go to his house and swim in his pool. He would make us hamburgers or go to McDonald's. I guess that was my start in basketball. It was great fun.

Darnell Valentine is one of the most honored basketball players in school history. A 1981 All-America selection as a senior, Valentine was a four-time all-conference selection and three-time Academic All-American.

Another strong male presence was Goose Doughty. We formed a relationship in junior high. He taught tennis at McAdams Park and was a mentor for many young kids. To this day, I can remember sitting in his house, watching NBA games on television. He would always comment on the play, pointing out mistakes and bad coaching decisions. His favorite comment was, "That was a rookie move." He'd be all fired up, and we would just sit and laugh. The kids of Wichita were fortunate at that time. There was so much nurturing going on, and kids were developing physically, mentally, and socially.

Coach [Lafayette] Norwood entered the picture when I was in high school at Wichita Heights. He had high expectations of a person and treated everyone equal. He actually became my guardian during the recruiting process and kept everything above board. He was not going to let me be bought. It came down to North Carolina and Kansas, and the pure virtue and honor of each program. Both were straight up with me, and I respected them for that. I had two great choices, so I could not lose. The great thing about Coach Norwood is that even though he was going to KU as an assistant, he left it up to me to decide where to go. KU was aware of that, as well. He was going there on his own merits. He was a good coach. But we had too good of a relationship, and that helped in my making the decision to go to KU. I also wanted to be able to play in front of my family. So you have the combination of my high school coach, staying in state, playing for a great program. I had all the support I could want. It was tough for North Carolina to overcome that.

There was a positive outcome of my recruitment for the city of Wichita. It had always had great basketball. The games in the parks were legendary. There were some great high school teams. But I don't think anyone got the national attention that they deserved until all of those schools started to recruit me. Schools from all over were recruiting me, and now they were seeing the talent of others. I think that opened up opportunities for people like Antoine Carr, Greg Dreiling, Ricky Ross, Aubrey Sherrod, and others. It was the beginning of a discovery that Wichita had good basketball players. It was a hotbed. I am just glad that the opportunities came for us.

149

That first year at Kansas was a great experience for me. What I remember most is the great leadership we had. The seniors were so strong—John Douglas, Ken Koenigs, Donnie Von Moore, Clint Johnson. Then you added the freshman core of Wilmore Fowler, John Crawford, and me. It was great chemistry. John Douglas may have been the greatest athlete I have ever played with. He was special. The UCLA game in the NCAA Tournament was a tough loss. We knew it would be a challenge to play them on the West Coast. The thing I recall about that game is we had 40 fouls playing a zone defense, and they had about 10 fouls playing man-to-man. But that's basketball. That's the way life is.

Playing at Kansas meant we played some great programs. We had some great games with Kentucky. They always had tough, talented players. In one game, we had a six-point lead with 30 seconds left and lost it. Sometimes the games are bigger than the players, and you have to have the right mindset to

finish it off. That was a moment of growth for us. It helped us understand
what it took to win, but it was a hard lesson.

To be named an academic All-American three times was an honor. My
education was important to me. It was the realization at an early age. Life is
fragile and athletics is fragile, and I wanted to be successful in everything that
I did. It was drilled into me at an early age. I had parents who stressed it. My
three older siblings had all gone to college. Coach Norwood stressed it in
high school. KU had the people in place in terms of academic support. It was
always important. The thing about it is you really don't understand or appreciate all of that until you are done playing and you have to go out and deal
with the world on a different playing field.

I liked watching the NBA to see how the best players did it. I go back to
the days of Hal Greer, Archie Clark, Walt Frazier, Earl Monroe, Nate
Archibald, and Jo Jo White. I loved Jo Jo's game. He was so smooth. He
would come back to KU in the summer and play with us. He was amazing.
Here he was, a person who had been in the league for 10 years, and he was
coming back and playing with us every day. He kept in such good shape. He
looks like he could play today. He was a person I emulated. What I appreciated is he was so committed to helping us develop as players and people. I
never got a chance to play against him because he retired just as I was enter-
ing the league.

I had some physical gifts. It was part of the gene pool, but I always thought
of myself as a hard worker. I always wanted to be the best-conditioned athlete. When I would meet fans or other people when I was not in uniform,
they would say, "Hey, you're the guy with the big legs." In the time I played,
the shorts were a bit shorter, so people could see my legs were developed.
With the long shorts that they play with today, no one would have been able
to notice. That might have been the only benefit I had of playing then. I took
care of myself then. I exercised a lot. I still exercise, not to the extent that I
did in the past, but I am in still good shape at 48 years of age.

It was a tremendous honor to represent the United States on the Olympic
team. I thought at the time it was unfortunate that we did not get to play. It
was unfortunate that politics interfered with athletics. You would hope that
that would not have happened. It would have been an incredible experience
to play on an international stage. But they did a tremendous job in making
us feel as if we were representing our country. We played exhibition games
against some NBA teams [including a win over a collection of some of the

players from the 1976 Olympic team]. Dave Gavitt [Providence's head coach] was the head coach and Larry Brown was the assistant. Larry made you feel like he was coaching you and only you. When you look at the thousands of people he's touched, he makes you feel like he was your coach and yours only. I enjoyed playing for him, and obviously he is a part of the Kansas tradition.

Playing at Kansas was an honor and a privilege. The heritage that I was and am a part of is more relevant now that I am done and can reflect back on it. I am really proud and thankful that I got to play at Kansas. After you are done and look back at it, you realize the stature of the program, and you count your blessings. The longevity of the program is amazing. Coach Williams was phenomenal in making sure that the KU family stayed together. He would call me on occasion and send me Kansas gear. I am always wearing stuff that says "Kansas." With all that he had going on, to take the time to do that was great. I really appreciate that. Coach Self is the same way. That is what is great about the coaches and the program. They are so inclusive. They appreciate those who are part of the program, whether they coached them or not. It's class, that's what it is.

It was a proud moment to go back and have my uniform hung up there with the others like Wilt, Jo Jo, Clyde Lovellette, Danny Manning. It was a blessing. I loved it, and it was a reconnection. It was a wonderful, overwhelming, and satisfying day. To be able to share it with my wife and daughter was great. Even though my daughter did not know what Daddy did in those days, she now has a pretty good feeling he did something good.

Allen Fieldhouse was home to me and always will be, in a sense. I love watching games on television. It takes me back to when I played. That place was great. It was difficult for any team to come in there and have success. The Kansas State and Missouri games were insane. It did not matter, the quality of the teams. It was always a competitive game. Kansas State had Mike Evans and later Rolando Blackman. There were some pretty intense games. Missouri was the border rivalry, and they had Larry Drew from Wyandotte. He beat me in the state finals my junior year, and the year after, we beat them badly. We had a really good game.

LYNETTE WOODARD
WOMEN'S BASKETBALL
1978–1981

WHO WAS THE FIRST KU BASKETBALL PLAYER to have a jersey number (31) retired and displayed in Allen Fieldhouse?

It's not Clyde Lovellette, Wilt Chamberlain, or Danny Manning. The answer, perhaps a surprise to some college basketball observers, is Lynette Woodard. Of course, it should be noted that a department-wide sanctioned jersey retirement system was not established at KU until the mid-1990s and no other basketball numbers—beyond Woodard's—had been retired up to that point.

But let the record show that Woodard's achievements on the basketball court leave no doubt that she belongs in that inaugural class of distinguished KU players who merit rafter recognition in the storied home of the Jayhawks.

In 2004, she was inducted into the Naismith Basketball Hall of Fame, an honor that speaks volumes about her career accomplishments. Woodard holds the all-time women's collegiate scoring record with 3,649 points. To put that number in perspective, only one other male or female NCAA Division I player—Pete Maravich of LSU with an 18-point advantage—scored more career points.

She has also been inducted into the Women's Basketball Hall of Fame and the National High School Hall of Fame. Woodard was the first woman to be inducted into the Academic All-America Hall of Fame.

Woodard's college career came at a time when the three-point shot didn't exist and before the NCAA began sponsoring women's events, which occurred the season after her graduation in 1981.

Woodard, a four-time All-American, led KU to three straight Big 8 championships during her career and a combined 108–32 record. In 1980 Woodard was selected as one of 12 on the Olympic women's basketball team, but due to the U.S.-led boycott, her team did not participate. However, Woodard led a second Olympic women's basketball team to a gold medal in 1984.

After her senior season, Woodard received the Wade Trophy, which went to the nation's top female player.

In 1985, she beat out 25 other aspirants to become the first female member of the Harlem Globetrotters and played two years with the team before competing professionally on Japanese and Italian teams.

In 1997, she was signed by the Cleveland Rockers of the newly founded Women's National Basketball Association (WNBA). The following year, she was selected in an expansion draft by the Detroit Shock.

Woodard retired from playing in 1999 and returned to the University of Kansas as an assistant coach to Marian Washington, her college coach. She also served as athletics director for the Kansas City (Missouri) School District from 1992 to 1994 and has worked as a stockbroker in New York City.

She's currently a representative with a securities firm in Overland Park and is active as a motivational speaker and clinician at youth basketball camps.

★　★　★

THANK GOODNESS COACH [Marian] Washington continued to stay after me and was persistent in recruiting me to attend the University of Kansas. My decision to take that bus ride to Lawrence was probably the best one that I've ever made.

It wasn't easy to get me motivated to make the trip. KU was not a high priority on my list of college choices when I was a senior at Wichita North High School. Actually, I didn't have much of a list. The concept of playing basketball in college or of even attending college was not something I had seriously considered before my senior year.

The focus of my world in Wichita was my neighborhood, my school, and playing basketball. The thought of attending college ranked right up there with making a trip to the Moon.

In my mind, my future path would be a job at the telephone company or work at Boeing or Beechcraft after I graduated from high school. From my perspective, the people who had nice things worked at these places.

The entire recruiting process for women's basketball was considerably watered down compared to what it is today. As I said, I didn't understand what it was all about. My knowledge of college was very limited. There was no one advising me at the time in terms of my future.

I got a lot of recruiting letters as I continued to have success on the basketball court. As a result, I began to realize that maybe there were other options in front of me. I watched and learned from some of the guys on the boys' basketball team. But I didn't really understand why they were so excited when they were being recruited to play basketball in college.

Coach Washington was among many college coaches who had written to me with promotional material about their respective programs. She also called me and came to Wichita to visit with me. I had met her once before, when she passed out the player medals when we won the state championship my sophomore year at Allen Fieldhouse.

She was pushing me to take that bus ride to Lawrence on a recruiting visit, and I told her that I was interested. The notion of getting on that bus, however, and riding it up to Lawrence was as appealing to me as a trip to see the dentist. I made up all kinds of cockamamie excuses to not do it. Eventually, something convinced me that I needed to go see what Coach Washington was talking about. More than anything else, I recognized the sincerity in her voice and decided that I needed to take the visit.

Coach Washington picked me up at the bus station when I arrived in Lawrence. It was late afternoon, and she took me on a quick drive around the campus. I was immediately impressed with the buildings, the landscape, and how nice everything looked.

It was like a little city in my eyes. I woke up the next morning, and I remember that it was a perfect spring day. I still remember seeing the beautiful tulips in full bloom as I walked throughout the campus.

Coach Washington had lined up a lot of people for me to meet. I talked to faculty members, students, and I even met the chancellor, Archie Dykes. I couldn't believe how nice all of those people were to me and how they made me feel comfortable. There was so much to like about KU.

I was very aloof, or guarded, at that time. I didn't exactly understand what was happening, but I pretended that I did. This was all new, and I wasn't sure

Lynette Woodard was a four-time All-American at the University of Kansas and the first female to play for the Harlem Globetrotters. In 2004, she was inducted into the Naismith Basketball Hall of Fame.

what was expected. I was totally removed from the realities of my universe. But, as a result of that trip, it became clear in my mind that I liked KU. If I was going to move out of Wichita and attend college, I thought that I could be comfortable in Lawrence.

I returned home and kept to myself about the entire experience. I didn't want to be influenced by others. No one was really giving me advice on what to do, and I didn't know much about college. I just knew that, down deep inside, when the right school came along, I would know it in my heart.

I did tell my brother that I really liked KU and that I might decide to go there. The response I got back from him made me nervous. He really questioned why I would go to Kansas. But I didn't want anyone to sway my decision. I just knew it felt right.

I took another visit to the University of Texas. But I didn't have the same feelings. When I got back, I called Coach Washington and told her I wanted to come to KU and play basketball for her.

As it turned out, I was the very first female to receive a full scholarship to play basketball at Kansas. Of course, I didn't understand that at the time. I knew that, if I was going to play basketball in college, I had to get a full scholarship. It never occurred to me that it would be handled any other way.

I arrived at the University of Kansas in the fall of 1978 as someone with a very limited understanding of the opportunities available to me. KU opened up a world of possibilities. It made me believe that anything could be possible.

Those four years helped unlock the doors of a whole new and exciting world I didn't know existed.

My first memory of sports is just the memory of play. I enjoyed playing. Every time I and my brother or friends and neighbors were around to go out and play, it was usually some type of competitive sport. It may have been kickball or dodgeball or tumbling. My brother, Daryl [two years older], and I were closest in age. I had an older sister and younger sister, but it was my brother who was most important in my childhood.

He created the opportunity for me to play games. I played follow-the-leader with Daryl and was always at his side.

Basketball entered the picture sometime around the fifth grade. Daryl introduced me to a game we called "sock ball." We rolled a sock tightly together and made believe it was a basketball. There was a little crack at the top of the bedroom door, and that served as our target, or basketball goal.

We also had the small bathroom wastebasket, and we'd create an imaginary line and shoot from there with the sock.

We were very competitive. We'd get into arguments, usually when I beat him. We knew all of the players from the Missouri Valley Conference, the Pac-10, and professional basketball. He would tell me about all of these players, and that's how I learned all about the world of basketball.

When we would play our game, we would each have five names of star players written on a piece of paper. Whenever that sock went through our version of a goal, we would mark a score down next to one of the players. That was our game.

I was Austin Carr, Lew Alcindor, or Sidney Wicks of UCLA, or someone like that. The radio broadcaster for Wichita State in those days was Gus Grebe, and Daryl would pretend to be Gus, broadcasting our games as we played. That's basically how I learned to play basketball and how I got interested in the game.

I played in the neighborhood on playgrounds and in school. There was also a point when we got a hoop in our backyard, and the game came to our house. At that time, there were no organized teams for me. Or, if there were, I didn't know about them. They started to have teams at the community center on Saturday, but it was not well organized. You never knew if the coach would show up or not, or even if there would be a game.

When we would play in the neighborhood, it was always with my brother's friends. When we got the hoop in the backyard, we got kicked out of the house, then all of his friends came over. If there was room for me on a team, he would call me out to be on the team. Otherwise, I had to watch.

They never really did accept me as a legitimate player at their level. Of course, when they were short of players, I was invited to participate. I really never thought of it in terms of if I was good enough to compete with them. I just wanted to play.

In junior high school, I started playing more often at the neighborhood recreation center. There was an older gentleman, his name was Mr. Blanchard, who would help organize the neighborhood boys and girls and create opportunities for games at the center. He'd pick up the kids and take them to the rec center gym. Normally, the guys would have all of the baskets for their games. One was reserved for the girls to play.

157

I was invited to play for the junior varsity high school team when I was in the ninth grade at Marshall Junior High School. But I turned down that opportunity. My gym teacher contacted the high school coach and suggested I should play. Winning trophies was always a big incentive for me in those days, and there were no opportunities to win a trophy playing for the junior varsity team. I never seriously considered playing junior varsity basketball. In my mind, I had a better situation playing at the recreation center.

I wasn't a serious student in high school. But I was a good student because my mother always told me, "You don't pass, you don't play." That was enough incentive for me. I knew if I did well in school, I could play basketball.

I wasn't considering playing basketball when I started high school. In my world, that really wasn't a big deal. I remember one day there was an announcement over the public address system that there would be a meeting for anyone interested in trying out for the girls' team. Between classes one day in my sophomore year, some of my friends came up to me and said, "Hey, are you trying out for the team?"

They encouraged me, and I guess I got caught up in that excitement. I just came along to the meeting because of them. It didn't interest me very much, to be honest.

To my surprise, when I got to the meeting, there were a lot of girls there. I usually played basketball with the boys, and I didn't realize there would be that many girls interested in playing. The girls I played with at the rec center attended other schools for the most part. I stayed with it and made the varsity team.

Our first game was against Bishop Carroll. I started and had a fantastic game, but I didn't know it was fantastic.

I was actually upset because I missed a lot of easy layups, and in my mind it was a bad game. But afterward, everyone was running up and congratulating me on how well I played. I scored 30 or 40 points, I don't remember exactly. I wasn't happy with the way I had played because I missed a lot of shots.

We won two state championships—my sophomore and senior year. My junior year we lost in the championship game to Hutchinson by a bucket. We played that same team again my senior year and got the win that year.

When I look back at my years at KU, I think about living in Oliver Hall and all of my friends. Allen Fieldhouse was just across the parking lot. It was easy for me to navigate my way to the gym and to class.

158

I became a serious student in college. I took as many classes as I could handle during the school year and in the summer. In fact, I basically had enough credit hours to graduate in three years. I took just enough hours my senior year to be eligible to play. If I could do it all over again, I would have started work on my master's degree.

Coach Washington had to fight the battles in terms of standing up for women's basketball. I kept my focus on playing.

It means a lot to me that I attended the University of Kansas. It's one of the greatest academic institutions and one of the most beautiful campuses in America. This is home for me, and the KU Jayhawks are mine. I'm proud of my school and its rich tradition.

We all have our dreams. We may not always know how to tap them. Life and experience can open the door to achieve them if you want them badly enough. Sometimes, you can reach those dreams by happenstance. But I know that you can reach them if you focus and make the commitment.

The
EIGHTIES

WILLIE PLESS

FOOTBALL

1982–1985

KANSAS HEAD FOOTBALL COACH Don Fambrough noticed a familiar look-ing package on his desk when he arrived for work one day. It was a videotape sent by Dr. David Fretz. A Kansas graduate, Fretz was based in Alabama and had sent the football staff tapes of high school athletes in the past. While Fambrough was appreciative, none of the featured players had ever made it to Kansas. The stars stayed home to play for Alabama or Auburn, while others were not quite at the Division I talent level.

But dutifully, Fambrough popped in the tape and was pleasantly surprised by what he saw. An undersized linebacker playing for Anniston High School was making virtually every play. Fambrough instructed assistant coach Mike Sweatman to call Fretz to make sure no other school saw that film. In Fam-brough's mind, if Pless was going to play anywhere, it was going to be Kansas. The deal was sealed on his campus tour and subsequent in-home visit by the Jayhawk coaching staff. Even a late charge by Alabama head coach Bear Bryant could not dissuade his desire to be a Jayhawk.

Other than Fretz and the Kansas staff, not many gave Pless a chance to suc-ceed. If he had listened to those around him, he probably never would have amounted to anything. He would not have been Kansas's all-time leading tackler with 633. He never would have played 14 seasons in the Canadian Football League. And his name certainly would not grace halls of fame for the CFL and KU. But the only thing Pless listened to was his heart. At 5′10½″

and 206 pounds, he made a name for himself on the gridiron with grit, intelligence, and quickness.

Despite not playing for a national power, Pless earned All–Big 8 first-team honors as a junior and senior (1984 and 1985). He, along with Oklahoma's Brian Bosworth, were selected the two linebackers for the Big 8 Conference's all-decade team. He was the defensive MVP of the 1985 Blue-Gray All-Star Game. Professionally, he played 14 seasons in the Canadian Football League, becoming its all time leading tackler in 1994 with 1,241. Success followed Pless to the CFL. His exploits gained him the reputation of being one of the best—if not the best—defensive players in the history of the league. He accumulated career totals of 84 quarterback sacks, 39 interceptions, and 39 fumble recoveries, earning him the CFL's Most Outstanding Defensive Player Award five times. He was selected an all-star 11 times during his 14 year-career, playing for the Toronto Argonauts (1986–1989), B.C. Lions (1990), Edmonton Eskimos (1991–1998), and Saskatchewan Roughriders (1999). During that time, he played in 18 playoff games and three Grey Cups, winning one championship. Pless and his wife, Rhonda, who is also a KU graduate, live in Edmonton. He is in sales for a valve manufacturer in the oil and gas industry. Pless returned to Lawrence on September 1, 2007, to be inducted into the KU Ring of Honor at Memorial Stadium.

★　　★　　★

I THINK THE [HIGH SCHOOL] COACHING STAFF was a little confused about where to play me because of my physical attributes. I was probably one of the smallest nose guards in high school football at about 5′9½″ and 180 pounds—if that. I used my quickness and intelligence. I shared time with a senior, so I was not playing all the time. I am not sure what made the coaches think I could be a linebacker, but during my junior year they moved me there. It may have been that they were just experimenting. I liked playing on the kickoff team. It was a good way to get the nervousness out of my body. I loved to run down and make the first hit. Once that happened, I did not worry about being smaller than the others.

No one was really looking at me for major-college scholarships. Some smaller schools were, but even they did not know where to put me. The prototype linebacker was 6′3″, 230 pounds. But I was very fortunate to have Dr. David Fretz—"Daddy" Fretz, as I call him—send some tapes up to KU. I still stay in close touch with him, and our families have vacationed together. When I went to Kansas on my visit, I just fell in love with the place. I fell in love with the people. I remember one of the first persons I met was our football secretary Carole Hadl. She always had a big, warm smile. Elvis Patterson was my host and made me feel comfortable right away. The campus sold itself. I had never seen anything that big and that beautiful before. To be a part of that was an honor.

When I made my verbal commitment to Kansas, I was going to be a man of my word. I did not have anything signed, but that did not matter. But then came the high school all-star game, and we were playing against some pretty high-profile players, including Bo Jackson, who went to Auburn. I had a good game defensively, but had a solid game offensively, too. I think our defense limited Jackson to 16 yards. There were lots of stories that some Division I schools were after me following the game. I understand Bear Bryant said I grew two or three inches that day. It did not matter what Coach Bryant or any other coach would have said. I had committed to Kansas and was not going to back out.

Coach Fambrough visited my house during the time Kansas had traveled to Birmingham for the 1981 Hall of Fame Bowl. He told me Kansas would provide me a good education and everyone treats everyone else like family. He held true to those promises. To this day, I have never regretted going to Kansas. It was a wonderful time for me. Lawrence is home for me. If I had to move back to the States today, it would be to Lawrence. Who knows what the future holds? I may end up there again someday.

The first year at Kansas, I played mostly special teams. The second year is when coach [Mike] Gottfried came in. We played that wide-tackle-6, so they moved me out as a linebacker. But I was more like a defensive back, jamming receivers. I was not really in the tackle box. But after the first game, assistant coach [Ron] Zook came to my room and wanted to see me. I thought, *Oh, boy. What have I done now?* We had given up quite a few rushing yards, so they wanted to try me at inside linebacker. They put me and freshman Darnell Williams inside. From that day on, I was a starter at Kansas. I did not care who had the ball, I just wanted to hit someone. I just wanted to play my best every time I stepped out on the field.

We were poor when I was growing up. We had five kids in the family with one parent working. It was difficult. But we had a lot of love and were not lacking for food and the basics. Being the youngest, I got a lot of hand-

Willie Pless ranks as the all-time leading tackler in both KU history and Canadian Football League history. The undersized linebacker has been honored as an inductee in both the KU Athletics Hall of Fame and the CFL Hall of Fame.

me-downs. By the time they got to me, they were about worn out. It's never fun to be the youngest in that case. But absolutely, I would not have been able to go to college had I not had a scholarship. Growing up, I always wanted to be a pro football player. I always had a football in my hands and spent a lot of time at the Boys and Girls Club to stay away from bad influences. I was small and not a great student. Not bad, but not great. There weren't many who gave me a chance to make much of myself. I wanted to prove them wrong.

I was fortunate as a freshman at KU. John Wooden, who owned the Wagon Wheel Cafe, met me on my recruiting trip. He said to me, "I want to make sure you make it through school." At the time, I was not sure what he meant. But when I arrived, he called me and told me he was coming to pick me up. I went to his house, and he had a desk set up for me. I had to do all of my school work before I could leave. It helped me develop study habits. I was not spending a lot of time out in the streets partying. So I have to take my hat off to the late John Wooden, because he made sure my butt was there studying. At that time, I said, "I hate this crap." But it definitely helped me make it through school. I was a decent student in high school. But college was harder. I had to buckle down. [Pless would go on to earn first-team Big 8 Conference and GTE Region VII all-academic first-team honors in 1985.]

The one game that stands out for me was the game against Oklahoma my senior year [1984]. They were ranked No. 2, and we upset them 28–11. That was the game Troy Aikman started as a freshman for Oklahoma. It was like a bowl game for me, since I never went to a bowl. I still remember that game to this day. It was such a great atmosphere around us. At first, the crowd was not that big. But then the fans started coming in to the stadium from nowhere. I remember their tearing down the goal posts and taking them off to Potter Lake. It was beautiful. The stars were aligned. But I don't want to take anything from our team. We played hard and were flying around everywhere. We had a pretty good team. It was quite a memorable day for us.

I was not drafted by NFL. They wanted the Brian Bosworth type, who came out in the same class I did. At 5′10½″ on my tiptoes, I just did not fit what they wanted. They knew I could hit, but they did not think I could play linebacker. They were probably going to move me to defensive back, and I did not want to play there. In the Canadian Football League, American players weren't drafted, but their rights were territorial. My first team, I believe it was Saskatchewan, did not think I could play. So they traded me to the Toronto Argonauts.

The Argonauts put me in the lineup in the first exhibition game against the Hamilton Tiger-Cats. They tried to run the counter trap that I had seen a million times run by Nebraska and Oklahoma. So I stuck the back and was in the lineup ever since. The toughest thing to figure out in the Canadian Football League was all of the motion going on. After I figured that out, it was just a matter of playing football. I was an inside linebacker. As in college, I watched a lot of film. I was a student of the game. I made plays because of my instinct, quickness, and preparation. I picked up tendencies and learned a lot about the teams we were playing. I think that is a major reason for my success as a player.

It did not matter whatsoever that I did not play in the NFL. But I wanted to give it a chance so that when I was 50 or 60 I would not regret not trying. It looked like I was going to make the team in Kansas City. The team had cut most of its linebackers, and it looked like I was going to make the team. But I hurt my back in an exhibition game against Buffalo and could never recover. I actually missed the whole season.

I cannot complain about anything in my career. High school was great. Obviously, Kansas was special. Being called one of the best defensive players ever in the Canadian Football League and one of the youngest to be named to the Hall of Fame is an honor. I guess the only drawback were the winters in Canada. Being from Alabama, I thought it was cold in Kansas. But in Canada, wow! I remember when I signed with Toronto, I asked my GM, Hugh Campbell, if it was always cold in Canada. He said, "Don't worry, you will adapt to it." I still haven't and probably never will.

TRACY BUNGE
SOFTBALL ★ HEAD COACH
1982–1986 ★ 1997–Present

TRACE BUNGE ARRIVED AT the University of Kansas in the early 1980s as a promising softball player from Bartlesville, Oklahoma, and left four years later as the school's first NCAA softball All-America selection.

She entered the university at a time when women's athletics at the collegiate level was in a critical stage of development. Bunge's success on the field helped her sport gain respect and fueled its growth in both funding and fan appeal.

The daughter of an All-American basketball player at the University of Maryland and sister of an all-conference women's basketball player at the University of Arkansas, Bunge qualifies as one of the school's outstanding performers. She was inducted into the KU Athletics Hall of Fame after her senior season.

"I loved the pressure of pitching, of being in the circle and in control of the game," said Bunge, who completed her 12th season in 2008 as head softball coach at KU.

After her successful career as a collegiate player, she went into coaching, serving stints as an assistant coach at Iowa State and Yale and head coach at Ohio University. Along the way, she continued her playing career during the summer months and was a teammate of some of the great softball players in the history of the game.

Tracy Bunge (center) was the second softball All-American in KU history and the school's first to earn the distinction since the NCAA sanctioned the sport.

She returned to her alma mater as the school's eighth head coach in the mid-1990s and continued to be a meaningful influence on the significant growth of the program. In 2006, under Bunge's direction, KU won the Big 12 Conference softball title and advanced to postseason play.

★   ★   ★

It has been said that every little girl's first hero is her dad. That was certainly the case for my big sister, Kim, and myself.

My dad [Al Bunge] was a standout basketball player at the University of Maryland. He was a 6′8″ All-American center for the Terrapins in the late 1950s and early '60s.

Like everyone in my family, I loved sports and had a strong interest in following the teams at Maryland. It didn't take my dad long to understand that his two daughters were anxious to follow in his footsteps and get involved in sports.

My sister grew to 6′3″ and was an all-conference basketball player at the University of Arkansas. She has a son and daughter who are both major-college athletes. Her daughter, Krista, played four years of basketball at Oklahoma, and her youngest son, Michael, is 6′10″ and a basketball player at Arkansas.

My father worked for Phillips Petroleum after college and played several years for the Phillips 66ers, the traveling AAU team sponsored by his company. His boss was Bob Kurland, who had a pretty impressive college and professional basketball career. You will find his name enshrined in the Naismith Basketball Hall of Fame. My dad was 6′8″ and Kurland was over 7′, so they needed tall ceilings in the company office.

I was born in Redbank, New Jersey, but we moved to Atlanta, Georgia, and that's where I started school and first got involved in sports. My dad never pushed his daughters to play sports. He just encouraged us to do the things we enjoyed and to work hard in school.

168

One day my sister arrived home and announced she was going to play basketball. Of course, I wanted to tag along and also join a team. Dad helped us learn the fundamentals, and we both loved to play the game.

I was first introduced to organized softball in the fifth grade when I played on a Little League team. My dad was transferred to Bartlesville, Oklahoma, headquarters of Phillips Petroleum, after my sixth-grade year, and that's where I first became serious about playing sports.

Basketball remained my first love, but I also enjoyed softball and soon found there were a lot of talented young softball players in the Bartlesville area. I got involved with a group of players coached by a local youth sports enthusiast, Lew Ambler, who wanted to develop an American Legion softball program much like the boys' baseball program that was already in existence.

My best friend in Bartlesville was Cindy Cooper, and she suggested we both try out for this new traveling softball team. We were both just 13 years old and soon discovered we were attempting to make the roster of an 18 and under team. Somehow, we made a good impression and were the two youngest players on the squad.

I wanted to be a pitcher, but I didn't have a clue how to pitch. There was an older gentleman in the community, Don Brisban, who had been a highly successful pitcher in a fast-pitch league. He started tutoring me when I was in the eighth grade and helped me understand the fundamentals of pitching.

Over the next four or five years, Cindy and I played with a variety of traveling teams in Bartlesville. My senior year, we had some amazing talent, including a bunch of girls that went on to play major-college softball. Cindy, in fact, was a three-time All-American at Texas A&M.

I also played on the high school team. We finished second in the state playoffs my sophomore season and won the state tournament my junior year.

Just before the start of my senior season, I dislocated my elbow in a practice session, and the doctors told me I might never be able to pitch again.

Keep in mind that sports medicine was not as advanced as it is today. There were not a lot of rehabilitation options at that time. As a result, I didn't pitch on my high school team my senior season.

Meanwhile, basketball remained my first priority. I played basketball three years in high school and at 5′11½″ I was the offensive center, or post. Girl's basketball in Oklahoma had not advanced to the five-on-five, full-court concept. It was still played with girls designated as offensive players and defensive players, and six starters on a side.

169

About four months after my elbow injury, I felt healthy enough to return to pitching and started throwing again in the summer league. We had an excellent group of players and placed third in the Amateur Softball Association national tournament.

My success in softball attracted the attention of a lot of outstanding collegiate programs. Recruiting, however, was not very sophisticated. My parents and I traveled to several college campuses, and it turned out that the University of Kansas felt like the best fit for me.

When I visited KU, I immediately felt comfortable with the campus and with the people. I didn't feel that way at Oklahoma or Oklahoma State. Creighton was also one of the top programs in the country at that time, but it snowed when I visited the campus. As a result, I crossed Creighton off my list.

Bob Stanclift was the head coach at KU and had developed a good program. The plan was for me to come in and be part of a one-two pitching punch with Rhonda Clark, who had already established her credentials as a top collegiate pitcher.

Right before the start of my freshman season at KU, Bob called me and said he had good news. He told me that I'd be pitching a lot more than originally planned because Rhonda had decided to transfer to another school.

I finished that first year with a 23–8 record and a 0.63 earned-run average, and our team went 33–9.

In addition to pitching, I was also pretty good with a bat in my hand. The equipment we used was nothing like it is today. Our bats were like tree trunks. I used a bat that was in the range of 33 ounces. Most girls today use a bat that is 26 to 28 ounces. Pitching really dominated women's softball in those days.

Women's athletics was still in the process of development at the collegiate level. We played at Holcom Park, an off-campus site, my first two years, and our fan base was mostly friends and family. We traveled in university vans that would occasionally break down on long trips.

But I really enjoyed my four years as a student at Kansas. I can remember walking down the hallways in the athletics department, and I was amazed that someone like Larry Brown, the men's basketball coach, knew me by name. Larry was always friendly and seemed to be interested in how we were doing.

Danny Manning was playing at KU while I was there, and we became friends. Danny liked to brag that he had been a hotshot baseball player and that he wouldn't have any problems hitting my pitching.

One evening we were in Allen Fieldhouse waiting for a junior varsity game to end before we started practice. Danny came in and sat down beside me. He started yakking about how he'd have no problem hitting my pitching. Finally, after several minutes, our assistant coach suggested we see if Danny was as good as he claimed.

We went upstairs into a batting cage, and I threw him about 25 pitches. He didn't touch one of them with his bat, and I never heard another word from him about women's softball being easy.

Danny became a fan of softball and remains a fan and a good friend today. After I came back to KU as the head coach, he drove over to practice one day and gave me a big hug and welcomed me back to the athletics department. He's one of our biggest supporters.

By the time I was a senior, I was excelling as both a pitcher and hitter. I had 15 shutouts as a pitcher and I also hit nine home runs that season. I became the school's second All-American softball player—making the team as a utility player—and the first to earn the distinction since the NCAA had sanctioned the sport. Jill Larson was the school's first AIAW All-American.

I was uncertain about my future. I was getting a business administration degree, and my parents felt I'd do something in the business world. I can remember one of those life-changing moments my senior year when I figured it all out. My pitching coach at KU, Gary Hines, and I were meeting in Allen Fieldhouse. It was one of those crisis moments for a college student. I was probably crying and in a panic about my future.

Gary put me at ease and said all of the right things. I figured out that I wanted to stay involved in the game of softball and that coaching might be my best avenue.

With Gary's advice and the help of Coach Stanclift, I was able to get my first coaching job the next year. I went to work for a former KU player— Deb Kuhn—as her assistant coach at Iowa State and spent five enjoyable years on her coaching staff.

I remained active in the summer months in fast-pitch softball leagues. I played for the St. Louis Classics for three years and alongside some of the best softball players in the Midwest.

My coaching career, meanwhile, was on the move. I took a job as assistant coach at Yale and worked under Kathy Arendsen, who was considered, at that time, to be one of the best amateur softball players in the world. She had gained fame when she struck out Reggie Jackson on national television during the major league baseball strike season.

The experience at Yale turned out to be a dream come true. I was able to join a summer league team called the Raybestos Bracketts, which was the premier team in women's college softball.

Our coach was Ralph Raymond, who would later coach two U.S.A. teams to gold medals. I was a teammate with some of the all-time great players, such as Dot Richardson and Lisa Fernandez. As I remember, we had seven future Olympians on the team.

Of course, I hardly played on that team. I was the fifth pitcher and the backup at first base. But what a great experience it was.

The senior women's administrator at Yale was Barbara Chesler, and she was a great supporter of the softball program. After two years at Yale, she came to me and suggested I was ready to be a head coach. She handed me information on an opening at Ohio University.

I interviewed at Ohio University and was hired for the job. The program was in bad shape. They had never experienced a winning season and normally finished last or next to last in the conference.

With the support of a terrific athletics director, Harold McElhaney, and with my assistant, Roanna Brazier (also a KU softball player and graduate), we turned the program around quickly and won the Mid-American Conference title in our second year.

I remember reading about the opening at KU while I was coaching at Ohio University. Things were really going great for me at the time. We were having success and had great support. As a result, I didn't seriously entertain the thought of changing jobs.

Shortly after the job opened up, I received a phone call from Betsy Stephenson, who was the associate athletics director at KU heading the search for a new softball coach. She wanted to know why I hadn't applied for the job.

We had a four-hour phone conversation, and I spent the first 30 minutes explaining how I felt being the head coach at Ohio University. Betsy then spent the rest of the conversation convincing me to consider coming back to KU.

I went back and decided to apply for the job. I visited campus and met with Betsy and AD Bob Frederick and got excited about coming back to KU. I had not been back to campus very often in the 10 years I'd been gone.

I was very impressed with the total commitment I found in the softball program. I quickly discovered it would be a great opportunity for me to return to my alma mater as the head coach. I've never regretted that decision.

Being a Jayhawk is a very special feeling, and I am so fortunate that I've been able to be both a player and coach at the university. KU is about connecting with people, and I'm proud to be a part of a great tradition.

MICHAEL CENTER
TENNIS ★ COACH
1983–1986 ★ 1987, 1990–1996

BY HIS OWN ADMISSION, Michael Center was better at basketball than ten-nis, but coming off a state singles title at Manhattan (Kansas) High School, he believed his best chance to succeed in college was to play tennis. By the time Center had won his state championship and other junior titles, most colleges had already doled out their scholarship money. His only options were Kansas State and Kansas.

Spurning the pull of the hometown fans, Center accepted an offer from the Jayhawks and went on to win the 1985 Big 8 Conference number-two singles championship and qualify for the NCAA championships in doubles in 1985 and 1986. He is the first Jayhawk to win 40 matches in a season, and the league singles title was the first for the school since 1979. Center was a mem-ber of head coach Scott Perelman's first recruiting class, and together they built the program from a doormat to being nationally ranked. The Jayhawks placed fifth in the league in Center's freshman campaign and improved to third in 1984, with consecutive second-place finishes in 1985 and 1986.

As an assistant coach to Perelman in 1987, Center helped to guide Kansas to its first league title since 1965 and first ever NCAA team qualification. Center would work for the United States Tennis Association for two years, then return to Kansas to coach the women's program from 1990 to 1992. His 1992 squad won the Big 8 title and qualified for the program's first-ever

Michael Center was a standout tennis player for KU and later became head coach for both the women's and men's teams. In 1994, under Center's guidance, the women's and men's programs won league titles for the first time in school history.

NCAA tournament. Perelman accepted the head coaching position at Tennessee in the spring of 1992, and Center was named director of tennis and head coach of the men's team. In four years, his teams had an 83–28 overall and 29–2 league match record. From 1994 to 1996, Center's Jayhawks were undefeated in conference play and earned NCAA tournament bids. He was the Big 8 Coach of the Year in each of those seasons. In 1994, the women's and men's programs won league titles for the first time in school history.

Center would serve as a volunteer assistant coach at Stanford in 1997 and 1998, then head the Texas Christian men's program in 1999 and 2000. In the spring of 2000, Center became only the fourth head coach in the history of the Texas men's program. In seven years, he has led the Longhorns to a 134–52 overall record and seven straight NCAA bids.

Due to financial constraints, several universities have dropped Olympic sports in the past two decades. Among the casualties was the Kansas men's tennis program, with the Jayhawks eliminating the sport after the 2001 season.

★ ★ ★

MY DAD WAS A PROFESSOR AT KANSAS STATE, and I had lived there for most of my life, so I figured I needed to get out of town. I was the oldest child in our family, so we really did not know much about the recruiting process. Most of the other schools had made their [scholarship] decisions, so I made the decision to go to KU. I was recruited by Randy McGrath, who was an attorney in town and coaching part time. He ended up quitting before I got there, so I showed up on campus not knowing who my coach was. I walked into the office, and there was this short little guy sitting behind this desk with an afro about 18 inches high and a little curly mustache. He popped up out of his chair, shook my hand, and said, "I'm Coach Perelman and I like your size. Glad to have you." The next thing I knew I was jumping up and down the stairs of Allen Fieldhouse on one leg a million times and running around the track a hundred times. People were throwing up fairly regularly. You could say the program was taking a new direction.

My first sport was swimming. I first picked up a racquet when I was about 12 and hit around with my parents. I started playing some local tournaments when I was 13 or 14. So I was a late starter. I was an athlete playing tennis. I played my first year at KU, but was probably too high in the lineup for my skills. I think I played number-two singles, and I wasn't probably ready for that at all. But Coach liked my competitiveness. We were basically a bunch of Kansas kids.

It was hard, but I never thought of quitting. Every kid questions himself at times. But the times have changed a bit since then. If a coach told me to jump up the stairs of Allen Fieldhouse on one leg and back down on the other, I did it. I didn't have a cell phone to call Mom and Dad to complain. I was running as much as the kids on the track team. He [Perelman] was going to weed anyone out who did not want to compete or be a part of this. We worked very hard. For me, he was a great coach because I responded to that. He helped me become as good a player as I could have possibly been. He was great. We still talk today.

Coach Perelman was the head coach for the men and the women. One team would practice at 6:00 AM and the other at 10:00 PM. So you can imagine that he was getting about four hours of sleep each night. We did not have anything and were as blue collar as you get. We had the six courts just outside of Allen Fieldhouse and then had to share the inside courts at Alvamar [Racquet Club]. At the time, the rules were different. You could play for unlimited amounts of time. We played Baker and other schools in the area

175

two times a year. There were no limitations on the days of practice. We played from the first day of the season to the last day. We created a work ethic and were going to get better. As the years went on, we started to compete with the big boys—the Pepperdines, UCLAs, Oklahoma States. I give Scott all of the credit for taking the program from nothing to a national level. He was the reason.

We were getting better during my career, but we just needed more depth. That takes time, but you could tell, going from fifth to third to second two years in a row, that we were nipping at the heels of the top team, and at that time it was Oklahoma State. I was the assistant coach in 1987, and Mike Wolf [an All-American] was a senior. We had these two freshmen in Craig Wildey and Chris Walker from Michigan who helped put us over the top. Then a top junior in John Falbo came. The talent level started to improve. We could attract a higher quality player and had gained momentum. Scott was a great ambassador for the program and the school. He was tireless. Almost everything I do now as a coach I learned from him.

I won the 1985 Big 8 number-two singles title and played junior and senior years at the NCAAs. My senior year was a bit hard. I broke my ankle against UCLA as I went back to hit an overhead, so I really did not have a chance to do much. It was a great time to play college tennis. At that time, the top players all went to college and then turned pro. So I was playing against the likes of grand slam winners and top-ranked players such as Ricky Leach, Luke Jensen, Brad Pierce, and Grant Connell. After that, the group of [Pete] Sampras, [Michael] Chang, and [Jim] Courier emerged and became professionals. The mindset had changed that you did not have to go to college.

Things were always lively with Scott. Our offices were small cubicles in the same corner office with the baseball team, on the second floor of Allen Fieldhouse. You knew you were in trouble if you had to meet with Coach in Allen Fieldhouse. If he wanted to talk to you, you went up high in a corner. It could get loud and echo in there.

This is a true story. We were playing Wichita State at night indoors in Wichita. It was my senior year. Wichita State had been the dominant team in our region, but we had closed the gap. In fact, we had put together a string of wins against them, but the matches were close. So this was a big match for us. I was playing Stephen Salthouse and needed to win it or we were going to lose. I ended up losing in the third set 6–4, and I knew I was going to hear it from Scott. So I decided that I was not going to go sit it the back of the van so he would have to climb over everyone to get at me. I got in the passenger seat and figured I was going to take it like a man. Lo and behold, he got in the van and started screaming. He called me every name in the book. He was pointing his finger at me. It was midnight and it was dark, but I could see his face because it was beet red. He told me he couldn't even stand to look at me, so he got out of the van and just started walking. The funny part was that Kevin Brady said he was hungry and wanted something to eat. So I moved over and drove the team to a Wendy's around the corner. I dropped them off and figured I had better go find Scott. He did not have his wallet or anything. I knew I had to find him. So after about 20 minutes, I found him and told him to jump in. We had such a great relationship. I just said, "Hey, we'll be okay, just get in." We went and picked the guys up at Wendy's and drove to Lawrence that night. The next day we talked, and he apologized. I knew he loved us and would do anything for us. We can all laugh about it today.

I went to graduate school at KU and was an assistant in 1987, then went to work for the United States Tennis Association in Springfield, Ohio. Just after I left, KU had decided to split the program and have different coaches. Scott was going to coach the boys, and Eric Hayes was going to coach the girls. Eric was there for two years and then got a job at South Florida in August, right before school started. So I got this phone call at around 2:00 o'clock in the morning. I remember it to this day. It was August 8, 1989. It was Coach Perelmen, and he said, "Center, ya gotta come back. Ya gotta come back and coach the team." I said, "What?" At the time, I thought I was going to be an athletics director or some administrator in athletics. I had not thought about being a coach. And certainly not the women's team, because I had never coached women before. I told him I would think about it. Those jobs were not in high demand. They really weren't paying much, so there weren't people beating the doors down to coach at KU. But I decided to take the job. I took a pay cut. I remember [athletics director] Bob Frederick telling me my pay would be $18,000 and that my budget was $40,000 in the hole. He told me I needed to raise that back and more because my entire budget was $22,000. I started paying out of my own pocket for things like strings and grips. Not major expenses, but anything to help the program along. But those were three great years. I would never trade that experience.

I coached the girls three years, and then Scott left in 1992 to go to Tennessee. I was sad to see Scott leave. I wanted him to stay. I tried to talk him into staying, but he made the decision that it was time for him to move along. Bob Frederick gave me the choice of coaching either the men's or women's team. That was a tough decision for me. The women had been No. 15 the year before and would have been a top-five-ranked team the next year. We had a great group of girls coming back. We had Nora Koves, Eveline Hamers, Rebecca Jensen—I mean, we were loaded. I got really close to them. They were my recruits. It was a tough decision, but I decided it was best for me to take the director of tennis program position and coach the men's team. I was happy in some respects, but sad that I was not their coach anymore. I was responsible for the whole program, but we brought Chuck Merzbacher in to coach the women's team. He did a great job.

I left Kansas after the 1995–1996 season—the last year of the Big 8. I had gotten married and just felt that I had taken the program as high as I could. We were getting ready to go into the Big 12 and were top 10 in the country, but I felt we were behind to go into that environment. I felt this was the best time to make a career change. So I went to the West Coast and became a stockbroker. I thought I was done with coaching. It was time to get a real job. It was tough to support a family on a coaching salary. My office was half a mile from the Stanford tennis complex, so I called Coach Gould and told him I would be willing to be help out if he needed me. He was great. He let me help when my schedule allowed.

Kansas means everything to me. It changed my life. It gave me an opportunity to play tennis, to meet people, to grow up, and become what I am. Without KU, I don't know where I would be today. I am a coach because of all the support I have received from the players, coaches, and administrators at KU. I have a lot of pride in being a Jayhawk. At the same time, I have some disappointment that they don't have a men's tennis program anymore.

I remember getting a call from [athletics department employee] Nancy Hettwer in April of 2001, and she told me KU was dropping tennis. I just about fell out of my chair. I knew there were some issues, but I just did not think they would drop a program that had been having success and had produced some great people. For a Kansan like myself who wants to play for what I consider the flagship institution of the state, that cannot happen now. That was really sad. It would be great if they brought it back. I would do anything to help to bring the program back. I would help raise money. At this point, I don't see it happening in the short run. But tennis is not an expensive sport to have. Not compared to the others. There's always hope.

LARRY BROWN

MEN'S BASKETBALL COACH
1984–1988

LARRY BROWN SPENT FIVE SEASONS as head basketball coach at Kansas and culminated his tenure in 1988 by guiding the Jayhawks to the NCAA championship. Brown's 1985–1986 KU team also reached the NCAA Final Four. Brown, the school's sixth head coach, led KU to NCAA Tournament appearances in each of his five seasons and compiled an overall 135–44 record during his stay at Kansas.

Brown was a 1963 graduate of North Carolina, where he was an honorable mention All-American guard under former KU basketball player Dean Smith. He helped the 1964 U.S.A. basketball team win an Olympic gold medal and distinguished himself as a player, then coach in the American Basketball Association.

Brown, who has also coached UCLA, eight different teams in the NBA, and the U.S.A. Olympic team, was inducted into the Naismith Memorial Basketball Hall of Fame in 2002.

★　★　★

AS A SOPHOMORE AT NORTH CAROLINA, I played in what they called the "Sunflower Classic." We played our first game in Lawrence and our second one in Manhattan. I can remember when we played in Allen Fieldhouse, they didn't have typical team benches. You sat in the bleachers, and they didn't have enough seats for all of us, so I had to sit in the second row. I remember telling my mom about the fact I didn't even make the first row! But, there was tremendous excitement and enthusiasm there. Coach Smith let me know about the history and talked about Phog Allen, Adolph Rupp, and James Naismith.

I once played for John McLendon, who's one of the great coaches of all time and was a student of Naismith's at KU. He was an assistant Olympic coach in 1964. Coach McClendon actually offered me my first coaching job. He was at Kentucky State at the time, and after the Olympics, he asked me to come to Kentucky State with him. But I still wanted to play and was playing for Goodyear at the time.

McLendon was a phenomenal coach and a better person. He told me a story from his days as a student at KU. He jumped in the pool at Kansas, and the next day, they emptied the water out of the pool. I think it took them over a day to fill it. He jumped in again, and they emptied it out again. He told them they were going to run out of water because he wasn't going to stop swimming. He was a pretty incredible man.

I came to Kansas because of Coach [Dean] Smith. I was fortunate enough to have the opportunity to play for him and had heard so many stories about the University of Kansas. Monte Johnson came to see me, I think, because of Coach Smith's recommendation.

I was in New Jersey and was just uncomfortable being a pro coach. I told the team's owner, during the second year, that if a coaching opportunity presented itself in college, I'd like to pursue it. He didn't think that there was any college job that would be as good as a professional job.

Monte was phenomenal to me. He loved KU. I don't know if anybody loved KU as much as Monte Johnson. My background was North Carolina, and that means you have an entire Carolina family that's pretty special. But when I went to Kansas, that family was equally special.

I agreed to come to KU without knowing the terms of my contract. Monte was the kind of person I knew would treat me fairly. I never got into coaching for money. I remember when I got my first job at North Carolina, Coach Smith paid me $6,000, gave me $1,000 for summer camp, and told me he overpaid me. He said, "If you get into coaching for money, you're in it for the wrong reasons." I've been overpaid my whole life.

I felt Monte was a genuine guy. When you meet somebody like him and you find out how much he loved that university, it's easy to say you want to be a part of it. I was treated fairly there my whole time. I never wanted

Larry Brown points to his college coach at North Carolina, Dean Smith, as the primary reason he ended up becoming head coach at the University of Kansas. Smith, also a former Jayhawks player, recommended Brown to KU's athletics director at the time, Monte Johnson.

for anything. When you're a college coach and you work for a man who gives you every opportunity to be successful, you don't worry about things like that.

Ted Owens did a phenomenal job while coaching at Kansas. I think my job was made a lot easier because of the recruiting class of players he left behind. I didn't come to Kansas with an empty cupboard. We had some really good players. I believe in the tradition of the game. I respect the game. It was an honor being the coach of the University of Kansas because of what it means to our sport.

I remember the first game I coached at KU. I walked up into the stands and met people who had been going to games there since the arena was built and before. I found out how special Kansas basketball is to everyone.

When you're the coach at the University of Kansas, you realize who was there before you. You understand you are part of a tradition that includes Wilt Chamberlain, John McLendon, James Naismith, Phog Allen, and Dick Harp. It's hard not to respect and appreciate the tradition. I was always uncomfortable saying I was the coach at Kansas. I always felt there was only one coach there, and it was Phog Allen. The rest of us were just following along. It was an honor to coach there. The five years I spent at Kansas were about as special as anytime in my life.

182

My best team at Kansas, by far, was the 1985–1986 team. If you remember, when we lost to Duke in the semifinals of the NCAA Tournament that year, we had three or four guys foul out. We also lost Archie Marshall in that game to an ACL injury and almost won the game, anyway. That team was the best. The 1987 team might have been equally as good or better, but we didn't have Archie.

The 1988 season was incredible. We were down to nine players and had to get two football players, and they contributed to our success. I think the best player in the nation won a national championship for our school. Danny [Manning] was incredible. We lost five games in a row that year. The last three teams to beat us that year were Kansas State, Duke, and Oklahoma— and the last three teams we beat to win the championship were Kansas State in the regional finals, Duke in the semifinals, and Oklahoma in the finals. So, I think, it was already written before I even started coaching that we were going to win.

One of the things I remember is the pregame meal before the national championship game. ESPN was showing our last game against Oklahoma in

Norman. We lost the game, and Danny had fouled out. I remember the players looking at the game and saying, "Hey, we're better than them." I got real excited hearing them talk about that. Normally, I never let our team watch our opponents. I saw them watching that game and convincing themselves they would beat them.

Danny made some unbelievable sacrifices for Kansas, and you can appreciate it now with kids coming out early. But, after his junior year, Danny had a chance to turn pro. I met with him, and he told me he had three goals when he came to Kansas. One was to get his degree, two was to win a national championship, and three, hopefully, would be to be the number-one pick in the NBA Draft.

He decided to come back, and we won a national championship. He got his degree and was the first pick in the draft. So it was pretty neat the way it turned out. But he's as good as they get. I don't think there's ever been a better college player, and I think he's going to be an unbelievable coach.

I didn't want to leave Lawrence. I was having some family issues at the time. That's the only reason I left. Monte left, and that was difficult for me because he hired me, treated me with respect, and gave me every opportunity to be successful. But I was having some family issues, and that's the only reason I left.

I think Kansas benefited by my leaving. The guy who followed me did extremely well! I'm really proud of what Roy [Williams] did at KU. And the guy who followed Roy [Bill Self] is pretty special in his own right.

There's nothing like coaching a game in Allen Fieldhouse. I don't think anybody can feel any better than knowing you're the coach of the University of Kansas. It doesn't get any better than that.

GLENN TRAMMEL

SWIMMING

1986–1989

A FEW PIECES OF PIZZA and a couple lines of bowling. That's essentially what it took for Glenn Trammel to become a Jayhawk. A nationally ranked junior and two-time state champion swimmer from Topeka High School, Trammel went on to earn All-America honors eight times. He was the first University of Kansas swimmer to eclipse 20 seconds in the 50-yard freestyle, recording a 19.85 in finishing fourth at the 1989 NCAA championship meet. That still ranks as the third-fastest time in Kansas history. His 43.47 in the 100-yard freestyle and his 49.24 in the 100-yard backstroke remain as school records. As a senior, he was selected by the Kansas athletics department as its Male Student-Athlete of the Year.

His coach, Gary Kempf, called him one of the greatest leaders he ever coached. "Glenn is the person who I felt turned our program into the real deal," Kempf said. "He was a phenomenal athlete. He was a stubborn athlete. He knew he was going to be pushed and he knew he was going to be asked to do something he had never done before. The team looked up to him. There are people who are natural leaders, and Glenn was one of those. The best memory I have of Glenn is when he suffered a devastating defeat in the Olympic Trials the summer before his senior year. He had as much talent as anyone. But he did not let the defeat define him. He returned for his senior season and took on a new event that led us to a national ranking. I can't say enough about what he did for the team and the program."

Today, Glenn Trammel is the chief information officer at Delta State University in Cleveland, Mississippi.

★ ★ ★

I HAD BECOME A HIGH SCHOOL ALL-AMERICAN as a junior and senior, so I had several opportunities to go different places. All the Big 8 schools, plus Tennessee, California, Arkansas, and SMU had offered me scholarships. I still took my visits because I needed to see what was out there. Some of the schools did things that you just don't do. Tennessee called me on Thanksgiving day during dinner, demanding an answer. On my visit to SMU, from the moment I got to the airport, it was one big party. That's great for a weekend, but I wanted to know about the school and the program. Essentially, it came down to the fact that Kansas treated my like a normal person. I stayed in the dorm with the swim team, ate pizza with them, and went bowling—normal college stuff. My swim club coach Jed Blankenship had swum at Kansas, so I had known Gary [Kempf], and was familiar with the program and the school. That and the fact that my parents could watch me made the decision easy.

I was about six years old when I started swimming. I remember playing baseball with my dad one day, and I noticed some kids running to the pool. I was upset because I had been told we couldn't swim because the pool was closed. We went over to the pool to check it out and found that they were having a big swim meet with some of the neighborhood teams and the country club teams. I watched it for a while and thought that was pretty cool, so the next day my mom went and signed me up for our neighborhood swim team—and the rest is history.

The 1988 Olympic Games were in Seoul. That winter, I had been invited to participate with the national team in a training camp in Hawaii—all expenses paid for two weeks. That was a big deal. The training was intense, but we were in paradise. Some of the other people there were Matt Biondi, David Berkoff, Tom Yeager, Pablo Morales, Summer Sanders, Janet Evans—so some of the biggest names were there. The trials were in Austin later that year. Austin was probably my second favorite pool, behind the one in Indianapolis where they had the NCAAs. It seated 10,000 people. It was fast. The summer between my junior and senior year was clearly one of my life learning experiences. I had another good NCAA meet [as a junior], and my sole attention was on the Olympic Trials. I really let the media and other things like that get to me. In fact, I have a framed copy of the front of the sports section at home. It has two big stories. One has a picture of Danny Manning winning the Naismith Award, and the other is me trying to make the national team. It was a cool layout because it looked like Danny was looking down at me and I was looking up at him. But things really snowballed on me. I did not anticipate the buildup. I was trying to shrug it off as another meet. The area media really built it up, and I let that and other things get to me.

The truth is I got to Austin and I just missed it. I knew I could swim with Berkoff. I knew I was better than him. My best time in the 100 backstroke that year would have put me on the team. I would have been the top back-stroker and would have gone to Seoul. It would have been a dream come true. But I just missed it. I got caught up in the moment and the whole four to five months in training. But I learned some pretty good life lessons and immediately turned around and started applying them. I remember getting out of the pool and being met by my dad. He pulled me over to the side and told me, "I want you to look to the east and I want you to look to the west." I was just a dumb teenager, so I wanted none of it. But he repeated it. So I did it. He said, "Every day the sun comes up in the east and goes down in the west. And how you choose to use that day is up to you. But when it is over, it is over. It is yours to learn from and not let those mistakes happen again. Or you take those successes and learn how to duplicate them in the future." Later that night Gary [Kempf] cornered me. He essentially said the same thing. He told me I could let it get me down for the rest of my life or I could learn from it and move ahead for my senior year and the rest of my life. He said the successful people use events such as this to propel them to greater successes. So my senior year was all about that. I decided to not get uptight and just have fun.

We never won a Big 8 championship as a team, but we were always right there. Nebraska had great teams, too. Both of us were ranked in the top 25. It always seemed something strange would happen at the league champion-ships. Nebraska would get a transfer in from South Africa at semester, or we'd have a relay team get mysteriously disqualified. Our senior year [1989], we felt we had the better team. But we knew we would have to do some things differently to win. Gary and the coaching staff put the plan together. The real crux of the plan was they were going to take me out of my traditional events, the 100, 200 backstroke, 200 IM [individual medley], and a couple of

Glenn Trammel was an eight-time All-American swimmer at the University of Kansas. His head coach at KU, Gary Kempf, credits Trammel with having a major impact on the success of the school's swimming program.

relays, and put me in the 100 backstroke, 100 freestyle, and some other events. We had some other guys whom we thought could win—and they did—and we thought we could take some points away from them. I surprised everyone in the 100 freestyle—A) because I was entered, and B) because I won it going away and made the NCAA championships. To me, that meet stands out because everyone sacrificed to do what was best for the team. I swam events I had never done before. Every single day of my senior year, I was determined to win every single set, regardless of which event. It became apparent that I was a pretty good freestyler.

Unfortunately, we didn't win the Big 8 meet. We did have a relay team and another person get disqualified. Those were two key disqualifications that were very controversial. They cost us the title. The meet was at Nebraska, and we felt they were "homer" calls. But we did finish 13th at the NCAAs. At the NCAA championships, I was fourth in the 50 freestyle, an event I had never swum competitively before, and finished third in the 100 freestyle. I had a great chance to win it, falling just a few hundredths of a second out of first.

I'm a proud Jayhawk. My office wall has my framed All-America certificates around a Jayhawk logo, and my diploma is next to that. I have a watercolor print of the Phi Delt house on the wall, too. So I am never really far from KU. People who come in my office quickly know where I am from. I truly enjoyed my time there. I just absolutely loved the experience. We went to all of the football games and all of the basketball games, and other sporting events that our schedules allowed. The environment was great. The bottom line is, the University of Kansas, the people, the faculty, the administrators, and students were all pretty down-to-earth folks. You could go down to Wescoe Beach and get engaged in some interesting conversations, not necessarily with people you knew or had in class. You could just hang out. We had letter jackets, but people didn't know us like they knew Danny Manning or Milt Newton. But people treated them and us like normal people. There was a great energy. There seemed to be a lot of involvement from the students. It was a great place to learn and meet people.

Thank goodness for ESPN Plus. It's a wonderful thing. I can keep up with KU, watching the basketball games. My family knows not to bother me when they are on television. I miss it, but the memories are great, and I still stay in touch with my friends and teammates. It was a great time.

KEVIN PRITCHARD

BASKETBALL

1987–1990

KEVIN PRITCHARD WILL FOREVER be remembered in Kansas basketball lore as being one of the significant components of the "Danny and the Miracles" Jayhawk team that shocked the nation, winning the NCAA championship in 1988. Moved to point guard midway through the season by head coach Larry Brown, the 6'3" Pritchard averaged 10.6 points as a sophomore and led the team in assists. He scored 13 points, hitting six of seven field-goal attempts, in helping KU defeat Oklahoma 83–79 to capture the NCAA title.

Pritchard played his final two seasons under Roy Williams and led the team in scoring during the 1989–1990 season when the Jayhawks finished with a 30–5 mark and ranked fifth nationally. He was a two-time academic all-conference selection and was named to the All–Big 8 team in 1990. He concluded his career with 1,692 points, to rank among the top 10 all time in KU history. He also finished his career ranked among the leaders in assists, steals, and three-point field goals.

After concluding his playing career both in the NBA and overseas, Pritchard remained involved in basketball at the administrative level. He became general manager of the Portland Trail Blazers and has played a significant role in helping rebuild that franchise.

★   ★   ★

During Kevin Pritchard's playing career at KU, he learned his basketball skills under two Hall of Fame coaches—Larry Brown and Roy Williams.

I CAME TO LAWRENCE ON A RECRUITING VISIT with my high school coach and my dad, and it was a weekend when KU was playing Oklahoma. I remember we were seated behind the bench, and on the first play of the game, Danny Manning broke loose and dunked the basketball. I looked up at my dad and my coach, and we couldn't hear each other because it was so loud. We were so fired up. Even now, thinking about it, I get tingles. That was the split second I knew I wanted to attend the University of Kansas.

I had been coming to basketball camps at KU during the summers through high school, so I already had an attachment to the program.

I was there when Ted Owens was running the camps, and then coach Larry Brown. I went through the recruiting process with several schools, and it came down to the place and the coach. Obviously, the place was unbelievable. You see Allen Fieldhouse—the way the crowd gets into the game and the atmosphere—and you know it's special. It didn't take me long to realize that playing for Coach Brown and with someone like Danny in a place like Allen Fieldhouse was an opportunity I couldn't turn down.

My first game in Allen Fieldhouse was against the Russian national team, and they were loaded. They probably had four or five guys go on and play in the NBA. I came in the game, off the bench, and I think I turned it over the first three times. I was as nervous as I could be. I had never been nervous before a game prior to that one.

I started playing better after that. Coach Brown, right before, came over to me and said, "Look, son, you're going to play, you know. So you better get used to playing. Either you're going to get used to it now or you're going to get used to it later, so let's figure out how to do it now."

I remember walking out before the game, 30 or 40 minutes before tip-off, and the crowd was going crazy, and I knew this was exactly where I wanted to be playing during my basketball career.

I've often been asked over the years what clicked with the 1988 team that drove it to a national championship. I think there were some turning points. We really struggled in the middle of the season. There was a point when Coach Brown called me into his office and said, "You're going to be the point guard. We're going to put Jeff Gueldner at the two and Milt [Newton] at the three." And, of course, it didn't take hold immediately. It took the three of us a while to get accustomed to playing and blending with Danny and Chris [Piper].

The thing was, we defended like crazy. We helped each other on defense, and our job was to get Danny the ball in the right position on offense and for us to make shots when we were open. It was something that we had to get comfortable with, and it didn't happen overnight. But, once we did, I felt like there was unbelievable growth. We had some practices in there that were fantastic, and we started gaining confidence in each other.

One of the keys to our success, of course, was Danny's taking it upon himself to take a larger role within the offense. Danny would rather make the passing play for a score than actually score. I remember many times Coach Brown would tell him, "You've got to get up shots and you've got to make shots. You've got to force the action." The rest of us made some shots from the outside, and it opened him up from the inside.

We won our first NCAA Tournament game, and the second, and all of a sudden, we realized we were just playing basketball. We didn't have the burden of winning the championship. Instead, we were just going out and having fun. When it got to the championship game against Oklahoma—a team that had beaten us twice during the season—we felt we had the ability to win.

I remember right before the game, talking to the guys and looking around the locker room. I thought we were going to win. There was no doubt in my mind we were going to win.

During the first half of the game, Coach Brown kept telling us to slow it down. But we had opportunities, and we kept making opportunities. They kept pressing, and we kept breaking the press, and it led to some easy buckets. When we went into the locker room at halftime, we were about dead. Coach Brown told us, "You think you're tired? They're more tired, and you just have to keep pressing on, and we're going to win this game."

I remember going out in the second half, and I was tired but determined to give it all I had. I decided to dig down deep and try to play the best defense, make those guys work for everything, and then get the ball to Danny on offense. When I had shots, I knocked them down. Danny had an unbelievable game, but a lot of guys really showed up in that second half and in that game in terms of offensive production.

There was a transition period after Coach Brown left and Coach Williams took over the program. We all knew that Coach Williams would be good for us, but we were thinking, *We just had one of the hardest coaches in the world.* Coach Brown was really hard—he's great—but he's very hard. And, of course, we just figured we would railroad this new coach.

Coach Williams came in and told us we would only practice two hours a day, which was different from Coach Brown. I soon found out those two hours would be the most intense two hours that I'd ever been through in my life. Even though he's a nice guy and he coaches out of love and respect, he's hard, gritty, and a winner.

I believe it was our fourth practice of his first year, and he made us run for an hour and a half. People were throwing up all over the place, and he just kept saying, "You've got to run again; you've got to run again."

I talk about that practice with him to this day. I rely on that experience because it allowed me to push myself further than I ever thought I could. We ran and we ran and we ran, and it was a great experience. I know with his teams today that he uses that tactic to serve as a stimulator for his team.

Coach Williams was unbelievably organized. He makes every single day as full as possible in making the team better. Whether that's talking to players or flying across the country, he's special in that way because he has great stamina.

My experiences at KU, and the people I came in contact with in Lawrence, have remained important in my life and my career. From Coach Owens, who had a big impact in my life going through those camps, to Coach Brown, Coach Williams, and people like R.C. Buford—they've all been a big influence on me. I also talk with Coach Self all the time. It's a fraternity and a very special one I feel privileged to be a part of.

One thing about basketball, which I think is important to realize, is that the game has a gray area. There's no black and white. There are no absolutes in terms of how you play the game. There is a gray area in the game and you get a feel for all of those styles and you grab the best of each of them. What's great for me is, I know I could pick up the phone today and say, "Coach Brown, I need some help," or, "Coach Williams, I need some help," and they'd be right there for me because I'd be right there for them.

ROY WILLIAMS

MEN'S BASKETBALL COACH

1988–2003

IT'S NO COINCIDENCE THAT Roy Williams threw up the night before he accepted the head coaching job at the University of Kansas and, once again, 15 years later on the night he made the decision to leave Lawrence and return home to North Carolina.

Both decisions cut deep into the soul of a man whose value system is cemented in the concepts of love, family, devotion, and loyalty. Leaving his beloved North Carolina, both the school and the state, was painful when he made the decision in early July of 1988 to uproot his family and become the head basketball coach at Kansas.

He found it equally difficult and heartbreaking in mid-April of 2003, after carving his place in the storied history of Kansas basketball, to leave KU and return home to revive a program in serious need of great leadership.

When he was recently inducted into the Basketball Hall of Fame, he suggested that he should be enshrined as a "Tarhawk," a combination of the mascots representing the two schools who dominate his coaching résumé.

"I love two schools. I wanted to coach both, but couldn't," said Williams during the press conference announcing his return as head coach at North Carolina.

Williams left a lasting legacy in Lawrence. After spending 10 years as an assistant coach on the staff of KU alum Dean Smith at North Carolina, he was, in the minds of some longtime fans, a curious choice by athletics director Bob

Frederick to replace Larry Brown as the school's seventh head basketball coach. He was untested and somewhat of a mystery to many KU loyalists who expected a more established name to be announced as the choice to lead the defending national champions.

Frederick, operating under the handicap of an impending NCAA penalty during the search process, saw something special in Williams. Dick Harp, the former KU head coach who was working on the staff at UNC, had planted the seed on behalf of Williams a few months earlier when he suggested to Frederick that he should keep the North Carolina assistant in mind if Brown were to ever bolt Lawrence for greener pastures.

Frederick's decision will go down as a meaningful one in the history of Kansas basketball. Williams took four KU teams—1991, 1993, 2002, and 2003—to the NCAA Final Four, and is one of only three coaches in history to lead two schools to the national championship game. He guided KU teams to a combined 418–101 record and captured nine conference championships.

The Jayhawks were ranked as high as second nationally in 11 of the 15 seasons he coached at KU. Throughout his time as the Jayhawks' head coach and in the years since he's moved back to North Carolina, Williams has listed coaching in Allen Fieldhouse as one of the greatest thrills of his career.

"For 15 years, every single time I walked through that tunnel onto the court at Allen Fieldhouse, I felt cold chills," said Williams in remembering those moments.

Williams was born in Asheville, North Carolina, which is also the birthplace of author Thomas Wolfe, who wrote *You Can't Go Home Again*.

Williams did return to Tobacco Road, but will forever be remembered for his stay in Kansas where he quickly learned what it means to be a Jayhawk and, in many respects, enhanced the pride of being one.

During the 2008 NCAA Final Four, Williams found himself in the awkward position of being on an opposing bench against a KU team, as the Jayhawks' and Tar Heels' road to the national championship intersected in the semifinals in San Antonio. Williams had been on record when he left KU with his philosophy of not wanting to face his former school unless it was a forced meeting during the NCAA Tournament.

The drama of Williams versus his former team proved to be an intriguing pregame storyline, which both Williams and KU coach Bill Self downplayed as much as possible.

Roy Williams spent 15 seasons as head coach of the Jayhawks, guiding his teams to nine conference titles, four NCAA Final Four appearances, and a combined 418–101 record.

Kansas prevailed in the encounter, and two nights later, in the national championship game, Williams was seated in the stands behind his former team's bench with a Jayhawk-logo sticker affixed to his shirt, giving clear evidence of his love and loyalty for Kansas basketball.

★   ★   ★

JERRY GREEN, A CLOSE FRIEND and the first assistant coach I hired when I came to Kansas, once told me, "It's amazing, you get guys who play so hard they'll pull the dadgum nails out of the floor."

That was a compliment that means as much to me as any I could possibly receive. Hard work is a value I was taught by my mom. I've never seen anyone work any harder than she did to make a life for her family.

I grew up just outside of Asheville, North Carolina, in the small town of Biltmore. I can remember that my sister, my mom, and I lived in a two-bedroom home just down the street from Biltmore Elementary School. I would spend hours there shooting baskets on the outdoor courts or the gymnasium in the school.

My friends and I would stop by Ed's Service Station, and everyone would spend 10¢ and buy a Coca-Cola. I didn't have 10¢ to spend, so I usually just drank water.

My mom found out about it and, as I've told the story many times, would leave a dime for me on the corner of the kitchen table every single day. She wanted to make sure her son could also have a Coca-Cola to drink, like his friends.

I remember seeing her take in other people's laundry, and she would spend hours at the ironing board. She charged 10¢ for shirts and 10¢ for pants. She worked long and very difficult days to pay the bills.

I attended T.C. Robertson High School, where I played basketball and baseball. My high school coach was Buddy Baldwin, and he had a great influence on my life and my coaching career.

But I had a full academic scholarship offer to study engineering at Georgia Tech. One of my teachers, coincidently, was Coach Baldwin's aunt, and she thought I should take the scholarship and go to Georgia Tech.

I had decided by the time I was a high school senior that I wanted to be a coach. My heart told me that attending the University of North Carolina would be the best choice for my future.

My basketball playing career as a Tar Heel lasted one season. I played on the freshman team for Bill Guthridge in 1968–1969, and that helped whet my appetite for a career in coaching. Over the next three years, I was a regular visitor to Coach Smith's practice sessions, where I would take notes. It proved to be my classroom for coaching, and I was learning from the best teacher in college basketball.

I started my coaching career at Charles D. Owen High School in Swannanoa, North Carolina. I coached basketball and golf for five years and ninth grade football for four seasons.

My wife, Wanda, and I had a pretty nice situation. She taught English at another local high school, we purchased our first home, and our family was expanding. Wanda gave birth to Scott while I was coaching in high school.

But, after five years, I was presented with an opportunity to return to North Carolina as a part-time assistant basketball coach. We were making a combined $30,000, had a house payment and a family to support. My paycheck at North Carolina was going to be $2,700, and I don't think Wanda felt it was a wise choice, considering our financial obligations. Thankfully, I had an understanding wife, so we packed up the U-Haul and headed for Chapel Hill.

198

I needed to find creative ways to put food on the table and provide for my family. As it turned out, I was able to supplement my income by distributing copies of the coaches' television shows and by selling team calendars.

I delivered videotapes of Coach Smith's television show and the football coach's show to the affiliate stations around the state of North Carolina. I would wake up at 5:00 AM every Sunday for five years and drive a round-trip total of 500 miles. I was paid $105, minus the cost of my gas.

Another task that proved to be financially rewarding for me was the selling of North Carolina basketball calendars. I started in the summer of 1979 and would drive 9,000 miles over the next few months selling the team calendars.

As the years rolled by, my responsibilities increased, and I was able to play a more significant coaching role at Carolina. That opened the door for me to get a few head-coaching offers, but none that seriously interested me.

When the Kansas job came open in 1988, both Coach Smith and Coach Harp told me they had mentioned my name to Bob Frederick.

Bob eventually called and asked to meet with me at the Atlanta Airport. We had a good talk, but I knew that Bob had his eye on some coaches with more experience than I.

Wanda and I were on a family vacation—our first in four years—in Bermuda when I received a phone call from Bob. He wanted me to fly to Lawrence to interview with the search committee. With Wanda's blessing, I cut our vacation short and made my first visit to the KU campus.

During the drive from the airport in Kansas City to Lawrence, we stopped along the interstate so I could get something to eat. I wasn't feeling very good and thought a sandwich might help.

I threw up several times after I was dropped off at the hotel and before I was picked up by assistant athletics director Richard Konzem to drive over for a meeting with the search committee.

Bob has told the story many times that the night before I arrived in town, he was getting ready for bed, and his wife, Margey, asked him whom he was going to hire. Bob didn't respond immediately, and Margey finally said, "You're not going to hire that no-name assistant coach from North Carolina, are you?"

Bob told her, "Yes, I am!"

After meeting with the committee and talking with Bob, I started to understand what Coach Smith and Coach Harp meant when they told stories about the tradition of KU basketball. Bob offered me the job, and I had no doubts that I wanted it.

199

A few weeks later, I had to face my team and tell them the NCAA had found the school guilty of NCAA infractions, and we would not be eligible to play in the postseason tournament. We were also presented with severe recruiting limitations. I'll never forget the look on the faces of our players and how painful those days were for them. I quickly learned the difference when you move 24 inches on the team bench into the role of head coach.

We won our first game at the Great Alaska Shootout against Alaska-Anchorage and started the season 13–1. However, in the second half of the season we lost several key players to injuries and went through a four-week period when we had an eight-game losing streak.

That team handled the adversity and became a cohesive, tough group of players, and I'll always remember them as one my favorite teams. They accepted a punishment they didn't deserve and did it with dignity. The players on that team helped set the tone for the following years by believing in what we were teaching and using that belief as a powerful tool in achieving success.

Being on the sideline at Allen Fieldhouse for those 15 seasons was an experience I will always treasure. From the very beginning, I felt the deep pride and passion Kansas fans had for their teams, and that knowledge motivated me in a way that's difficult to properly put into words. I wanted to return that passion back to them by giving everything I had within me to make our players and our team successful.

It was ignited every season when we had the Late Night event and I'd walk out on the court through the tunnel greeted by a chorus of students chanting my name over and over. That gave me cold chills. I loved that connection with our students.

It was the emotion that drove me every single day for 15 years to give my heart and soul to the responsibility of being head coach at Kansas.

I always felt we had a great home-court advantage because opposing players and coaches could also feel the intensity of just how much our fans cared. I know it had to weigh on their minds when they came into Allen Fieldhouse and feel the overwhelming strength of that emotion. Allen Fieldhouse is a monster for opposing teams to deal with, and it's the great fans that make it that way.

I look back on our 62-game, home-court winning streak and take tremendous pride and satisfaction in being a part of that achievement. It happened because of great players and passionate fans who united in a common cause.

Being at Kansas was such a huge part of my life in so many ways. I had the opportunity to coach in Allen Fieldhouse and work with talented players such as Jacque Vaughn, Nick Collison, Kirk Hinrich, Paul Pierce, Raef LaFrentz, Mark Randall, and so many more who became a part of my extended family.

It was such a meaningful chapter of my life, and I'll always take pride in being a part of the Kansas basketball tradition.

The

NINETIES

DAVID JOHNSTON
TRACK
1990–1994

His unwavering dedication to the University of Kansas was born, in part, through a deeply rooted family heritage that was fueled by a first-grade teacher and later sealed by the lessons learned from a competitive rivalry with his best friend in elementary school.

David Johnston will eagerly tell you that the blueprints for his journey from childhood to adulthood were embedded in his DNA at birth. Later experiences while growing up helped light his journey to Lawrence.

"It's a pursuit I carried on my sleeve for a long time," notes Johnston, a proud member of the fraternity of track and cross-country All-Americans produced by KU.

Johnston wrote the script for his place in the KU track and cross-country annals at the start of his senior year when he filled out a questionnaire supplied to all of the team members by the coaching staff.

Under a listing asking for individual goals, he simply wrote, "All-American."

Johnston had set his ambitious sights on that meaningful achievement from the moment he announced his intentions, along with twin brother, Peter, to be a Jayhawk following a successful cross-country and track career at Lawrence High School.

He embraced that goal each year he competed in the Jayhawk pink-and-blue singlet, but it was not until his final season that he felt his athletic maturity would allow the dream to become a reality.

An elementary school teacher once labeled David Johnston a "Missouri mule" because he was born in Joplin, Missouri. Johnson, a product of a loyal KU family, found the tag insulting, and it served to inspire his dedication to the University of Kansas, where he would become a proud cross-country All-American.

In his apartment, located across the street from Memorial Stadium, he posted pictures of seven KU cross-country and track legends on the walls: Glenn Cunningham, Wes Santee, Billy Mills, Jim Ryun, Herb Semper, Al Frame, and John Lawson. It served as a daily reminder of the proud tradition of KU track and cross-country and the footsteps he hoped to follow.

He would later note, when asked about days on Mount Oread, that it was a pursuit that served to define both his college experience and ascension into maturity at a critical stage of his life.

"For me, it was becoming All-American," said Johnston. "Not so much the athletic distinction, it was more the idea of being an All-American... something that would define me.

"What I learned later was that it wasn't a single race that made me an All-American, even though I was fortunate to run the race of my life the last time I put on a Kansas uniform. I realized that I became an All-American long before that, supporting the idea that the journey is often more important than the destination.

"Perhaps that's what it means to be a Jayhawk. It's about the way you conduct yourself and pursue your goals, with integrity, diligence, and passion every day. Not a day goes by that I don't think about my KU experience. I may not be able to articulate exactly what it means to be a Jayhawk, but I know how much it matters to me."

★   ★   ★

204

I GREW UP IN PITTSBURG, KANSAS, where I attended elementary school. My father was a graduate of the University of Kansas, and we were a loyal KU family. I believe the first word out of my mouth may have been "Jayhawks."

One of the more defining moments early in my childhood that helped ignite my passion for being a Jayhawk occurred, strangely enough, in the first grade at Lakeside Elementary. My teacher was reading to the class from a publication called *The Jayhawker Book*, which offers information about the history of the state.

From the book, she read that people born in Kansas are called "Jayhawkers," and people living in the state are called "Kansans." At that point, she asked all of us to raise our hands if we were born in Kansas.

Every hand in the room shot up. The only child left not raising his hand was me. My mother and father, being such loyal KU people, had driven across the state line to Joplin, Missouri, so I could be delivered by a KU Medical School graduate who happened to be working at the hospital there.

My teacher quizzed me about my birthplace, and I reported that I had been born just across the border in Missouri.

"That makes you a 'Missouri Mule,'" was her response.

You can imagine how my classmates reacted to that. It was probably 10 seconds of snickers, but as far as I was concerned, it was years of torture that probably inspired me to be a little more Jayhawk as I grew up.

A close childhood friend and next-door neighbor was a boy named Barry Coleman. He came from a big Missouri family and, as it turned out, became a bit of a rival in sports while I was growing up in Pittsburg. As fate would have it, he was the best athlete in our elementary school. He eventually would be my roommate at KU.

It didn't matter if he played tennis, football, or any sport, I had to try and beat him. He was the best athlete, and beating him rarely happened.

Around the age of 10, I received a phone call from Barry around 6:00 AM on a Saturday. Barry and his mom were headed out on a 5K run that concluded in the Pitt State football stadium, and I was invited to join them. Neither one of us was an active distance runner at that point in our lives. But I wanted to run and try and beat Barry.

So I showed up and ran the race with the two of them. It was a lot of fun until the end. We entered the stadium at the same time for the finish and had to race around the turn to the finish line, and he beat me by one second.

That one narrow loss to a Missouri fan, no doubt, fueled my passion for running the rest of my life. It wasn't long after that race when another opportunity came along. They were entered in a race in Joplin and had a one-mile fun run attached to it, which we both entered. That time, I beat *him* by one second.

It was around that time that my father started taking the family to Lawrence to attend the Kansas Relays. We had been going to football and basketball games already and certainly were no strangers to KU. My dad had served as a track manager for the legendary KU track coach, Bill Easton, and was once chair of the KU Student Relays Committee. He knew many of the KU greats, such as Al Oerter, Wes Santee, and Al Frame.

I was 11 years old when we moved from Pittsburg to Lawrence in 1983. My dad became president of the University State Bank, which later became Commerce Bank. Running became an important part of my life as I continued to grow and mature.

I attended Lawrence High School and ran both cross country and track.

Our cross-country meets were at Rim Rock Farm, which is also the home course for the KU team. I've probably run that course about as much as anyone. Living in Lawrence, I never wavered from my ambition to attend KU, and running was my way to be an active Jayhawk.

I was under the delusion in high school that winning the Jayhawk Invitational, which was run at Rim Rock, as a senior would be my guaranteed ticket to become a Jayhawk. In my mind, they would have no choice but to offer me a chance to run for them. I made winning the Jayhawk Invitational my senior year as high a priority as the state championships, because it would legitimize my hopes for running for KU.

Fortunately, I did finish first. Had I finished second, I would have questioned if I was good enough to run for KU. Having won it, I felt it solidified my credibility to compete at the college level.

I was undefeated in my primary events my senior year. I had a good career at Lawrence High School, and we won two state championships. Individually, I won six state championships, five in track and one in cross country.

I was being recruited by many outstanding schools and was offered the opportunity to visit the University of Arkansas. They are to track and field what Notre Dame is to football. While I had no interest in going there, you have to listen when the top program in the country recruits you.

I took the trip to Arkansas and distinctively remember that I never saw the inside of an academic building. The coach, John McDonnell, sat me down at the conclusion of the trip and said—and I'm paraphrasing—"Look, we're going to win national championships the next four years. You can either choose to be a part of that or not."

206

I responded back that I'd rather try to win a national championship at the University of Kansas because it would be much more meaningful to me.

My recruiting visit to KU went great. My host was Ladd McClain, who had been one of my biggest high school rivals. We also had the opportunity to meet with a faculty member from our academic area of interest, which was journalism for me. Ladd attempted to show me around the campus, but I actually had a better understanding of where to find the J-school building.

I knew in high school that I wanted to build a career promoting KU. I knew I wanted to make a living telling people great things about the University of Kansas. KU had the best journalism school in the country, and it seemed to me that learning advertising would be a good fit for me.

Gary Schwartz was the head coach at KU. Coach Schwartz, along with an assistant coach, Mike McGuire, came to visit Peter [twin brother] and myself at our home. This was the point we would be told what KU was going to offer us to attend and be a part of the team. We had decided that we wanted to go as a package. Peter was also a strong runner in high school.

Of course, when Gary asked if we would sign, we immediately said yes. There was no question about it. We did stipulate one condition on agreeing to sign with KU. We wanted to have a press conference announcing it in the same location where KU always had its major press conferences. We wanted to sign our papers in front of the big Jayhawk banner.

That was my suggestion, and I wanted to do it the week of the Kansas Relays. I'm not sure any media turned out for the signing, but that didn't matter to me. I just wanted to announce it publicly in front of the Jayhawk. That was unique in those days, particularly for someone who was not a basketball or football star.

College is a life-changing experience for anyone. People have often said that, "You come to college and you are part of KU. When you leave, it becomes part of you." I think that holds true for everyone.

There was a cross-country meet my junior year that I would call my breakthrough race. I didn't win the race and, in fact, finished 15th, as I remember. But this was a major cross-country meet. I looked around me and saw so many great runners, including All-Americans.

On the advice of our team psychologist, David Cook, I had written a plan of how I would run the race. I followed that script, and it helped me control the outcome. I realized that I could run with all of the great runners. That's when it hit home that I could do this and achieve my goals.

207

To become an All-American, you have to finish among the top 25 American runners at the national championship. Plus, you first have to qualify to make it into nationals. They take the top teams and the top three individuals not on those teams. That meant, to assure a position at the finals, I had to at least finish among the top three individuals.

My best friend and teammate, Michael Cox, and I found ourselves running side by side at the two-mile mark. I turned to him and said, confidently, to "take it if you've got it." That's what we would say to a teammate. I was running my race and was where I wanted to be at that stage.

Michael looked over and said, "This is my plan. I'm where I want to be."

Our plans, as it turned out, were identical. We had counted heads and knew where we stood and who we had to beat to be among the top three individuals. With a mile to go in the race, we set our sights on the one person we needed to beat, and it turned out to be the number-one runner from Kansas State.

We kicked it in gear and passed him on either side. Michael and I crossed the finish line second and third, and I can't describe how good it felt.

I kept a lot of scrapbooks that tell the story of my running career and my days in college. In fact, I have about 24 scrapbooks in my house.

My wife and I have two little girls. Our first daughter, now four years old, is named Sydney. We liked that name partly because it was a host Olympic city. My other daughter was born the day before the opening ceremonies in Athens, and we were tempted to call her Athena or something like that. But we didn't take it to that extreme. We named her Sophia.

Sydney may one day be a runner. When she was three years old, I was running a 5K that finished on Jayhawk Boulevard. As I was approaching the chute and finish line, she broke loose from her mother and came running after me. I grabbed her hand and we crossed the finish line together.

The next year she wanted to run with her dad in the same race. So we ran the race together, and at about the halfway point, I thought she would not be able to finish. I looked down and suggested we go home and have ice cream.

"But, Daddy, you are not supposed to quit in the middle of a race," she reminded me. I smiled and we continued to run until we crossed the finish line.

I guess there might be another runner, perhaps another Jayhawk, in the family.

MATT GOGEL

GOLF

1991–1994

Y OU MIGHT SAY MATT GOGEL took advantage of a mulligan at the beginning of his collegiate career. A graduate of Tulsa's Bishop Kelly High School, the pull of national power Oklahoma was too much to resist. But after redshirting a year, Gogel calls the decision to transfer to Kansas "one of the best ones of his life." Attending KU was not totally foreign to him, however. His family lived in Lawrence from 1976 to 1982, while his mother, Celeste, earned her undergraduate degree and his father, Tony, his master's from KU.

Gogel burst onto the scene as a freshman, winning medalist honors at the 1991 Big 8 Golf Championships. He became the first Jayhawk to win such honors since Bob Richards did so in 1956 and only one of five such Kansas champions of all time. He followed that up with 12th-, third-, and sixth-place finishes in his career—resulting in All–Big 8 honors four times. As for the team, Gogel's tenure was among the most successful. Under the direction of longtime coach Ross Randall, the Jayhawks were third, fourth, and second twice at the conference championships. Kansas finished runner-up to national power Oklahoma State, losing by 1 stroke in 1993 and by 5 strokes in 1994. In 1993, Gogel earned All-America honors with a 34th-place individual finish, as the Jayhawks placed 15th as a team.

As a professional on the PGA Tour, Gogel won the 2002 AT&T Pebble Beach Pro-Am, after finishing second to Tiger Woods in 2000. His 12th-place finish at the 2001 U.S. Open at Southern Hills Golf Club in Tulsa was

Matt Gogel became the first Jayhawk in nearly 40 years to win medalist honors at the Big 8 Conference Championships when he took first in the 1991 tournament. He would later earn just over $4.5 million from 1994 to 2007 on the PGA Tour.
Photo courtesy of Getty Images

his best finish in a major. For his career, Gogel has earned just over $4.5 million from 1994 to 2007. In 177 regular tour career starts, he had 32 top-25 and 16 top-10 finishes.

Today, he and his family live in Kansas City, where he is a partner in the insurance brokerage firm of Matthews, Gogel, and Craddock. He also is doing some broadcast work for The Golf Channel in its coverage of PGA Tour events.

★   ★   ★

I WAS KIND OF A LATE BLOOMER in the junior golf world. I had won some junior tournaments in Oklahoma but really did not have any national exposure. When I was 13, I began playing in some local tournaments, but it wasn't until I was 15 or 16 that I really played earnestly in junior competitions. That is pretty late compared to some of the top juniors today. I started playing some national events during my senior year and won a tournament in Florida during Thanksgiving break. I was being recruited by some schools before winning that tournament, mainly Oklahoma, Oklahoma State, and Tulsa, because they tend to contact the junior champions in the state. But winning that tournament in Tampa opened up recruiting on a national scale and gave me some choices. I visited Oklahoma, Kansas, and LSU, and was going to go visit New Mexico but passed on that because I thought I had narrowed my choices and knew what I wanted to do.

It was a tough choice because my parents both had degrees from KU, and Alvamar was as good a course as you could want to play on as a collegian. Oklahoma was the number-one team in the nation and in the process of winning the national championship my senior year in high school. Ultimately, I went to Oklahoma with the blessing of my parents. When I got there in the fall of 1989, I sensed some things were not quite right. It was just a different culture, and I could sense some disconnect. I told my parents over break that I wanted to leave, but they made me stick it out and told me to honor the scholarship for a year. Late in the season, I told Gregg Grost, the Oklahoma coach, that I was going to transfer after the year. He had heard some talk that I was considering it and was upset because five players left that year. But he did grant me my release, and that allowed me to go to KU without having to sit out a year.

I was playing okay in the fall at Oklahoma and was probably going to play in some spring events. But I knew in my heart I was going to transfer, so I did not want to use up any eligibility. It became a redshirt year. I could tell from the first moment I was at KU that it was going to be a good fit. At Oklahoma, it was just golf and school. It was a bit of a factory. I can respect that to a degree. But, at the same time, I was freshman in college, and I needed an opportunity to experience college life. We had mandatory 7:00 AM team breakfasts, classes had to be scheduled in the mornings, and you could not join a fraternity. I thought that was just not right. It was an amazing culture change at KU. I had known some of the guys on the team and was able to join a fraternity, so it was a breath of fresh air.

211

There was a bit of controversy my senior year at Kansas. Oklahoma said that I had actually played in a competition while I was there, so my eligibility should be exhausted. Oklahoma said I had played in a team booster fundraiser they had every year with the University of Texas the same weekend as the OU-Texas football game. I never really felt that I was going to lose a year, but the NCAA and Big 8 just wanted to make sure they got a full explanation. It was not a competition. I guess hard feelings lingered.

Kansas hosted the Big 8 championships my freshman year at Hallbrook Country Club in Kansas City. I was the individual medalist and really did not know that a freshman shouldn't be the champion. It was a tough course, but I had only played it maybe once in the fall when we hosted the rest of the league for a one-day preview. I don't think I played it in the spring in advance of the tournament. I did not sense I had an advantage. College is a funny competition because you play with the other school's players in the same slots. So I was paired with Colorado, and not Oklahoma or Oklahoma State, where the power was. I think I was two or three on the team. I really did not know what was going on at the time. I was just out there competing.

We had a great group of guys during my time at KU. The team included Jeff Moeller, John Hess, Brad Bruno, Casey Brozek, and Jay Hepler, and the next year Tyler Shelton came in. We all kind of grew up together. The tournament that meant a lot to us was the Western Intercollegiate in Santa Cruz. It was where [head coach] Ross [Randall] had grown up, and we wanted to do well for him. We won several tournaments, but you always feel you could have won more. We finished second to Oklahoma State at Prairie Dunes Golf Club two years in a row for the Big 8 championship, losing by a shot my junior year and a few strokes as a senior. It would have been nice to get those. We were one of four teams invited to go to Japan and compete in a tournament. It was based on your previous year's performance. I won that event, and that meant a lot.

212

KU means so much to me. It is a wonderful place and has so much to offer it basically recruits itself. I met my wife, Blair, in the fall of 1992 and made numerous lifelong friends. Kansas is respected and known everywhere. I think it is an amazing story that everywhere I went—and I don't mean just the United States, I mean the world—everyone knows about KU. My caddie can attest to that. One year at the British Open, I was heading to the driving range and someone yelled, "Rock, Chalk, Jayhawk!" to me, and my caddie just dropped the bag and shook his head. Obviously, there are people who travel to Phoenix, so he also heard it at the Phoenix Open and other places. But he could not believe it happened in England. It makes me feel good. I consider it to be a special family. It was always a thrill for me when I was out on the tour to hear or see a reference to KU. It was awesome to see the KU people. It was comforting, in a sense.

I developed a pretty good relationship with Coach [Roy] Williams because he loves golf and with Coach [Joe] Holladay, given his Tulsa roots. The week after I won at Pebble, I came home and went to a game. It happened to be my birthday. It was also Bobby Knight's first game at Allen Fieldhouse with Texas Tech. They presented me the game ball at a timeout, and then the band played "Happy Birthday." That was great. After the game, Coach Williams told me he'd wanted to shake my hand at the time, but his team got off to a bad start, and he needed to "chew my dadgum guys out."

We ended up killing them, so it all worked out. When he went to North Carolina, I'd see him at tour events in Greensboro and Charlotte, and we'd hook up and talk. I've gotten to know Coach Self a little, but I think with his family being younger, he does not get to play as much. I remember when he first got the job at KU, I sent him some golf balls with his name on them. I ran into him a year later at my club in Kansas City, and he showed me the box and said, "Look, I still have the balls you gave me." I said, "Coach, if you still have those balls, you aren't playing enough golf." I'm excited with what he has done at KU, and I'm sure we'll hook up on the course someday.

I really wasn't sure if I could play past college when I was being recruited, even though I'd had some success. I won the Oklahoma state junior title in 1990 the summer before I came up to KU, and then qualified for the U.S. Open in the summer of 1992. It was then that I thought, *Hey, I could be pretty good at this and might be able to do it for a living.* I played a practice round with Tom Watson and Fred Couples at the U.S. Open. I was not at their level, but it didn't seem like I was too far off. It was at that point I put my energy into being a professional.

I had a good run on the tour beginning in 2000. After finishing second at Pebble in 2000 and winning it in 2002, I tied for 12th at the 2002 U.S. Open at Southern Hills in Tulsa. It was my best performance in a major. At the Open, I remember it was hotter than hell. We were pregnant with our first child. After my sister graduated from high school in 1994, my parents had moved to Raleigh, North Carolina, so I had been back to Tulsa maybe one other time. It had been five or six years since I had been back. It was familiar to me, but at the same time, it wasn't like I had lived on that course. We had some rainstorms that week, so I had to finish my second round Saturday morning, then go out and play my third round that afternoon. I think it was that nine on Saturday morning that got me. I was 4 over par right there, and I think I finished the tournament at 3 over par. That nine kept me from having a chance.

I played well in 2003 and really well at the end of 2004. What was frustrating about 2004, and I remember talking with Tom Watson about it, was being in the hunt for four straight tournaments late in the year but just not being able to finish. It was frustrating. When a person has success, the confidence increases so much and it means so much in helping you win. You cannot overstate that.

213

RAEF LaFRENTZ

BASKETBALL

1995–1998

MONONA, IOWA, IS A TINY COMMUNITY in the northeast part of the state where agriculture is the dominant industry. But, for a few years, it could have been argued that travel and tourism were the economic engine. That's because nearly every major-college basketball coach came to woo Raef LaFrentz, one of the nation's top prepsters, to play for them.

Ultimately, Roy Williams and Kansas won out for the services of the agile 6′11″ LaFrentz. From 1995 to 1998, Kansas would go 123–17, including a 58–0 mark at home, and win four conference titles. LaFrentz would become the third pick in the 1998 NBA Draft by the Denver Nuggets, but not before earning consensus All-America and Big 12 Player of the Year honors twice (1997 and 1998).

At the time of his graduation, he ranked among the school's top 10 in scoring, rebounding, career field goals and attempts, free throws and attempts, field-goal percentage, and blocked shots. His 2,066 points and 1,186 rebounds at the time trailed only Danny Manning's totals of 2,951 and 1,187, respectively. Those exploits have earned him entry into the Kansas Athletics Hall of Fame, and his No. 45 jersey is retired, hanging in the rafters of Allen Fieldhouse. LaFrentz has played for the Nuggets, Dallas Mavericks, Boston Celtics, and Portland Trail Blazers since his graduation.

★ ★ ★

You had to have a reason to come to Monona, Iowa. If you were going to fly commercial, you had to fly into a place two hours away—Waterloo; Cedar Rapids; La Crosse, Wisconsin; Rochester, Minnesota. They are all small cities with small airports. So you had to do some driving if you were going to come see me.

Everybody came to visit. Duke was about the only one that didn't recruit me, because they had their front court assembled. But just about every other top program made contact, and most of them came to see me. They came whether they were invited or not. They just seemed to pop up at the high school or at the local restaurant. It was like everything in town was normal, and then all of a sudden—*boom*, a high profile coach just showed up. It was fun. The whole town got involved. Monona is about 1,500 people, so your business is everyone's business. Everyone was excited by the prospect of guessing who would be in town this week.

I guess I made a name for myself nationally for the first time at the AAU national tournament in Winston-Salem, North Carolina, between my sophomore and junior years of high school. I was a kid from small town Iowa, so no one really knew about me. I played really well in a game, and the Kansas coaches were there in the stands, so they learned about me early.

I knew that I wanted to remain in the Midwest, so my parents could come watch me play. After a while, I narrowed my choices to Kansas, Iowa, Notre Dame, and Missouri. I visited Notre Dame because I really wanted to go to a football game there. I canceled my Missouri visit, which I don't think made them too happy. They made it tough on me in Columbia for my four years. The crowd was always on us. I was leaning toward Kansas the whole time, but I felt I owed it to myself to look at other options, and I felt I owed it to the home state to look at Iowa. I was never really a huge Hawkeye fan, but I had friends who went there. I did go to an Iowa State game on an unofficial recruiting visit, but that was so I could get good tickets for the Kansas game. I had to sit behind the Iowa State bench, but deep down I was cheering for Kansas. There were a lot of unhappy people with me when I announced I was going to KU, but anyone in their right mind would have made the same decision I did. [Among those who expressed public displeasure was legendary Iowa football coach Hayden Fry. He chastised LaFrentz's decision and said he took it "personally" that a resident would leave the state to attend school. Williams shot back, saying, "I don't know if Hayden Fry knows a jump shot from a crab block, whatever a crab block is."]

The dead honest answer is that, as great as the University of Kansas is and as nice as the people there are, the decision came down to one thing and one thing only—Coach Williams. He was relentless in my recruitment. I was comfortable with him, and he was honest in telling me how I'd fit in there. I had never been to the state of Kansas before my first visit to the campus. I came down on an unofficial visit my junior year and spent a weekend, going to a practice and a game. I learned quickly why Kansas was so special.

My first impression of Allen Fieldhouse was that it was an old building. Initially you did not get the feeling it was anything special. But once you experience a game, your mind changes rather quickly. The crowd and the students were unbelievable. We play the games, but the Kansas people create the environment. It's the best environment that I have ever played basketball in and the best that I have ever seen. I feel fortunate to have played there four years.

When you are in the locker room before the game, you know exactly what is going on. The fans are loud. The band is wild. You can feel the electricity in your body and in your soul. It gave us so much confidence, a feeling like we could not lose. But you have to learn how to harness all of that. You get so excited, so amped up that, by the time you take the floor, you can be gassed after about two and a half minutes. As a player, you feed 100 percent off the crowd. Running out of the tunnel is exhilarating. The first time is off the charts. You don't ever get used to the adrenaline rush. Even as a senior, you still feel it. By the time you are an upperclassman, you learn how to manage it, but it is still there. It never gets old or any less thrilling.

The University of Kansas is a special place with special people. It was a place where I grew up as a person. For me, it was a time for great emotional growth and maturation. I think that was due to the people I was around. Coach Williams put us around quality people and gave us the chance to grow from high school boys to college men.

I think my parents had as much fun during my time there as I did. It was a 16-hour round trip from Monona to Lawrence and back. So that lasted one year. They rented Rex Walters's [who was playing in the NBA] condo for three years. It was a vacation for them. They were both retired school teachers, so during the season they lived in Lawrence. They met a lot of great people and became good friends with some people down there. They still keep up with some of them.

It was a typical day of practice. We were going through a spirited workout, and there was a loose ball. I dove for it, and Jacque Vaughn did, too. He

During his four-years with the Jayhawks, Raef LaFrentz helped KU to a combined 123–17 record and four conference championships. At the time of his graduation, he trailed only Danny Manning in career points and career rebounds at KU.

jumped on me and landed on my head and jammed my tooth into the court. I ended up taking a chunk of wood out of the court. But then he rolled over again, and my forehead hit the court. My eyebrow was sliced open, and I had to have it stitched up. Coach Williams made sure they left that mark on the floor when they refinished it because I think he felt it showed that even the big men at Kansas get after it. It was across from our bench, just below the free-throw line, across the lane.

There were two games that stick out for me in Allen Fieldhouse. Probably the first one was my sophomore year when we played UCLA the year after they won the national championship. We were down 20 points in the first half and 15 at halftime. We got after them in the second half and came back to win by 15. We just smoked them. It was the loudest building I have ever been in. I think the UCLA players were shell-shocked. Once Jacque hit the spin move in the lane, that was all she wrote. It was the closest I had come to losing a game in Allen Fieldhouse.

The other was against Missouri. It was a nationally televised game. As far as an individual performance, that game stood out for me. I think [Missouri head coach] Norm [Stewart] was ticked at me still for canceling my recruiting visit. I had 31 points, including a follow-shot dunk that got the crowd going. It was a pretty physical game. I am sure they are good guys, but during the game they weren't. It was always good to beat Missouri.

I think the class above me, my class, and the one below never went to the Final Four. However, I only lost 17 games there in four years. I never felt my record or my experience was a failure. Sure, advancing to a Final Four would have been great. But if I had to trade places with someone on another team that had made the Final Four, I don't think I would have. I enjoyed the guys, I enjoyed the coaches, and I enjoyed Kansas. We were successful. That is why I decided to come back for my senior year. I am glad I made the decision I did. It wasn't to win the national championship. You can't put a price tag on the experience I had at KU. I am not going to let not making it [to the Final Four] detract from a great experience. The NCAA Tournament is a one-and-done situation.

I appreciated the opportunity and my experiences at KU when I was going through it. But being 11 years removed and looking back on it, I really appreciate it. I'll credit Coach Williams for most of that. I haven't been able to come back much because of my schedule, but you never forget those nights in Allen Fieldhouse.

Being in the NBA, I get a chance to see quite a few people with KU ties. Absolutely, I look forward to seeing any guy from KU, whether I played with him or not. I know them all. One thing you find out is that there's also a lot of coaches and other people in the NBA who have been at Kansas. There is a pride factor among us all.

218

The
NEW
MILLENNIUM

NICK COLLISON

BASKETBALL

2000–2003

THERE'S A GOOD REASON Nick Collison's No. 4 hangs in the rafters of Allen Fieldhouse. The Jayhawks' second all-time leading scorer (2,097 points) and third all-time leading rebounder (1,143), he was selected the 2003 Collegiate Player of the Year by the National Association of Basketball Coaches and the 2003 Big 12 Conference Male Athlete of the Year, in addition to piling up other accolades and awards. In his four years at Kansas, the Jayhawks were 113–29 with two Big 12 titles and appearances in the 2002 and 2003 NCAA Final Fours. The 2003 squad fell to Syracuse 81–78 in the NCAA title game in New Orleans. Collison was a first-round selection and the 12th overall pick in the 2003 NBA Draft by the Seattle Supersonics. His jersey was retired on November 25, 2003, at halftime of the Jayhawks' 81–74 win over Michigan State.

★   ★   ★

You might say that love played a role in Nick Collison coming to Kansas. Sure, Collison was attracted to the university from the first step he set foot on the campus. And the pitch he heard from Roy Williams sealed the deal. But had Cupid's arrow not landed close to him, perhaps the Iowa Falls, Iowa, native would have never been a Jayhawk.

"Going to Kansas is probably the best decision I've made, and the time there was the best four years of my life." —Nick Collison

"A high school friend of mine and his family were going to a game at Kansas my sophomore year, and they asked me to come along," Collison said. "My friend's sister was dating Raef LaFrentz at the time. I knew about how good Kansas was, but growing up near Iowa City, I followed Iowa more closely. The first impression I had was that the [Allen] Fieldhouse was kind of old and a little dark. But the crowd was unbelievable. It was an early-season game, but it was completely packed and everyone was going wild. That was quite a first impression.

"I met the coaches after the game and [assistant coaches] Neil Dougherty and Matt Doherty later came up to Iowa Falls to watch me practice the night before KU was playing Iowa State in Ames. They kept contact with me, and Coach [Roy] Williams offered me a scholarship after we won the state title my junior year. Everyone was saying that the only reason I came to Kansas is because Tom Davis was fired at Iowa. But that was not the case. I had never made any type of commitment to anyone. I liked Iowa growing up, but Tim Floyd was the coach at Iowa State, and I was also considering them. But I knew I had to make the decision that was best for me. I narrowed it to Kansas and Duke after my junior year. I was always leaning toward Kansas, but I felt I had to go through the process. I visited Duke, but I did not get the same feeling I got from the players, the coaches, and the atmosphere at Kansas."

As is the case with most former student-athletes, specific games do stand out, but it is the cumulative experience that leaves the most enduring impression on them.

"Going to Kansas is probably the best decision I've made, and the time there was the best four years of my life. Everything about it was positive. The campus was great, the guys on the team and the coaches were family, and the fans—especially the students—were awesome. You probably appreciate it even more when you're gone. You won't play in a better environment than Allen Fieldhouse.

"What made it great for me was that my family got to experience it, too. My dad was my high school coach, but he quit coaching so he could come watch me play. I remember they made a lot of trips between Iowa Falls and Lawrence [630 miles round trip]. Sometimes they would sneak out of school an hour or two early, come to the game, make the trip back in the early morning hours, then get up, and go to school. It was tough on them, but I am sure my little brother, who was in grade school at the time, thought it was cool. He got a lot of TV time."

Collison was understated as a person, but his play on the court spoke volumes for his talent, competitiveness, and leadership. Few would argue that his senior season at Kansas (2002–2003) was the most dominating for a Jayhawk since Danny Manning led the Jayhawks to the 1988 national title. He averaged 18.5 points and 10 rebounds per game, shot 55.4 percent from the field, blocked 74 shots, and recorded 16 double-doubles. If there were any games that stood out for Collison, they came his senior season in a 90–87 win over No. 3–ranked Texas in Allen Fieldhouse and a 69–65 win over Duke in the NCAA Sweet 16 in Anaheim, California. Against the Longhorns, Collison recorded a 24-point, 23-rebound performance that earned a standing ovation from ESPN announcer Dick Vitale.

"I've been fortunate to see lots of great performances during my career as a broadcaster," said Vitale. "On Monday night, I saw Nick Collison put forth one of the most special efforts I've ever seen. There have been very few occasions where I got up as a broadcaster and gave a player a standing ovation. David Robinson of Navy was one, and Collison on Monday night when he fouled out with a minute-plus left."

"I remember we needed to beat Texas if we wanted to win the conference title," Collison said. "We had stunk it up in a loss at Colorado [60–59] earlier in the week, then gave up the big lead in losing to Arizona [91–74] in Allen Fieldhouse on Saturday. We played Texas on Monday night on ESPN, so we did not have much time to prepare. We started out slow [trailing by 12 points midway through the first half], and you kind of got the feeling of, 'Here we go again.' But we really turned it on. Everyone played great that night. Kirk [Hinrich] hit some huge shots and made some big plays. The thing I remember about my game is it just seemed like the ball was a magnet. Texas had some size, but it seemed like I was able to get to every ball. The bad thing was I fouled out with about a minute left."

223

Against Duke, the Jayhawks trailed 54–53 late in the game, but Collison scored 12 straight points to extend the lead to 65–59 with 3:15 left in the game. He would finish with 33 points and 19 rebounds in playing all 40 minutes. To say Collison ran over Duke would be accurate, both literally and figuratively. As he bullied his way to the basket on one occasion during the Jayhawk run, he stepped on a Duke player, much to the surprise (and pleasure) of KU fans.

"That was a big game. Of course, we beat Arizona two nights later to go to the Final Four, but Duke had our number [six wins in seven previous meetings] and was considered to be the top program at the time. I just tried to keep moving and stay aggressive. I know I was pretty tired after the game. I know a lot of people got fired up when I stepped on Casey Sanders, but it was not intentional. I remember we lost at Iowa when I was a freshman when

I missed a shot on a layup because I was concerned about landing on some-one. After that, I vowed never to worry about what or who was below me. I was going to make the basket no matter what."

Collison is one of a multitude of Kansas basketball players who return to Lawrence on occasion to play pickup games and meet up with friends. It has become the home for many who have completed their collegiate and/or professional careers.

"The great thing about Kansas is the family atmosphere," Collison said. "The players who came before you and the ones who came after enjoy each other. The games we play in the summer are pretty competitive. I wish I could make it back more, but the NBA schedule keeps me busy, and I have a family now. But you never lose the memories. My family stays close to it, too. They go see KU when they play Iowa State in Ames. My time at KU may have been as fun for them as it was for me."

Collison's play, appreciated by Kansas fans, also left an indelible impression on the coaches, both his and his opponents'. As he and fellow senior Kirk Hinrich exited the game on Senior Day on March 1, 2003, in a 79–61 win over Oklahoma State, Cowboy head coach Eddie Sutton jogged over to the Kansas bench to shake both their hands in appreciation for what they had accomplished.

"I just wanted to go down there and tell them that they really brought a lot of class to the University of Kansas and the Big 12," Sutton said. "They are great players. But I am glad I don't have to face them anymore."

"Nick Collison is as good a student-athlete as you would ever want to coach, but he is an even better person," Roy Williams said. "He means so much to me and he means so much to Kansas basketball."

NICK REID

FOOTBALL

2002–2005

To get a feeling of how much Nick Reid wanted to be a Jayhawk, all you have to know is he committed to Kansas despite it not having a head football coach. Reid was an all-around athlete at Derby High School, earning all-state honors as a quarterback/defensive back in football, an all-league decathlete, and a three-year starter in basketball. He was regarded by many to be the top high school football player in the state as a senior.

At Kansas, Reid began as a strong safety in fall camp before his freshman season, but his tenacity and attacking style prompted the staff to move him to outside linebacker. It also earned him the admiration of Jayhawk fans, the respect of his opponents, and the scorn of opposing fans. He would go on to start the final six games of the season and earn *Sporting News* Freshman All-America honors. His stock skyrocketed from there, earning honorable mention All–Big 12 Conference status as a sophomore, first-team recognition as a junior, and Big 12 Defensive Player of the Year honors as a senior. He played in 48 games, starting in 40, recording 416 tackles (254 solo), 41 tackles for loss, 14 quarterback sacks, three interceptions, 14 broken-up passes, six forced fumbles, and one fumble recovery. The Jayhawks ranked in the top 10 nationally against the rush his senior year.

Jayhawk head coach Mark Mangino credits Reid for setting the tone in rebuilding the Kansas football program. Noting that Reid's motor never quits

Nick Reid was a two-time all-conference selection as a linebacker for the Jayhawks and was named the Big 12 Conference Defensive Player of the Year in 2005.

running, Mangino called him "a player who made a difference in our program and one of the finest defensive players ever to play at the University of Kansas. I appreciate the fact that he came to play every day and never took a play off. His leadership qualities are what every coach wants."

Reid did not fit the typical mold of a professional football player, but he remained undeterred in signing a two-year free-agent contract with the Kansas City Chiefs. He was a late cut prior to the 2006 season. Not one to give up, Reid signed with the Frankfurt Galaxy of NFL Europe and earned a starting role as the team fell just one win shy of winning the 2007 league title. He was second on the team in tackles and earned league player of the week honors once. All this with playing the last eight weeks with a broken nose that hampered his breathing. Given the option of having surgery and missing a significant portion of the season, he continued to play. That decision should come as a surprise to no one. The Chiefs invited him back for fall camp for a second year in 2007.

★ ★ ★

I COMMITTED TO KANSAS EVEN THOUGH the school was between coaches because I felt like it was a great time to be a Jayhawk. I knew Chancellor [Robert] Hemenway was going to bring in a coach who wanted to win. I wanted to be a part of the building process and a part of turning the football program around. My first football letter was from Oklahoma. I thought it was the coolest thing in the world to be recruited by a program of that stature. After that, the letters started rolling in mostly from schools in the Big 12, but also some others from across the country. I actually had a lot of interest from schools in track and field to compete in the decathlon. However, I knew all along that I wanted to play college football. I also received some interest in basketball, but most of those letters came from smaller schools in the Midwest.

When it came down to signing, the two options I considered for football in Division I were Kansas and Oklahoma State. After talking it over with my family, we decided that Kansas would be the place for me. It was also not too far of a drive for my family and friends to come see the games.

I have always been a fan of KU and the city of Lawrence. I came up to Lawrence and competed in a couple of the Kansas Relays when I ran track in high school. So I got a look at the campus. Also, my sister went to school there her freshman year, so I would go up and hang out with her and really get a feel for the college atmosphere. I also grew up watching KU basketball. I was a huge fan. My Biddy Basketball coaches, Rex Smith and Scott Ritchie, were the biggest fans in the world. That rubbed off on me. We would always get together and watch the games and eat pizza. I thought Jerod Haase was an awesome player. I loved how he would sacrifice his body and do anything to get the ball. He really played with intensity, and that was the intensity that I wanted to have. No matter what kind of sport I was playing.

It seems my playing style got opposing fans riled up. I did pride myself on playing hard. I'm not really sure why opposing fans hated me so much. But I do remember it starting a long time ago. In high school basketball games, people would chant things at me to try to get under my skin. And I remember before a big football game we had, the opposing team made a life-size replica of me and threw it on a bonfire they had at a pep rally. It seems to me that people just love to hate me. I really think I am a pretty nice guy.

My time at KU was outstanding. I wouldn't trade it for anything. I wouldn't change one thing. I made some amazing friends who will be life-long friends. I received an education from one of the premier schools in the country. I was a part of building a successful football program. To be a Jay-hawk is a truly wonderful thing. With all the tradition and success that surrounds KU athletically and academically, just to be a small part of it is a big deal. To be able to tell people you have a diploma from the University of Kansas is something to be truly proud of.

My first year was difficult. We lost a lot of games by close margins. You could tell the program was improving. Being a part of a program that started off 2–10 and finished with two bowl berths and a top 10 defense nationally against the rush tells you how far we came. We had a great group of guys, especially on defense. My fellow linebackers, Kevin Kane and Banks Flood-man, were the best. We had played together for so long we really knew how the others would react in any situation. Aside from being so close on the field, we also hung out off the field. I believe that is where the real trust was built, and that carried over to the field. I knew that any one of those guys would go to battle for me, and they knew I would for them, as well. We really weren't the most athletic group, and we weren't highly recruited.

228

I enjoyed every time I suited up to play. Even though Kansas is not as well-known for football, I thought we had good support. Memorial Stadium could get pretty wild. My junior season, the Kansas State and Texas games stood out. I remember K-State hammering us 64–0 my freshman year, but we turned around two years later to beat them. It was a great feeling because we had lost 11 straight games to them. That same year, Texas came to Lawrence ranked No. 6 in the nation. I remember this game so well because of one play. We were ahead 23–20 late in the game. It was fourth down and 18 yards to go. The play had broken down, and Texas quarterback Vince Young took off and scrambled. I missed a tackle that probably would have sealed the game for us. I was crushed, but it helped me to learn how to take the bad with the good. Things happen, and you have to learn how to put them behind you and move on.

The Nebraska game at Memorial Stadium my senior season was truly a day to remember. We snapped a 36-year drought and beat them badly at home. We made some great plays on offense, defense, and special teams. We broke open the game in the second half to win 40–15. I remember people coming up to me after the game and thanking me for doing it and being a part of it. It really made me feel special, like we had accomplished something. Missouri was a big game for us because of the rivalry. I think we were underdogs every time we played, but we beat them three out of the four times we played. Missouri quarterback Brad Smith was in the Heisman race in 2005, and I think we held him to under 30 rushing and not much more passing as we won 13–3. It just seemed like every year they really thought they were better than us, and every year we put it to them. We had no problems getting up for Missouri. Before those games, former Kansas head coach Don Fambrough would come in and give us a speech. Let me tell you, he really knew how to get us fired up. He would start off by telling us that Kansas was a free state and Missouri was a slave state and how Quantrill came over and raided Lawrence. Just the way he told the story and the emotions he showed in his dislike toward Missouri made every one of us want to run through a brick wall for him. He really knew how to get us going and get us ready to play.

We had our fun. Coach Mangino was a disciplinarian, but he also realized we were college kids. He knew we were going to be ready to play. Before every game, my fellow linebacker, Darren Rus, and I would play tricks on Banks Floodman. Banks would get so excited to play that he would get dry heaves before the game. To add a little more drama to it, we would always hide some of his equipment right before we were getting ready to go out on the field. The look on his face was priceless. He would freak out, and we would eventually tell him or play the hot/cold game with him until he found it. He was a really good sport about it and never really got too bent out of shape.

MARK MANGINO

HEAD FOOTBALL COACH

2002–Present

MARK MANGINO RESTORED THE PRIDE and national respect in Kansas foot-ball in 2008 by leading the Jayhawks to the most successful season in the school's history. He earned consensus National Coach of the Year honors after guiding KU to a 12–1 record, including a victory over third-ranked Virginia Tech in the Orange Bowl and a top-10 national ranking. Under Mangino's guidance, the Jayhawks' remarkable emergence into the national spotlight became one of college football's top stories.

KU's rise to prominence in college football circles was a testament to a coaching philosophy Mangino brought to the KU program when he took over as head coach in 2002. It marked KU's third bowl appearance under Mangino, as he rebuilt a program that had won just two games the year before he arrived and had suffered through six consecutive losing seasons.

Mangino's pedigree as a coach has impressive roots. He learned his trade while serving as an assistant coach at various stops during his career under Jim Tressel, Bill Snyder, and Bob Stoops, all former National Coach of the Year winners.

He also worked his way into a successful college coaching career without the benefit of playing college football. Prior to his arrival in Lawrence, Mangino served as one of the primary architects in the rebuilding process at Oklahoma (1999–2001) and Kansas State (1991–1998). As assistant head coach and offensive coordinator at OU, the Sooner staff took a program that was 5–6 in 1998 and carved out seasons of 7–5 (1999), 13–0 (2000), and 11–2 (2001). He won the 2000 Frank Broyles Award as the top assistant coach in college football.

Overall, Kansas State and Oklahoma were a combined 102–30–1 and ranked in the top 25 nationally in eight of 11 seasons during Mangino's involvement on the coaching staff.

★ ★ ★

MY PARENTS INSTILLED THE PRINCIPLES of hard work, loyalty, and discipline in me, and I channeled those values every opportunity I had on the sandlot fields around Mahoningtown, a neighborhood of New Castle in western Pennsylvania.

Those principles have served as the foundation for how I've lived my life, raised my family, and approached my career in coaching.

I was raised in a working-class, Italian-Catholic community, where many people worked in the steel mills or the railroads. Life was somewhat challenging in my neighborhood, and competition provided an outlet for kids to learn leadership skills and develop confidence. I suppose that's where my path into coaching started. I enjoyed playing baseball, football, or about any game we could organize with friends.

Some of my favorite childhood memories are from those years when my brother, Matt, and I played for a Connie Mack baseball team that was managed by my dad [Thomas]. I was a pretty fair catcher/third baseman on my neighborhood teams, and it's accurate to say that baseball, while I was growing up, was my first love.

Like a lot of kids, my dad had a strong influence on me and my life in sports. He was an all-state football player and received a scholarship to play football at Penn State. He was limited, however, after suffering a knee injury late in his senior season of high school and was unable to continue playing after his initial season at Penn State. My dad was a big, athletic man and was called "Bear" by his friends. It was a nickname that I later inherited.

Despite the injury setback, my dad stuck with his education and was the first in his family to earn a degree. He went into social work and later served as executive director of children and youth services in Beaver County. He was also a helping hand in the neighborhood. My dad and mom [Connie] would offer advice to neighborhood families who were impacted by injuries on the job in the steel mills or railroads. They assisted people with their legal problems or getting workman's compensation.

I learned a lot about loyalty from the examples set by my parents.

While I enjoyed playing baseball, football took over as the primary focus of my sports attention in high school. In my early teens, I was a good player for the neighborhood, average for my high school football team, and above average for our baseball team. I always liked the strategy aspect of sports and paid a lot of attention to understanding how teams should be coached. I had a scholarship to play football at Youngstown State, but I spent too much time playing and traveling with baseball and softball teams in the bush leagues and not enough time with my studies. As a result, I wasn't able to play in college.

Without the benefit of a playing career on my résumé, my path to college coaching was launched under different circumstances.

I had to postpone my coaching career plans and college education for a while. I got married and started a family. I did a variety of jobs to supplement the family income, including working as an emergency first responder for the Pennsylvania Turnpike Commission. Eventually, I went back to Youngstown State and got my degree in 1987. I always thought that I would end up coaching high school football. My first coaching job, in fact, was serving as an assistant coach at New Castle High while I attended Youngstown State.

Later, while I was in school at Youngstown, I was approached by Bob Dove, then an assistant coach at the school, about helping coach the offensive line. That was an opportunity I couldn't turn down. I worked on the coaching staff at Youngstown under Bill Narduzzi and then stayed on the staff when Jim Tressel took over as head coach. From there, I went to Geneva [Pennsylvania] College as offensive line coach and offensive coordinator. In 1990, I accepted the job as head coach at Ellwood City [Pennsylvania] High.

I heard about an opportunity for a graduate assistant position at Kansas State and had a childhood friend, John Latina, who was already on the staff there. Another former high school teammate, Nick Rapone, was the secondary coach at Pittsburgh and was talking with me about coming there to be a graduate assistant.

Kansas head football coach Mark Mangino won virtually every national coach of the year honor during the 2007 season.

I was impressed with what I heard from John and from my interview with Bill Snyder at Kansas State. I was sold on Coach Snyder and decided to start my college coaching career in the Midwest. My wife, Mary Jane, and I packed up a Ryder truck and took our two kids, Samantha and Tommy, to Manhattan. It proved to be one of the best decisions of my life.

I soon learned that graduate assistant coaches don't make much money. Mary Jane worked as a teacher's aide in a Manhattan elementary school. We were living in the basement of Coach Latina's home for a while and were struggling to pay our bills. Eventually, I went to Coach Snyder and told him that I wasn't living a lifestyle that was fair for my family.

We were broke, had to get credit cards, and we were running up debt like crazy. I told Coach Snyder that I really liked the job and the experience, but we were flat broke, and I was going to have to look for a job elsewhere.

He said, "Mark, you just continue to do the job you're doing, and good things will happen." Then he said, "Trust me." So I looked at him, and I thought, *Well, he's a man of his word, and he's never said anything that's not true. He's always been up front.* And then, almost four months later, he hired me full-time as recruiting coordinator.

I had a great experience at Kansas State and developed a lot of my philosophy working with Coach Snyder. Of course, that led me to Oklahoma, where I had the opportunity to work under Bob Stoops. Bob had served on Coach Snyder's staff at K-State, and we had become good friends.

While leaving Manhattan was difficult, I was convinced that adding another coaching stint to my résumé—particularly one at Oklahoma—was in the best interest of my coaching career. My years at OU were enjoyable and rewarding. We won a national championship in 2000, and that vindicated, without question, my decision to join Bob Stoops at OU.

234

Of course, our success in Norman opened the door for new opportunities. I certainly had aspirations to be a head coach at a major-college program, and that chance came knocking on my door late in the 2000 season when the University of Kansas approached me about its vacancy.

My first opportunity to make an impression on the group of individuals charged with searching for a new football coach at Kansas came on the morning following one of the most disappointing losses I had experienced at Oklahoma.

That memorable defeat came on a cold November day in Norman, our last regular-season game of the 2001 season, when we were upset by our in-state rival Oklahoma State, 16–13. We came into the game with an 10–1 record, ranked third in the country, and with our sights set on a conference championship.

Less than 24 hours later, I was scheduled to receive a phone call from the search committee at Kansas. I was well aware that it would be a phone conversation that could easily impact my coaching future and the lives of my family members.

Apparently, I made a favorable impression on the search committee. Shortly afterward, I was invited to meet with a smaller group of Kansas athletics department leaders—athletics director Al Bohl, and associate athletics directors Richard Konzem and Doug Vance—in an Oklahoma airport hotel meeting room.

While I felt the interview went well, I had a few lingering doubts about whether this was a move I wanted to make at this point in my career. Coach Stoops was not only my boss, but also a good friend and someone I deeply admired. I was very happy in Norman as the offensive coordinator at one of college football's most storied and successful programs. The future was bright, and my family was happy.

I later called Al Bohl, the KU athletics director at the time, and expressed that I had decided to pull my name from consideration. Al, however, was persistent and pleaded with me to reconsider that decision. I had actually made contact with him, I later learned, while he was in the middle of an interview with another candidate. He made some strong promises about the type of commitment and resources that he would put forth in building the Kansas football program.

There was no question in my mind that I was ready to be a head coach at a BCS school. I had worked under the direction of two of the best coaches in the game in Coach Stoops and for 11 seasons under Bill Snyder at Kansas State. I served as assistant head coach and offensive coordinator during our national championship season at OU in 2000. We had won at least nine games and played in a bowl game in each of my final six seasons at Kansas State.

235

Following several phone conversations with Bohl over the next couple of days, I decided the Kansas opportunity, despite my reservations, was a step I couldn't turn down. I knew there would be a lot of challenges at Kansas. However, I had been part of coaching staffs that developed the blueprints for successful rebuilding jobs at both Kansas State and Oklahoma.

Beyond the opportunity to be a head coach, the job had added appeal. My family and I had always been impressed with Lawrence. In fact, my daughter, Samantha, was already a student at KU.

So, after I evaluated all of the positives of the decision and consulted with Coach Stoops, I accepted the job offer.

It didn't take me long to realize the magnitude of the challenges that I faced. The Jayhawks had won just three conference games over the previous two seasons, and it was apparent the program was mired in an atmosphere

where everyone involved—players, support staff, administrators, and fans—
didn't fully understand the commitment that was going to be needed to turn
the program into a consistent winner.

Early on in those first years, I became frustrated over the lack of a vision
for the football program and the unfulfilled promises made when I was
being courted for the job. However, Chancellor [Robert] Hemenway
helped us throughout the process and made it clear from the beginning he
wanted a successful football program at Kansas. His support was meaningful in helping me know we had a commitment from the highest level of the
university.

Gradually, with the hard work from a dedicated coaching staff, we started
making small improvements both on and off the field. We won just two
games in our first season, but I was convinced we were taking all of the right
steps to move the program forward.

As I told the media often during our first years on the job following a loss,
we just need to keep sawing wood. We stayed positive, kept our commitment
to building for the future, and didn't back down from the values we felt were
important in the building process.

I'll always remember those early years and the efforts of a lot of great
young men who helped pave the way in the building process at KU. Those
kids had faith in what we were telling them and set the tone for the program.
We made no promises or predictions. For the young men who bought into
it, things have worked out pretty well.

I'm forever thankful for the family values handed down to me by my parents and the experiences I had growing up in a community and a neighborhood that demanded a simple, but structured lifestyle—one that was defined
by the principles of hard work and perseverance. It has served well as a foundation for a career in coaching.

I'm also fortunate to have had the unyielding support of a loving and car-
ing family. My wife, Mary Jane, along with our children, Samantha and
Tommy, have made many significant sacrifices in support of my career in
coaching.

Being the head football coach at the University of Kansas has been a
rewarding experience and changed my life in many ways. The rewards come
daily in witnessing the transformation of our program into one that commands
national respect and seeing the impressive improvement of our facilities. I take

tremendous pride in watching our players mature on and off the field and gain confidence in their accomplishments as student-athletes.

When I arrived at KU, Coach Don Fambrough and John Hadl were among the first of many loyal fans and football alumni to impress upon me what it means to be a Jayhawk. I was immediately struck by the loyalty, pride, and love they exhibited in being a part of our football history. Both Coach Fambrough and John have been with the program, through the ups and downs, providing unconditional love to this university.

They serve as great inspirations to anyone who bleeds the KU colors and inspire me and all of our coaches to appreciate and understand that we represent special people and a special place. That's the message I carry forward as a coach and ambassador of the University of Kansas.

The Jayhawk is a symbol that illustrates pride in accomplishment. Simply stated, embracing what it means to be a Jayhawk is opening the door to a life-changing experience.

RUSSELL ROBINSON

BASKETBALL

2005–2008

BASKETBALL IS A NUMBERS GAME, but for Russell Robinson it was never important how many points he scored, how many assists he made, or how many steals he accumulated. As a point guard for the University of Kansas, the only numbers that really mattered were one, four, and 100. One representing the top ranking as 2008 national champions, four representing the number of Big 12 Conference championships Kansas won during his time as a Jayhawk, and 100 signifying the percent of effort he gave every time he stepped on the floor.

Robinson grew up in the Bronx, far from the rolling plains of Kansas. Homesick and a bit beleaguered as a freshman, he contemplated transferring closer to home. But encouraged by his parents to "establish his roots," Robinson dug down deep with greater resolve. He would start every game as a sophomore, junior, and senior (with the exception of Senior Night during his sophomore campaign). In recognition of his relentless pressure, cat-quick hands, and high basketball IQ, Robinson earned Big 12 Conference All-Defensive Team honors three consecutive years. Recruited by numerous schools in the East and South, Robinson eventually chose the Jayhawks over Georgia Tech. He has come to love his university so much that he has created his own personal hall of fame in his apartment. He has organized his rings, posters, newspaper clippings, and other paraphernalia to remind him of this special time in his life.

The numbers and accolades tell but part of the story. It is not too strong to say that no player during the Bill Self era was more admired by coaches, teammates, and fans than the heady Robinson. He wasn't flashy or boisterous. He never drew attention to himself, although a boyish, wry smile served as his equivalent to Red Auerbach's signature victory cigar.

"The point guard should be an extension of the head coach, and Russell is just that," Coach Self says. "The only important stat for the point guard is wins and losses. His job is to run the team. And as our record indicates, Russell does that pretty well. He isn't really flashy, and he doesn't do it with a lot of flair. But he is productive. Look at his defense. He creates havoc. When a team is forced to take a bad shot because the defense does not allow it to run its offense, often times that is because of Russell. There really is no stat for that, but when you look at the film, you realize it was because he would not let them run the play. You never question his effort."

Three times he was honored by his coaches and teammates with the Danny Manning "Mr. Jayhawk" Award, signifying his leadership and dedication to the program. As a senior, he earned Academic All–Big 12 Conference honors. And no player in Kansas received a louder ovation during the starting lineups than he did, when the public address announcer yielded to the fans to belt out Robinson's state of birth. The announcement of Russell Robinson, from "New York, New York" was anticipated by fans almost as much as the game itself.

Robinson also proved to be an expert prognosticator. Following the Jayhawks' 109–51 shellacking of Texas Tech on Senior Night, he stood at center court in Allen Fieldhouse and told fans that he expected them to join him in celebration of a national championship. One month later, Robinson and his teammates carried through on their end of the deal.

239

★   ★   ★

MY GOAL WAS JUST TO BE A PART of a great tradition and hopefully leave something with the program that has my mark. The program already has a hold. Hopefully, I can come back one day and people will remember me. No matter how many points I score or how many rebounds I get, the program is the program. It is as big as anything in college basketball. I just try to contribute as much as I can. Players like Aaron Miles, Keith Langford, Wayne

Russell Robinson earned four Big 12 Conference championship rings and added a
fifth ring to his collegiate basketball career collection when he helped the
Jayhawks to the 2008 NCAA national championship.

Simien, and Michael Lee are the ones I look up to. Those guys set the tone
for me my freshman year—introducing me to the KU tradition. And I've
been trying to carry it on for my years at KU.

After coming out here and visiting the campus and visiting with Coach
Self and his staff, I felt really comfortable and was able to make that jump
from New York City. Coach Self is a great guy—really intense, but really
friendly at the same time. But he knows how to get the best out of his players. And he pushes us to the max each and every day for us to get better. I

think guys respond to him really well. He just wants each player to excel individually, and he knows how to get the best out of his players.

The community here is great, and once I got here I felt like I couldn't pass on it. And the fans did a great job of accepting me and making me feel welcome. The tradition was a great part of my making the decision. I felt like I just wanted to be a part of that. You're not surprised when [basketball lettermen] alumni come back and play with you for a couple of days or just hang out. And that's always a great opportunity, just to talk to them. Every time they come back, you see them go back to their locker and relive their college experience.

It reminds me that I'm here for only four years, so I need to make the most of it. It is definitely a joy to turn on the TV and see KU alumni [in the NBA] representing the program so well. In the back of your head, you're just wishing, *Oh, that could be me one day*. So you just work hard every day. You think about it and look forward to doing well in practice, so hopefully you can be at that level one day. I just try to be a great role model for the community and the young kids growing up. Hopefully, they can recognize that and do it themselves.

241

Playing Texas on national TV in Lawrence [in 2007] was a great opportunity. The fans live for those types of games. *We* live for those types of games. Those are the games that we look forward to when we decide to come to KU. I think Coach did a great job of calming everybody down and getting everybody focused. We look to Coach. When he has a big smile on his face and he's happy, that takes a lot of pressure off us, and we were able to go out there and perform.

To put on that Kansas jersey, go out there and play in front of all those fans, and be seen all over the nation is definitely an experience I will remember for the rest of my life. Words can't really put into place how I feel when I run out that tunnel and hear 16,300 people yelling my name and chanting and grooving. It's a great, great feeling. I think every player in college basketball wants to be a part of something like that.

Hearing my name introduced at games, the way they do it, is a great feeling. The students are as loud or louder than the PA. I didn't know the PA didn't say, "New York." I just thought they [fans and PA] said it together. But, wow, that's a great feeling. You know the fans take a lot of pride in that, and it's something they enjoy doing. I will definitely miss that.

TODD REESING

FOOTBALL
2006–Present

TODD REESING ENDEARED HIMSELF to Kansas fans long before he threw his first pass as a member of the Jayhawk football team. Upon verbally committing as a high school senior, Reesing was quoted in the *University Daily Kansan* as saying, "After seeing Manhattan and Lawrence, there was no comparison. Kansas's campus was prettier, and their facilities were a lot nicer. I really liked Lawrence, and everyone I talked to convinced me it was the better school."

Reesing bided his time on the bench as a true freshman until halftime of the ninth game of the year (2006). With the Jayhawks trailing Colorado 9–0, he started the second half at quarterback and led the Crimson and Blue to a 20–15 win. He saw action as a reserve in the final two games and became the starter for good in the first game of the 2007 campaign. It would become the most successful season in school history, as Kansas went 12–1, tied for the Big 12 North Division title, defeated Virginia Tech 24–21 in the FedEx Orange Bowl, and finished ranked No. 7 in the nation in the Associated Press and ESPN/USA Today polls—the highest-ever final ranking for the program.

Reesing was the catalyst for an offensive explosion that saw him establish numerous school season and career records. In 2007, he completed 276 of 446 passes (61.9 percent) for school records of 3,486 yards and 33 touchdowns. As much as he moved the ball with his arm, his shifty feet and quick thinking made him a running threat, as well. He was a Davey O'Brien Award (nation's

Todd Reesing was on his way to a summer football camp hosted by Kansas State when he received a call from Kansas inviting him for a recruiting visit. Reesing quarterbacked the Jayhawks to the 2008 Orange Bowl victory over Virginia Tech.

top quarterback) semifinalist, a second-team All–Big 12 selection, and an academic all-league pick as a double-major in finance and economics. He set a Big 12 record with 213 consecutive pass attempts without an interception. Through his sophomore season, he has school career bests in passing yards per game (230.6), 300-yard passing games (five), and touchdown passes (33). But as impressive as the statistics, teammates, coaches, fans, and opponents quickly found it was the heady play of this gritty Texan that separated him from others.

Spurned by virtually every Division I school because of his diminutive size (5'11", 200 pounds), Reesing attended Lake Travis High School in Austin, Texas. He was the Class 4A Player of the Year as a junior, Central Texas Player of the Year as a senior, and graduated in the top 1 percent of his class.

★   ★   ★

I GOT OFF TO A PRETTY GOOD START with the fans after making that quote. Kansas State was the only school to offer me a scholarship at the time. Coach Snyder offered me a scholarship in the spring of my junior year. It really came out of nowhere because I really only spoke to him once. I didn't know if anyone else was going to take a chance on me, so I was pretty much resigned at that point that it would be my only offer. Kansas really wasn't recruiting me. But a family friend, the daughter of Pat Henderson, who used to be an assistant coach at KU, sent my résumé to the coaching staff in the summer following my junior season. One day, I got a call from [assistant coach] Tim Beck to see if I might be interested in Kansas. It so happened that I was actually in the Wichita airport when he called. I was visiting a high school friend and was then headed to a camp at Kansas State. I told Coach Beck I was actually on my way to Kansas State and could stop by on my way back. I arranged for my parents to send some videos to KU and then headed off to Manhattan for camp.

244

I went from the mini-camp at Kansas State and visited Lawrence for the first time. I was blown away when I got there. It was the first time I had set foot in the state, and all I really knew about Kansas was what I'd learned from being recruited by Kansas State. The staff gave me a tour of the athletic facilities and campus. I met some of the players who had stayed in town to work out and lift weights. All the time I was there, I was hoping I would get an offer. I knew it was the place for me. I talked with Coach Mangino, who told me that he liked what he had seen on tape. I later learned he first looked at the tape the night before my visit. I didn't work out or throw any passes for them. I think they had seen enough on tape. Right before I left, Coach Mangino said he would be offering me a scholarship within the week. That is when I knew I would be a Jayhawk. I really liked the campus and everything about it. I had committed to attending some other camps in the summer, so I carried through on those. Duke was the other school to offer me a scholarship.

Even though I had good stats in high school and was named player of the year, I wasn't heavily recruited because of my size. I would attend camps where I would throw farther, with more accuracy, and had a quicker release. But I would still get passed over, so it was a bit frustrating. I'm thankful Kansas did not let my size affect their decision. Even though I graduated from high school a semester early and came to Lawrence in the spring of 2005, the plan all along was for me to redshirt my freshman season unless there was an emergency. We had two good quarterbacks in Kerry Meier and Adam Barmann. But they had been nicked up with injuries late in the year, and we just weren't doing much against Colorado.

We were down 9–0 at the half. Earlier in the week, Coach Mangino asked me, if the right situation presented itself, would I be willing to play? I told him, yes. I was ready to play and wanted to see how I stacked up against Division I players. Right before half, one of the coaches told me that Coach Mangino wanted to see me. He told me that I was going to start the second half and that I would play the rest of the game. I just kind of said, "Wow." I don't know if I looked nervous or not, but he smiled and told me not to worry because we really couldn't play much worse. He said he was just looking for a spark. I guess that is why he gave me the nickname "Sparky." I remember sitting in the locker room, listening to the coaches but really wanting to get out there and stretch out and get warmed up. I hadn't done anything for about an hour. We went on to win the game, and it proved to me that I could play at this level. I think it was good for me to give up the redshirt because it gave me confidence going into spring ball.

My freshman year left a bad taste for our team. We were 6–6 and bowl-eligible, but weren't selected for a bowl. We were more upset in that we lost so many close games. We committed ourselves to not let that happen again. We had great offseason workouts, a great spring, and virtually everyone stayed in Lawrence to work out during the summer. We got stronger and faster, but we also grew as a team. I certainly did not think we would go 12–1, but I felt we would be pretty good. I think our whole team felt that way. We lost all of those close games the year before. We just needed to finish the job. We blew away our first four opponents at home, and I think that just confirmed what we felt. But you really never know for sure until you get into conference play. Winning at Kansas State was great for our confidence. That told us we could win in the Big 12 and win on the road. Things just started to snowball, and we just got more and more confident. We still played with a chip on our shoulder because no one was giving us the respect they gave the other teams that were ranked highly. We were a team. I think Kerry Meier was the best example of that. We were competing for the quarterback job, but we have always been great friends. He could have sulked when I was named the starter, but he went to the coaches and offered nothing but support and volunteered to help in any way. What we found out is that he was a hell of a receiver. He made some big plays for us.

We went into the Orange Bowl knowing there were a lot of people who still did not respect us. Virginia Tech was bigger and faster than us. We were just a bunch of average Joes. We didn't feel pressure because we were confident in our abilities. We felt it was a great opportunity for us and a chance to silence the critics. We had a great set of practices leading up to the Orange Bowl. But that was the story for the entire season. We were always well-prepared, and the players had the discipline to carry out the game plan. You have to give Coach Mangino and the staff a huge amount of credit for having us prepared for every game. I think it helped us that our defense stuffed Virginia Tech early in the game and we moved the ball well on offense. We seemed to have the upper hand the whole game. I think we just wanted it more than they did. It was a great way to end the season. But it also told us that we cannot let up. Winning the Orange Bowl doesn't guarantee we'll be good next year. That is why we don't say, "Let's continue this next year." Next year is a different year. We aren't continuing anything. We're starting over with a new team and new goals. I can't wait to get started.

It was a great year for us. The stadium was rocking every game, and the fans were unbelievable. I always heard that the fans here were just waiting for basketball season to start. But they were great to us, and the town, the university, and the alumni rallied around us. It was fun to be on campus—there was lots of energy. Lawrence is the perfect college town. The campus is gorgeous, the people are great, and there's live entertainment and other things to do. Growing up in Austin, it just seemed like the campus sprawled on forever, and there were traffic jams all over. You don't have those issues in Lawrence. KU is just a great place.

AFTERWORD

by Danny Manning

My FATHER WAS A PROFESSIONAL BASKETBALL PLAYER, so my family was accustomed to moving around. Still, it came as a shock to me when I found out that I would be moving from Greensboro, North Carolina, to Lawrence, Kansas, the summer prior to my senior year in high school. I must admit I was a bit conflicted. I was disappointed that I would be leaving my friends and what was projected to be a pretty good team. But at the same time, I was happy for my father in that he was getting the opportunity to work with one of the all-time best coaches at one of the most historic collegiate basketball programs.

It didn't take long for us to realize that the move to Lawrence would be one of the best things ever to happen to the Manning family. My dad had been out of basketball for a brief time, and being back in the game revitalized him. My mother and sister instantly made friends they would keep for life. I, too, fit in immediately as the students of Lawrence High welcomed me with open arms. I have maintained many friendships from my LHS days. I did not have a shortage of friends—especially after I committed to play basketball at Kansas. I realize the people at North Carolina and North Carolina State were upset when Larry Brown hired my father. But they had a relationship that dated back to the days of the ABA. And, believe it or not, my parents would have had no problem if I had decided to become a Tar Heel or member of the Wolfpack. But, after spending time in Lawrence and around the Kansas program, it was my decision to become a Jayhawk. I have never regretted that choice.

Although not growing up a Jayhawk fan, it did not take long for me to appreciate the passion they have for their school. Shortly after my father took the assistant coaching position, I read and heard a lot about the history of Kansas basketball. It really sank in during my senior year in high school, when the Lawrence High gym and even some games on the road would be packed with Kansas fans to watch a future Jayhawk play. I credit my high school coach Ted Juneau with helping me develop as a person and player at that time. There was pressure on both of us. I was trying to live up to the hype that had built up, and Coach Juneau was suddenly expected to not lose a game. I always thought that was unfair. After all, he won the Kansas Class 6A title the year before with my future college teammate, Chris Piper, leading the way. Coach Juneau really had nothing to prove. We ended up having a great season. To this day, Ted Juneau, his wonderful wife, Judy, and lovely daughter, Whitney, are a big part of our family.

Ironically, I lost the first game I ever played at Allen Fieldhouse, falling to Wyandotte High School 50–49 in the state title game. Wyandotte had future KU wide receiver Willie Vaughn and future Oklahoma basketball player William Davis. Kansas fans might remember that was the same night that Ron Kellogg hit a baseline jumper with 16 seconds remaining for the Jayhawks to upset Oklahoma and Wayman Tisdale at Kemper Arena to win the Big 8 Postseason Tournament. A few years later, we would get a chance to win a title at Kemper Arena against Oklahoma. I think we all know how that turned out.

248

Looking back, it seems like my career at Kansas went by in no time at all. I was fortunate to be a part of teams that had some success, albeit there were some trials and tribulations. There are some Kansas fans who think the 1985–1986 Jayhawk team was the best ever. That was my sophomore year. The program was coming off back-to-back NCAA Tournament berths for the first time since 1974–1975, so the fans were hungry. We had a veteran team, featuring Ron Kellogg, Calvin Thompson, and Greg Dreiling, plus Cedric Hunter and myself as starters. We had productive bench players in Archie Marshall, Mark Turgeon, and Chris Piper. An improbable NCAA Sweet 16 overtime win over Michigan State, followed by a regional final victory against North Carolina State, sent us to the Final Four for the first time since 1974. The Jayhawk Nation was in a frenzy. We entered our semifinal game against Duke on a 16-game winning streak. It looked like it was going to be number 17 when my good friend Archie Marshall hit a driving layup

Danny Manning was a two-time All-American at the University of Kansas, an Olympian, and an NBA All-Star. He concluded his collegiate career as both the Jayhawks and Big 8 Conference leader in career points and rebounds. In 1988, he was named College Player of the Year and led KU to a national championship.

249

to put us up by four with eight minutes left. We had the momentum. But Archie fell to the floor on the play and never got up. A torn ACL ended his season and demoralized us. We lost by four points. We were honored with a parade when we got back. It was a tough loss, but I found out how much Kansas fans appreciated the players and the program.

My junior campaign (1986–1987) was a bit of a rebuilding season, but we still managed to tie for second in the Big 8 and earn an NCAA Tournament bid. More than anything, Kansas basketball was a happening. It marked the third straight year every game had been sold out. The late-night practice to begin the year was anticipated for months. Students actually camped outside in the cold overnight for days, not to get a ticket, but to get a seat. The campus was alive and buzzing. It was great to be a Jayhawk.

Quite naturally, my senior season (1987–1988) was filled with great expectations. We were picked No. 1 by almost every media outlet. I remember a magazine took a cover shot with me next to a highway sign with an arrow pointing to the Kansas City exit. The Final Four was in Kansas City that year. The headline read "Goin' to Kansas City." Our team embraced the expectations. Our late-night practice before a packed Allen Fieldhouse was a giant pep rally. But the season started out with a thud. We lost two games at the Maui Classic. To be fair, this was a team that had much to prove. We had a good recruiting class, and Archie Marshall was coming off a medical redshirt season. We were going to be better at the end of the season than the beginning. We rebounded from the 1–2 start with seven straight wins, but just when it looked like we were starting to jell, Archie hurt his other knee at a tournament in New York City. He had landed on my foot and tweaked his knee. Archie was one of my best friends on the team. I was devastated.

We scuffled along for a while after that. We had a 55-game home-court winning streak ended by Kansas State, and after a loss at home to Oklahoma, we stood at 12–8. There was talk of the athletics department making contingency plans to host an NIT game. Things were not going well at all. For some reason, the team's chemistry had not materialized to that point. It may come as a surprise to many that teammates do not have to be best friends to achieve success. But the players must respect the team concept, and that means being unselfish. Coach Brown was more upset at our selfishness than anything else. Our fortunes turned on the road at Oklahoma State. Coach inserted Jeff Gueldner into the starting lineup and moved Kevin Pritchard to point guard. Both were extremely intelligent players. We should not be surprised that today Jeff is a successful businessman and Kevin is the general manager of the Portland Trail Blazers. Those adjustments, along with Milt Newton establishing himself as a starter, moved us in a positive direction.

Things began to click. We went 9–3 down the stretch. We lost a tough overtime game to Duke at home and on the road at Oklahoma—both teams were ranked. We lost a semifinal game at the Big 8 tourney to Kansas State.

Kevin did not play because he hurt his knee the day before. We felt good about our play to end the season, but at 21–11 we did not have high hopes about our NCAA Tournament chances. Surprisingly, we secured a No. 6 seed and headed to Lincoln, Nebraska, for the opening round. Little did we know that we would assume the role of Cinderella for the tournament. Kansas fans travel well, but even the Nebraska fans became Jayhawks after players from Xavier denigrated Lincoln in the local media. We blitzed them early and awaited a matchup with No. 3 seed North Carolina State. But the Wolfpack were upset, and Murray State stood between us and a Sweet 16 berth. The Racers pushed us to the end, but we held on. We were headed to Detroit, but instead of facing nationally ranked Pittsburgh, we got upstart Vanderbilt. The slipper fit us better than it did the Commodores, and we were just one win away from a trip to Kansas City. Ironically, Kansas State stood in our way. The Wildcats had won two of the previous three meetings during the season and were riding high following a win over second-ranked Purdue. The game was nip and tuck, but midway through the second half, we took over. Milt Newton clamped down on All-American Mitch Richmond, and Scooter Barry took over and had the game of his life. We were going to Kansas City.

We were the toast of the town that week. We brought our bus driver, Jimmy, down from Detroit with us. Coach Brown was so superstitious that he did not do anything different than he had the past two months. Final Four week was a blur. I won National Player of the Year honors and did media interviews nearly every waking moment. The authors of this book were our sports information directors and set up our media activities. I was as sick of them as they were of me by that time—media interviews not being at the top of my favorites list. Coach Brown did a wonderful job with us that week. He filled us up with encouragement. The media let us know that our last three losses were to Kansas State, Duke, and Oklahoma. If we were to win the national championship, our last three wins would have to be over—you guessed it—Kansas State, Duke, and Oklahoma. One down, two to go.

Friday of Final Four week is a great day. Fans can attend open practice free of charge. This was in the days of pre-dome Final Fours, so Kemper Arena was packed to the roof. Later I learned that Mickey Krzyzewski, wife of the Duke head coach, could not get into the arena because the fire marshal had closed off the doors. It was an electric atmosphere. Our Final Four practice was recorded as the biggest crowd ever at Kemper Arena. I don't know how

251

the games could be any more exciting. We met Duke in the semifinal game, and like the game earlier in the year, we jumped on them early. We were running on an adrenaline high. Unfortunately, halftime came and cooled us down a bit. Duke was making a run, but Kevin Pritchard hit an unbelievable fade-away shot, and we held on to win. Two down, one to go. The second semifinal game was great—from what I heard. We were back in the interview area for most of the game. I was rooting for Oklahoma. I wanted another chance at the Sooners. Most people thought that game [Oklahoma vs. Arizona] was actually for the national championship. Dick Vitale was signing his autograph during the week, followed by the statement, "Arizona over Duke."

Oklahoma beat us twice that year, both times by eight points. Nobody was picking us to win. Nobody, but us, that is. Coach Brown again had us prepared to play. He told us we could outsmart them. He told us to be patient. There was some history on our side. North Carolina State upset heavily favored Houston in 1983, and Villanova stunned Georgetown in 1985. If were could beat Oklahoma, we'd be mentioned in the same sentence. I was especially motivated by the fact that Archie Marshall, despite wearing a full-length brace, warmed up with us before the game. The intangibles were pointing in our favor. There was a lot of talk that I pulled the rest of the team aside and told them not to listen to Coach Brown, that we were going to run full bore with the Sooners. I told the guys that, if we had the chance on the break, take it to the hoop and force the action, enjoy the moment. I liked the Oklahoma team and really did not mind Billy Tubbs too much. They were a very talented and confident group, and they were likeable from an opponent's standpoint.

The first half was the best half of basketball I have ever been associated with. It was 50–50 as we celebrated the 50th anniversary of the Final Four. We shot amazingly well. We were psyched up in the locker room at half, but Coach Brown did not want us to run out of gas. He told us it was our turn to dictate tempo. He wanted us to run our offense and not get impatient. We fell behind 65–60 midway through the second half, and it looked liked the clock had struck midnight. But a late surge and key plays gave us an 83–79 win. We may not have had the best players, but we did have the best team. Three down, no more to go. We returned to campus and filled the football stadium half full. We had a parade. Once again, it was great to be a Jayhawk.

We were nicknamed "Danny and the Miracles," and I took that as a compliment to the team. It was not a one-man effort. We were a team in every aspect of the word. Credit first and foremost goes to the coaching staff. Several tough decisions had to be made. Some players had to be dismissed. The playing rotation was adjusted. We even got rid of the yellow jerseys. My teammates also deserve recognition. We became a cohesive unit. We played with heart and we played tough. But most of all, we played "Kansas Basketball"—play hard, play together, play unselfishly and unrelentingly!

There was a lot of talk during the season that Coach Brown and I were at odds. He was fairly open in that he wanted me to be more assertive. At the time, I did not totally understand what he was talking about. I thought he meant I needed to shoot more and be more selfish with the ball. That was not me. I felt I was at my best when I got my teammates involved. I was also not a rah-rah type of player, either. But I came to realize that the team was looking for me to put it in a position to win. I needed to take the responsibility to be a leader on and off the court. I am not sure I embraced it to the degree he desired, but everything worked out in the end. I had a good relationship with Coach Brown. He made me a better player and probably, and more important, a better person. Having my father as an assistant coach was special, as well. He instilled a strong work ethic. He pushed me, challenged me to be the best I could be on and off the court.

Although it was not as prevalent as it is today, players of that era were beginning to leave school early for the NBA with increasing frequency. There was much talk about my leaving after my junior season. I looked at all of my options, but my dad, a former NBA player, told me point-blank that I was not ready. That was the end of that discussion. My mother was a teacher and put a high priority on my going to school for four years. I thought it was the right decision then and am even more certain of my decision today. Even if we had not won the title, it was the right move. As much as I enjoyed the NBA, my years at Kansas were more enjoyable and fulfilling.

When I left KU, my dad left with Coach Brown to go to San Antonio and coach the Spurs. I was not sure what my long-term future held. All I knew was, I was going to play in the NBA, and hopefully for a long time. I figured that my days at Kansas were just a phase and they were now over. But as they say, "Once a Jayhawk, always a Jayhawk." I remained close to my friends from school, married my college sweetheart, and kept up on the scores of the team.

I came back as much as I could, which was not as much as I wanted, given my busy schedule, but Lawrence became my offseason home. I became one of those crazy Jayhawk fans.

It also helped to have Coach Williams leading the program. I had known him a bit from my days in North Carolina. He did a great job of leading the program. He was wonderful to the ex-players. He welcomed us back with open arms. We had some great summer pickup games with the players.

It was interesting timing for me when Coach Self was named to succeed Coach Williams. I was near the end of my career, and the thought of coaching interested me. I had known Coach Self from his days as a graduate assistant to Coach Brown, so there was speculation I would join Coach Self. Kansas could not have made a better decision than the one to hire him. He is one of the best coaches in the game. He's an even better person. I could not resist the calling. I joined the program in a non-coaching role in 2003–2004 and became a full-time assistant coach in 2007–2008. My excitement at being back in Lawrence and at KU is rivaled only by that of my wife, Julie, and my daughter and son. It is a great atmosphere in which to raise a family.

254

Several times, I have been asked what my best college memories are. Certainly playing the games was great. We had some epic battles against the nation's best. But to me, it was so much more. It was hanging out with friends. It was bonding as a team on road trips. It was Senior Night with Archie Marshall getting to take one last shot with his injured knee. It was sitting in the locker room before the game, hearing the sounds of the fight song, the "Rock Chalk Chant" and the sound of roaring fans coming through the walls. It was the deafening roar as we beat the Russians—in an *exhibition* game! It was the feeling of running out of the tunnel to warm up for a game in Allen Fieldhouse as the band played our school song. It was playing softball in the summertime. It was going to football games, bowling against the swimmers, sharing the thrill of victory and the agony of defeat with the other student-athletes in the training room. It was being mentored by coaches, administrators, tutors, and instructors. It was the basketball reunions, where hundreds of Jayhawks from all eras would share memories and swap stories. It was walking down the "Hill" with my classmates. It was all that and more.

So, what does it mean to be a Jayhawk? I don't know if I can give that question a succinct answer. First and foremost, it means that I attended a wonderful university in a wonderful community in a wonderful state filled with wonderful people. Second, it means I got to play in Allen Fieldhouse, the best arena in the world, before the best fans in the world. Getting to be a part of the Allen Fieldhouse experience again has been rewarding. I can tell you that opposing coaches and players are envious of what we have at Kansas.

Now, as an assistant coach, I have the honor of being a more integral part of the Jayhawk basketball family. It's almost as if I get to relive all of those experiences. But I also view my position as the opportunity to give back. I owe so much to so many people who helped me get to where I am today. I feel the obligation to build upon the foundation laid by the coaches and players who came before me.

So, what is it like to be a Jayhawk?

It's awesome.

—Danny Manning
Basketball, 1985–1988
Assistant Coach, 2007–present

Danny Manning might not be the best basketball player to ever don a Kansas jersey, but if he isn't, there aren't many others who can be mentioned in the same breath. Manning was virtually undefined on the court. He could handle the ball, bang with the big boys in the lane, shoot from inside and out, and pass like a point guard. Few teams had answers for him. His arrival at Kansas signaled a renaissance of Jayhawk basketball. Larry Bird, Magic Johnson, and Michael Jordan had elevated the popularity of the sport on the college level. Now Kansas had its own superstar.

Manning was the 1988 College Player of the Year and the NBA's first draft pick that same year by the Los Angeles Clippers. He was an Olympian, an NBA All-Star, and a two-time All-American. Statistically, he completed his career as the Big 8 Conference's all-time leading scorer with 2,951 points, and his 1,187 rebounds are a Kansas record. He played in 147 games, starting all but one. He scored in double figures in 132 games.

Manning's life as a Jayhawk came full circle with the Jayhawks' 2008 NCAA championship. It marked the 20th anniversary of the same title he won as a Kansas basketball letterman, playing the leading role in "Danny and the Miracles." His 2008 Final Four experience was further enhanced with his selection to the College Basketball Hall of Fame.

APPENDIXES

JAYHAWK TRADITIONS

THE JAYHAWK

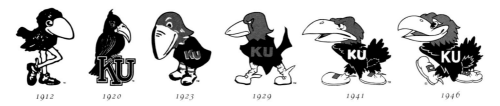

1912   1920   1923   1929   1941   1946

MASCOTS ARE BELIEVED to bring good luck, especially to athletic teams. Just about every college claims a mascot. The University of Kansas is home of the Jayhawk, a mythical bird with a fascinating history. Its origin is rooted in the historic struggles of Kansas settlers. The term "Jayhawk" was probably coined about 1848. Accounts of its use appeared from Illinois to Texas. The name combines two birds—the blue jay, a noisy, quarrelsome thing known to rob other nests, and the sparrow hawk, a stealthy hunter. The message here: don't turn your back on this bird.

During the 1850s, the Kansas Territory was filled with such Jayhawks. The area was a battleground between those wanting a state where slavery would be legal and those committed to a Free State. The factions looted, sacked, rustled cattle, stole horses, and otherwise attacked each other's settlements. For a time, ruffians on both sides were called Jayhawkers. But the name stuck to the free staters. Lawrence, where KU would be founded, was a Free State stronghold.

During the Civil War, the Jayhawk's ruffian image gave way to patriotic symbol. Kansas Governor Charles Robinson raised a regiment called the Independent Mounted Kansas Jayhawks. By war's end, Jayhawks were synonymous with the impassioned people who made Kansas a Free State. In 1886, the bird appeared in a cheer—the famous "Rock Chalk Chant." When KU football players first took the field in 1890, it seemed only natural to call them Jayhawkers. How do you draw a Jayhawk? For years, that question stumped fans. Henry Maloy, a cartoonist for the student newspaper, drew a memorable version of the 'Hawk in 1912. He gave it shoes. Why? For kicking opponents, of course.

In 1920, a more somber bird, perched on a KU monogram, came into use. In 1923, Jimmy O'Bryon and George Hollingbery designed a duck-like 'Hawk. About 1929, Forrest O. Calvin drew a grim-faced bird sporting talons that could maim. In 1941, Gene "Yogi" Williams opened the Jayhawk's eyes and beak, giving it a contentious look. It is Harold D. Sandy's 1946 design of a smiling Jayhawk that survives. The design was copyrighted in 1947.

In the 1960s, the Jayhawk went 3-D when the KU Alumni Association provided a mascot costume. Welcome, "Jay." In 1971, during homecoming halftime, a huge egg was hauled out to the 50-yard line, and fans witnessed the hatch of Jay's companion—"Baby Jay."

Today you'll find several Jayhawks on the Lawrence campus. A piece of birdlike iconography on Dyche Hall, erected in 1901, looks suspiciously like a Jayhawk. In front of Strong Hall perches a large 'Hawk, a statue with sleek, modern lines, gift of the class of 1956. Another, a striding, feathered bronze, greets visitors to the Adams Alumni Center.

COLORS

KU's COLORS HAVE BEEN CRIMSON AND BLUE since the early 1890s. Originally, the board of regents had decided to adopt the University of Michigan's colors, maize and sky blue. Maize and blue were shown at oratorical meets, and they may have colored the Kansas crew in rowing competitions in the mid-1880s.

But in 1890 when football arrived at KU, a clamor arose for Harvard's crimson to honor Colonel John J. McCook, a Harvard man who had given money for KU's athletic field. Faculty members who had graduated from Yale insisted that their academic lineage, and Yale blue, not be overlooked. In 1896, crimson and blue were adopted officially.

THE UNIVERSITY SEAL

KU's first chancellor, Reverend R.W. Oliver, chose the seal in 1866. It was redesigned by Elden Tefft, professor emeritus of art, for the university's centennial. It pictures Moses kneeling in awe before a bush engulfed in flames. The translation of the Latin inscription on the seal is, "I will see this great vision in which the bush does not burn." The story of Moses's vision is from the third chapter of Exodus in the Bible. Fire symbolizes knowledge in many stories and myths. Moses is thought to represent the humble attitude of the scholar who recognizes the unquenchable nature of the pursuit of truth and knowledge.

"ROCK CHALK CHANT"

KU's world-famous "Rock Chalk Chant" evolved from a cheer that a chemistry professor, E.H.S. Bailey, created for the KU science club in 1886. Bailey's version was "Rah, Rah, Jayhawk, KU" repeated three times. The rahs were later replaced by "Rock Chalk," a transposition of chalk rock, the name for the limestone outcropping found on Mount Oread, site of the Lawrence campus.

The cheer became known worldwide. Teddy Roosevelt pronounced it the greatest college chant he'd ever heard. Legend has it that troops used the chant when fighting in the Philippines in 1899, in the Boxer Rebellion in China, and in World War II. At the Olympic Games in 1920, the King of Belgium asked for a typical American college yell. The assembled athletes agreed on KU's "Rock Chalk Chant" and rendered it for his majesty.

Its lyrics are a refrain of "Rock chalk…Jay-Hawk…KU" repeated twice slowly and then three times quickly. It is usually preceded by the Kansas alma mater, "Crimson and the Blue," followed by the fight song, "I'm a Jayhawk."

ALMA MATER ("CRIMSON AND THE BLUE")

COLLEGE STUDENTS AND FACULTY used to make up school songs—and sing them. Many have faded away. In 1891, professor George Barlow Penny searched for a school song for the Glee and Mandolin Club to sing on a tour. Just before departure, he thought of Cornell's "Far Above Cayuga's Waters." Changing a few words, Penny taught it to the glee club. The campus has been singing "Crimson and the Blue" ever since.

Far above the golden valley
Glorious to view,
Stands our noble Alma Mater,
Towering toward the blue.

(Chorus)
Lift the chorus ever onward,
Crimson and the blue
Hail to thee, our Alma Mater
Hail to old KU.

Far above the distant humming
Of the busy town,
Reared against the dome of heaven.
Looks she proudly down.

(Repeat Chorus)

Greet we then our foster mother,
Noble friend so true,
We will ever sing her praises,
Hail to old KU.

(Repeat Chorus)

(Follow with "Rock Chalk Chant")

"I'M A JAYHAWK"

GEORGE "DUMPY" BOWLES, class of 1912, longed to make a big contribution to KU spirit. He wasn't football-sized, but he could write music. One of his musical shows had a song called "I'm a Jayhawk." Written in 1912, it became a hit with students in 1920. The 1926 glee club performed it nationally. (It was revised in October 1958 to conform with Big 8 Conference team names.)

Talk about the Sooners
The Cowboys and the Buffs,
Talk about the Tiger and his tail,
Talk about the Wildcats,
and those Cornhuskin' boys,
But I'm the bird to make 'em weep and wail.

(Chorus)
'Cause I'm a Jay, Jay,
Jay, Jay, Jayhawk,
Up at Lawrence on the Kaw
'Cause I'm a Jay, Jay,
Jay, Jay, Jayhawk,
With a sis-boom, hip hoorah

Got a bill that's big enough
To twist the Tiger's tail
Husk some corn and listen
To the Cornhusker's wail—
'Cause I'm a Jay, Jay,
Jay, Jay, Jayhawk,
Riding on a Kansas gale.

JAYHAWK ATHLETICS
HALL OF FAME

THE UNIVERSITY OF KANSAS ATHLETICS HALL OF FAME was established to formally recognize outstanding individuals and teams and to preserve the heritage and tradition of the University's athletics program. Individuals are eligible for the hall by achieving the following status: Olympic medalists; U.S. Olympic team member; world or American record holder; NCAA individual champion; consensus first-team All-American. Head coaches are eligible by coaching an NCAA championship team. Teams are eligible based on accomplishments for a particular season (i.e., NCAA Final Four, College Baseball World Series, College Softball World Series, or bowl team). Special admittance is the other criteria considered. Other individuals and teams may be considered for bringing national distinction and honor to the university.

INDIVIDUALS

Baseball

	Years
Jeff Berblinger	1990–1993
Stirling Coward	1964
Matt Gundelfinger	1978–1980
Josh Kliner	1995–1996
Steve McGreevy	1963–1965
John Trombold	1952–1954

Men's Basketball	Years
Tusten Ackerman	1923–1925
Charlie B. Black	1942–1943, 1946–1947
Charlie T. Black	1922–1924
B.H. Born	1952–1954
Bill Bridges	1959–1961
Wilt Chamberlain	1957–1958
Nick Collison	2000–2003
Forrest Cox	1929–1931
Ray Ebling	1934–1936
Paul Endacott	1921–1923
Howard Engleman	1939–1941
Ray Evans	1942–1943, 1946–1947
Drew Gooden	2000–2002
Gale Gordon	1925–1927
Charlie Hoag	1951–1952
Bill Hougland	1950–1952
Bill Johnson	1931–1933
Tommy Johnson	1909–1911
John Keller	1951–1952
Al Kelley	1953–1954
Dean Kelley	1951–1953
Bob Kenney	1950–1952
Raef LaFrentz	1995–1998
Bill Lienhard	1950–1952
A.C. Lonborg	1918–1920
Clyde Lovellette	1950–1952
Danny Manning	1985–1988
Ted O'Leary	1930–1932
Al Peterson	1925–1927
Paul Pierce	1996–1998
Fred Pralle	1936–1938
Dave Robisch	1969–1971
Ralph Sproull	1913–1915
Bud Stallworth	1970–1972
Darnell Valentine	1978–1981
Jacque Vaughn	1994–1997
Walter Wesley	1964–1966
Jo Jo White	1966–1969

Women's Basketball	Years
Angela Aycock	1992–1995
Tamecka Dixon	1994–1997
Lynette Woodard	1978–1981

Football	Years
Nolan Cromwell	1973–1976
Bobby Douglass	1966–1968
Ray Evans	1941–1942, 1946–1947
John Hadl	1959–1961
David Jaynes	1971–1973
Bruce Kallmeyer	1980–1983
Curtis McClinton	1959–1961
Mike McCormack	1948–1950
George Mrkonic	1950–1952
Willie Pless	1982–1985
Gil Reich	1952
John Riggins	1968–1970
Gale Sayers	1962–1964
Otto Schnellbacher	1942, 1946–1947
Oliver Spencer	1950–1952
John Zook	1966–1968

Softball	Years
Tracy Bunge	1983–1986
Sheila Connolly	1983, 1985–1987
Jill Larson	1978–1981
Camille Spitaleri	1989–1992

Men's Swimming/Diving	Years
Ron Neugent	1982–1983

Women's Swimming/Diving	Years
Michelle Rojohn	1993–1996
Tammy Thomas	1980–1983

Men's Tennis

	Years
Wilbur Coen	1931–1933

Women's Tennis

	Years
Rebecca Jensen	1992–1994
Nora Koves	1992–1995

Men's Track & Field

	Years
Lee Adams	1967–1969
Bill Alley	1959–1960
Gary Ard	1966–1967
Jim Bausch	1929–1930
Terry Beucher	1958–1960
Thorn Bigley	1968–1971
Les Bitner	1955–1956
Dick Blair	1954–1956
David Blutcher	1977–1979
Leo Bookman	2002–2004
Everett Bradley	1920–1922
Jeff Buckingham	1979–1980, 1982–1983
George Byers	1967–1969
Frank Cindrich	1952–1954
Clyde Coffman	1931–1932, 1934
Sam Colson	1970–1973
Glenn Cunningham	1931–1934
Cliff Cushman	1957–1960
Art Dalzell	1952–1954
Elwyn Dees	1933–1935
Bob DeVinney	1950–1952
Bill Dotson	1960–1962
Emmett Edwards	1971–1974
Kent Floerke	1956–1958
Allen Frame	1953–1956
Merwin Graham	1923–1925
Curtis Grindal	1965–1968
Herold Hadley	1962–1965
Theo Hamilton	1974–1975

Deon Hogan	1979–1981, 1983
Scott Huffman	1985–1988
Ron Jessie	1969–1970
Jan Johnson	1969–1970
J.W. Johnson	1967–1969
Randy Julian	1968–1970
Roger Kathol	1967–1970
Doug Knop	1968–1971
John Lawson	1963–1966
Eddie Lewis	1973–1975
Lloyd Koby	1952–1954
Mark Lutz	1971–1974
Brian McElroy	1970–1971
Richard McGlinn	1953
Billy Mills	1958–1961
Ralph Moody	1954–1956
Ray Moulton	1899–1900
Kevin Newell	1977–1979
Bill Nieder	1953–1956
Jim Neihouse	1970
Al Oerter	1956–1958
Ben Olison	1967–1968
Sanya Owolabi	1979–1981, 1983
Dwight Peck	1965–1967
Tom Poor	1923–1925
Terry Porter	1973–1974
Carl Rice	1916–1918
Michael Ricks	1980–1981
Scott Russell	1998–2002
Jim Ryun	1967–1969
Karl Salb	1969–1971
Wes Santee	1951–1954
Tom Scavuzzo	1971–1974
Herb Semper	1949–1952
Ernie Shelby	1958–1959
Don Smith	1951–1953
Randy Smith	1972–1975
Dennis Stewart	1969–1970
Charlie Tidwell	1958–1960

Jay Wagner	1974–1977
Cliff Wiley	1975–1978
Dick Wilson	1951, 1953–1954
Steve Wilhelm	1969–1971
Tom Yergovich	1964–1967

Women's Track & Field — Years

Sheila Calmese	1976–1979
Kristi Kloster	1993–1996

Wrestling — Years

Pete Mehringer	1931–1934

268

Special Admission — Role

John Bunn	Basketball (Naismith Hall of Fame)
Ed Elbel	Instructor
Max Falkenstien	Broadcaster
Jim Hershberger	Benefactor
Bob Lockwood	Gymnastics Coach
John McLendon	Student (Naismith Hall of Fame)
Ralph Miller	Basketball (Naismith Hall of Fame)
James Naismith	Men's Basketball Coach
Dean Nesmith	Athletic Trainer
John Outland	Football Coach
Don Pierce	Sports Information Director
Dick Reamon	Swimming Coach
Adolph Rupp	Basketball (Naismith Hall of Fame)
Marilynn Smith	Women's Golf
Dean Smith	Basketball (Naismith Hall of Fame)
Floyd Temple	Baseball Coach, Assistant Football Coach, Assistant Athletics Director
Jerry Waugh	Assistant Women's Basketball Coach, Golf Coach, Assistant Athletics Director

Football Coaches — Years

George Sauer	1946–1947

Jack Mitchell	1958–1966
Pepper Rodgers	1967–1970
Don Fambrough	1971–1974, 1979–1982
Bud Moore	1975–1978
Glen Mason	1988–1996

Men's Basketball Coaches — Years

Forrest Allen	1908–1909, 1920–1956
Dick Harp	1957–1964
Ted Owens	1965–1983
Larry Brown	1984–1988
Roy Williams	1989–2003
Bill Self	2003–present

Women's Basketball Coaches — Years

Marian Washington	1974–2004

Track & Field Coaches — Years

Bill Easton	1948–1965
Bob Timmons	1966–1988
Teri Anderson	1978–1980
Bill Hargiss	1933–1943
Brutus Hamilton	1930–1932
Stanley Redwine	2001–present
Gary Schwartz	1989–2000

Softball Coaches — Years

Kalum Haack	1988–1995
Sharon Drysdale	1973–1976
Bob Stanclift	1977–1987

Swimming Coach — Years

Gary Kempf	1977–2000

Baseball Coach	Years
Dave Bingham	1988–1995

Women's Tennis Coach	Years
Chuck Merzbacher	1993–1996

Wrestling Coach	Years
Leon Bauman	1929–1932

Administrator	Years
Forrest Allen	1919–1937
Gwinn Henry	1937–1942
E.C. Quigley	1943–1950
A.C. Lonborg	1950–1964
Wade Stinson	1964–1972
Clyde Walker	1973–1978
Marian Washington	1974–1979
Bob Marcum	1978–1982
Monte Johnson	1982–1987
Bob Frederick	1987–2001

TEAMS

BASEBALL

Year	Coach
1993	Dave Bingham

MEN'S BASKETBALL

Year	Coach
1922	Phog Allen
1923	Phog Allen
1940	Phog Allen
1952	Phog Allen

270

1953	Phog Allen
1957	Dick Harp
1958	Dick Harp
1960	Dick Harp
1966	Ted Owens
1967	Ted Owens
1971	Ted Owens
1974	Ted Owens
1978	Ted Owens
1986	Larry Brown
1988	Larry Brown
1990	Roy Williams
1991	Roy Williams
1992	Roy Williams
1993	Roy Williams
1995	Roy Williams
1996	Roy Williams
1997	Roy Williams
1998	Roy Williams
2002	Roy Williams
2003	Roy Williams

WOMEN'S BASKETBALL

Year	Coach
1981	Marian Washington

MEN'S CROSS COUNTRY

Year	Coach
1950	Bill Easton
1951	Bill Easton
1953	Bill Easton
1954	Bill Easton
1955	Bill Easton
1956	Bill Easton
1957	Bill Easton
1961	Bill Easton
1963	Bill Easton

| 1965 | Bill Easton · |
| 1989 | Gary Schwartz |

FOOTBALL

Year	Coach
1947	J.V. Sikes
1961	Jack Mitchell
1968	Pepper Rodgers
1973	Don Fambrough
1975	Bud Moore
1981	Don Fambrough
1992	Glen Mason
1995	Glen Mason

SOFTBALL

Year	Coach
1972	Pat Duncan/Nancy Eyler
1973	Sharon Drysdale
1974	Sharon Drysdale
1975	Sharon Drysdale
1976	Sharon Drysdale
1977	Bob Stanclift
1979	Bob Stanclift
1983	Bob Stanclift
1985	Bob Stanclift
1986	Bob Stanclift
1992	Kalum Haack

WOMEN'S SWIMMING

Year	Coach
1983	Gary Kempf

WOMEN'S TENNNIS

Year	Coach
1994	Chuck Merzbacher

MEN'S INDOOR TRACK & FIELD

Year	Coach
1965	Bill Easton
1966	Bob Timmons
1967	Bob Timmons
1968	Bob Timmons
1969	Bob Timmons
1970	Bob Timmons
1971	Bob Timmons
1973	Bob Timmons
1975	Bob Timmons
1978	Bob Timmons
1979	Bob Timmons
1980	Bob Timmons
1989	Gary Schwartz
2001	Stanley Redwine
2002	Stanley Redwine

WOMEN'S INDOOR TRACK & FIELD

Year	Coach
1979	Teri Anderson

MEN'S OUTDOOR TRACK & FIELD

Year	Coach
1932	Brutus Hamilton
1933	Bill Hargiss
1952	Bill Easton
1953	Bill Easton
1955	Bill Easton
1956	Bill Easton
1957	Bill Easton
1958	Bill Easton
1959	Bill Easton
1960	Bill Easton
1969	Bob Timmons
1970	Bob Timmons

1971	Bob Timmons
1972	Bob Timmons
1974	Bob Timmons
1975	Bob Timmons
1976	Bob Timmons
1978	Bob Timmons
1980	Bob Timmons

WRESTLING

Year	Coach
1930	Leon Bauman